FROM GENESIS TO APOCALYPSE

FROM GENESIS TO APOCALYPSE

INTRODUCING THE BIBLE

Roland J. Faley, TOR

Paulist Press
New York/Mahwah, N.J.

All artwork/maps provided by Lawrence Boadt, CSP

Cover design by Cynthia Dunne
Book design by Lynn Else

Library of Congress Cataloging-in-Publication Data

Faley, Roland J. (Roland James), 1930–
    From Genesis to apocalypse ; introducing the Bible / Roland J. Faley.
      p. cm.
    Includes bibliographical references and index.
    ISBN 0-8091-4217-1 (alk. paper)
    1. Bible—Introductions. I. Title.
BS475.3.F35 2005
220.6′1—dc22

                               2004024931

Published by Paulist Press
997 Macarthur Boulevard
Mahwah, New Jersey 07430

www.paulistpress.com

Printed and bound in the United States of America

CONTENTS

Contents

To William Morell, OMI,
and the Oblate School of Theology
in San Antonio, Texas, for many reasons
but especially for helping to bring this book to birth

PREFACE

No book about the Bible is comparable to the Bible itself. This modest contribution to its better understanding is no exception. It was written to give an overview of the scriptures as a whole in a single volume, with the hope that it might serve the needs of students of all ages in formal or informal settings.

This book was written with the realization that biblical research has taken giant strides in the course of the last century. Although Catholic scholarship was late in catching up with the developments that began in Protestant and Jewish circles early in the 1900s, it is safe to say that Catholics now find themselves on equal footing with scholars of other faiths. This is borne out by the fact that Bible translations are now an ecumenical endeavor, scholarly research is now undertaken jointly, and the major biblical associations, formerly sectarian, now cross denominational lines in terms of membership.

It is the belief of this author that authentic modern scholarship is a valuable aid to a better understanding of the scriptures. In incorporating the results of modern research, there is no attempt here to bypass any feature of the biblical message or to make its message more palatable to the modern age. Quite the contrary. The truths of both the Hebrew and Christian traditions now appear clearer and more challenging.

The unifying theme of the Bible, as Walter Eichrodt suggested long ago, is that of covenant. The bond made between God and people stands at the center of Old Testament theology. There is no book of the Hebrew Bible that does not revolve in some fashion around the Sinai covenant. The same is true of the covenant established in the blood of Jesus. It is the centerpiece of New Testament thought. When people ask how they can best teach the scriptures in an organic way, this author invariably suggests that covenant serve as the central theme around which a course rotates.

It is axiomatic to say that a book about the Bible is no substitute for an exposure to the Bible itself. The comments of a master chef about the contents of a gourmet dish can never equal that initial taste. Thus, throughout this book, at appropriate moments, the reader is referred to parts of the Bible to be read. These are in boldface type, presented in conjunction with the treatment of the particular book.

A number of people have been valuable enablers in bringing this book to life. I began my scriptural life as an Old Testament specialist and have completed it with a New Testament emphasis. Only this diversity provided the courage to attempt a work on the Bible as a whole. I am particularly indebted to my editors, Lawrence Boadt, CSP, and Joseph Scott, CSP, whose assistance proved valuable indeed. Theodore Bradower, TOR, has once again offered valuable help in preparing this manuscript for publication. In a very special way, I owe a great deal to my many students—in Pennsylvania; Washington, DC; Rome; New York; and Texas; and in both Catholic and Protestant schools of theology—who for forty years have been my companions on the biblical journey.

Roland J. Faley, TOR
Syosset, New York
January 2005

BOOKS OF THE BIBLE
AND ABBREVIATIONS

OLD TESTAMENT

Genesis *(Gen)*

Exodus *(Exod)*

Leviticus *(Lev)*

Numbers *(Num)*

Deuteronomy *(Deut)*

Joshua *(Josh)*

Judges *(Judg)*

1–2 Samuel *(Sam)*

1–2 Kings *(Kgs)*

1–2 Chronicles *(Chr)*

Ezra *(Ezra)*

Nehemiah *(Neh)*

Tobit *(Tob)*

Esther *(Est)*

Judith *(Jdt)*

Ruth *(Ruth)*

1–2 Maccabees *(Macc)*

Job *(Job)*

Psalms *(Ps[s])*

Proverbs *(Prov)*

Ecclesiastes (Qoheleth) *(Eccl [Qoh])*

Song of Songs *(Song)*

Wisdom *(Wis)*

Sirach (Ecclesiasticus) *(Sir)*

Isaiah *(Isa)*

Jeremiah *(Jer)*

Lamentations *(Lam)*

Baruch *(Bar)*

Ezekiel *(Ezek)*

Daniel *(Dan)*

Hosea *(Hos)*

Joel *(Joel)*

Amos *(Amos)*

Obadiah *(Obad)*

Jonah *(Jonah)*

Micah *(Mic)*

Nahum *(Nah)*

Habakkuk *(Hab)*

Zephaniah *(Zeph)*

Haggai *(Hag)*

Zechariah *(Zech)*

Malachi *(Mal)*

NEW TESTAMENT

Matthew *(Matt)*
Mark *(Mark)*
Luke *(Luke)*
John *(John)*
Acts of the Apostles *(Acts)*
Romans *(Rom)*
1–2 Corinthians *(Cor)*
Galatians *(Gal)*
Ephesians *(Eph)*
Philippians *(Phil)*
Colossians *(Col)*

1–2 Thessalonians *(Thess)*
1–2 Timothy *(Tim)*
Titus *(Titus)*
Philemon *(Phlm)*
Hebrews *(Heb)*
James *(Jas)*
1–2 Peter *(Pet)*
1, 2, 3 John *(John)*
Jude *(Jude)*
Revelation (Apocalypse) *(Rev)*

INTRODUCTION

From Genesis to Apocalypse

The Dome of the Rock

I.

THE HUMAN WORD

Through the ages there have been various ways in which human knowledge has arrived at the idea of a supreme being. The philosophical pursuit, know as *theodicy*, can lead to the knowledge of an ultimate intelligent being responsible for the creation and maintenance of the universe. However, in a sense, having said that, we have not said much. What sort of relationship exists between this god and the world we inhabit? What meaning does our life have and how does the supreme being relate to it? Is there really a human destiny and how is it attained?

For the believer, the answer to these and similar questions is to be found in revealed religion. Not only has God created humankind but he has engaged it in conversation. God's self-disclosure is contained in sacred writings that, in one form or another, contain the core beliefs of various world religions. For Jews and Christians, this God who speaks is found in the Bible, or, as it is frequently termed, the word of God. The latter expression is apt because it is through our words that we tell our own story and give people access to our inner self. The Bible, derived from many sources and spanning two millennia of human history, is the core of our insight into the design of God for his people, the manner in which they are expected to live, and the destiny prepared for them. There is nothing in the Judeo-Christian tradition more central than the Bible. This is not the God of the deists who keeps a safe and silent distance from the world. Nor is it the lofty and frigid unmoved mover of human reason. Rather it is a deity who by generous initiative has entered into a personal and deeply concerned relationship with his creation. In making sense of the largely unknown, he has revealed himself as protective, provident, and, above all, as saving. This is the story that the Bible tells in what is often referred to as "salvation history."

This message or revelation, as it is generally known, was captured by a people at given moments in history and in specific parts of the world. Therefore, if God's word is to be understood, we must strive to recapture the human dimension—the cultures, the modes of expression, and even the human limitations—that gave birth to God's design for humanity.

COVENANT

Our Bible is divided into two major parts, the Old and New Testament, or the Hebrew and Christian scriptures. The former is held as sacred by the Jewish people, whereas both Testaments form part of the Christian patrimony. The word *testament* means "witness" and is a key to the revealed message itself, a witness to the caring and saving action of God. This is centered in what is termed a *covenant*, a concept that is central to both Testaments. A covenant is nothing more than a bond or a pact between two parties of equal or unequal status. At a given moment in history God entered into a bond with the Hebrew people, termed in their language a *berith*. The partners were certainly unequal but it was a two-sided relationship. There was a strong commitment to adhere to God's law on the human side and the assurance of protection on the divine. The central moment of covenant making was that mediated by Moses on Mt. Sinai at the time of the Exodus (Exod 19–24), but it had its forerunners in the covenant with Abraham (Gen 15) and that with Noah in prehistoric times (Gen 9). For Christians the covenant is carried to another level in the bond established between God and his people in Jesus Christ. The Bible, then, is based on two major covenants, Jewish and Christian, one built on the other; it is the thread uniting the scriptures as a whole.

When God or Yahweh (which transliterates God's distinctive Hebrew name), entered into a covenant relationship in Hebrew history, he manifested his concern for a displaced body of people who had left slavery in Egypt and were made clearly "his own." In return for the protection and deliverance that Yahweh promised, the people were to live in a prescribed manner that would reflect the holiness of God. These norms of life are to be found in the major Hebrew law codes of the Old Testament, containing among many other laws the Decalogue or Ten Commandments. The new covenant is centered in the redemptive death of Jesus Christ on behalf of all people, with its corresponding mandate of love of God and neighbor. It is the covenant, then, that unites both Testaments.

SCRIPTURE'S HUMAN FACE

The biblical story of this God-humanity relationship begins in the nineteenth century BC and continues to the early years of the second century AD Yet this is not simply a historical recounting. Various types of literature and the imprint of the human authors round out the biblical picture; it is the task of interpretation to ferret out these sundry modes of writing and to assess their meaning. God's revelation reaches us through the faith community that first received it. Given that the word goes through a process of human refraction, we cannot understand the message fully without first attempting to understand the community that transmitted it. This is but to say that we have the word of God in the words of human beings. It means that we cannot take each word, phrase, or sentence as divine utterance enunciated by God himself. This would be to adopt a fatally flawed fundamentalist stance with no recognition of the Bible's human face. Such is a form of literalism that leaves countless problems of interpretation unresolved. It represents a mentality that believes that if the Bible states it, it must be so.

Every human culture has its strength and weaknesses. There are limitations present in every stage of human history. The fact is that a divine message has been channeled through many cultures over many centuries in the course of its composition. This means there were forms of expression used that are foreign to us today. It also means that there were limits on the grasp of reality imposed by time and place. It is only with the effort to understand the past, using the tools presently available, that we arrive at clarity and an appreciation of God's message. It is a task that is not always easy but is ultimately rewarding.

THE BELIEVING COMMUNITY

The Catholic Bible contains seventy-three books, forty-six in the Old Testament and twenty-seven in the New. Although a common Bible for Catholics and Protestants is much to the fore today, this sectarian distinction is made because Protestants and Jews recognize only thirty-nine books of the Old Testament. Books written in Greek, which frequently came from the Jewish Diaspora, were never part of the Jewish canon because it contained only books written in Hebrew. The Christian world, however, developing outside of Palestine, used a Greek translation of the Bible, known as the Septuagint, which included the seven books not found in the Hebrew Bible. Protestantism has followed something of a middle position by not according these seven books official or canonical status but recognizing them as sacred or apocryphal.

If the biblical books had all been written by individual authors, the task of interpreting them would still be culture bound but considerably simpler. The fact is that, although many books of the Bible bear the name of an individual author, they have all been fashioned and formed within communities, whose beliefs and outlook they bear. We speak, for example, of the first five books of the Bible as the books of Moses, whose archetypal presence stands at their center. Although Moses was undoubtedly a principal recipient of God's revelation and probably the initiating force behind these volumes, the five books in their final edited form are centuries removed from Moses and quickly betray the presence of various traditional sources that are embedded in their final form. They are more the books of a believing Jewish community over many centuries than those of a single patriarchal figure.

All of this means that in speaking of the Bible's composition, we are speaking of many hands at work and a cultural world with an outlook that spans many centuries. Because we have no independent account of how these books were composed, we are limited and often bound by conjecture; this means that our conclusions are often somewhat tenuous, even though they give us very reliable working hypotheses; however, to bypass this effort would leave us impoverished in grasping the full measure of God's intended message.

BIBLICAL CRITICISM

As we have seen, the Bible is intimately linked with particular times and cultures, and to grasp the intended meaning in interpreting the text it is important to determine the era of composition, the various modes of literary expression, and the major external influences that have played a part in conveying the scripture's message. In the matter of the Hebrew scriptures, this means coming to grips with early Palestinian (Canaanite) culture, the life and practices of the Israelites themselves, and the later influences brought to bear from Assyria, Babylon, Persia, and Greece. The history of the Hebrews themselves spans almost two millennia and the written literature approximately nine hundred years. The New Testament, on the other hand, covers a period of only about one hundred years. To understand the Christian scriptures, it is important to know not only Jesus of Nazareth but also the life and times of the early Christians and the influences brought to bear by the Jewish and Greco-Roman cultures of the time. All of this falls within the scope of what is termed *biblical criticism*.

We do not use the word *criticism* in the same way it is customarily used in modern speech, where it has a dominantly negative connotation. Rather in biblical circles it is used in the way in which we speak of music or art critics. The latter's task is to determine whether a given work or performance meets certain determined standards. These will usually center around a composer's or painter's intuition and intent. So, too, the biblical critic is interested in the author(s)' original intent, which cannot be determined in a vacuum. It requires a knowledge of the history and literature of the times, the ways in which people ordinarily expressed themselves, and the manner in which they transmitted their knowledge. The instructed ear listening to a Brahms symphony is concerned with an accurate presentation of the composer's intent. The biblical critic tries to evaluate the meaning of the biblical text in a similar way in asking what the text intends to say. In fact, the keynote of all biblical criticism is fidelity to the author(s)' intent. The major forms of this pursuit are textual, historical, literary, form, and redaction criticism.

Textual Criticism

The sources of the Bible as well as the completed text itself were, as has been indicated, transmitted over centuries. These written texts were hand-copied in their original language, very often under very primitive circumstances, and passed on to subsequent generations. How can such an arduous and fallible task assure us that the text we are reading today accurately reflects the original? The task of determining accuracy is the work of *textual criticism*. The text being analyzed, often referred to as the "received text," is viewed in the light of other copies that have been handed down to verify the correctness of what is written. In the case of a hand-copied text, the possibility of mistakes is real. Very often it is possible to correct errors in words, phrases, or verses on the basis of comparison with other texts in the same language or in some cases from translations from the original text (Hebrew, Aramaic, or Greek) into other ancient languages. It is essential that a textual critic have a good working knowledge of the original language of the text with which he or she is dealing.

Why do these texts need such careful scrutiny and why is there the need to make corrections where necessary? Because it is the original text as it came from the author(s)' hand that bears the note of authenticity. The closer we come to that the better. As in any mortal pursuit, to err is human. In the course of transcribing, copyists have made mistakes in a word or have duplicated a line. In other instances they misinterpret a phrase or a verse. Sometimes, in the interests of explanation, they will add to the text or try to highlight it in what is called a *gloss*. In Isaiah 11:2–3, for example, there is a list of various gifts that a future descendant of David will possess. They are actually six in number, but because one is given an unintended repetition ("fear of the Lord"), the Greek translation (Septuagint) renamed one of the duplicate "fears," piety, and we end up with what is traditionally termed "the seven gifts of the Spirit."

The importance of textual criticism lies in the fact that we are dealing with a book that lies at the center of two important faith traditions, and therefore the accuracy of what is presented for belief has the highest priority. It is a painstaking but essential task to remain as close as possible to an original text.

The discovery of the now celebrated Dead Sea scrolls in 1947 shed considerable light on the Hebrew text of the scriptures. A common consensus holds that the scrolls found in the caves of Qumran near the Dead Sea in 1947 represent the library of the Jewish sect known as the Essenes. Many books of the Hebrew Bible are represented among the Qumran findings, at least partially, and, coming from the first century before Christ, the texts are almost one thousand years older than any previous texts in our possessions. They have proved helpful in making adjustments and clarifying the later text, which has long served as the basis of vernacular translations. Most important, though, in comparing the Qumran texts with the "received text," we realize how carefully the text we have long used has been transmitted. The differences, in short, are not major.

In conclusion, it can be said that the skilled pursuit of textual criticism has rendered a high level of certainty that we are, in the main, reading the text as it was finally edited centuries ago, and

Caves of Qumran

that translations made from the original languages can be assured a high level of accuracy. Because many of our manuscripts of the New Testament are only a few centuries removed from their original authors, the problem is much less complex and accuracy more easily attained. The Old Testament spans a much longer period of time, although we are reasonably assured that in reading the books of the Bible today we are in direct touch with the original author.

Historical Criticism

No book is ever written in a vacuum. To read Margaret Mitchell's *Gone with the Wind* is to learn much about Confederate life during the Civil War or to read the novels of

John Steinbeck is to glean important insight into American rural life in the early part of the last century. Books are rooted in a determined culture at a given historical moment. Historical criticism is then faced with a twofold task. The first is to determine how well the author portrays the historical period in question. The second is a greater game of mystery: to determine the period of composition from the text itself in seeing how historical events have helped to shape and form the biblical writing. In both there is required a careful reading of the text itself and a knowledge of the history of the times.

It may be helpful to look at a few examples. In the book of Jonah, we read that the citizens of Nineveh, the capital of the extensive Assyrian empire, were converted (almost miraculously) to faith in the Lord of Israel (Jonah c. 3). Yet secular history, which has well documented the Assyrian era, gives no indication of such a mass conversion nor was Yahwistic faith to be later found in that part of the world. This historical irreconcilability then helped to shed light on the literary character of the Jonah story as a "faith parable" not a piece of ancient history.

In the account of Joshua's invasion of Canaan, the capture and destruction of Jericho figures prominently (Josh 5–6). The historical evidence, however, provided by archeology, shows that Jericho was destroyed centuries before this period and was unoccupied at the time of Joshua's conquest. Again, historical data sheds light on the literary character of the book, which is basically a theological statement on the land's consignment to the Hebrew people as a pledge of Yahweh's fidelity. The mode and manner of the conquest are secondary and the ruins of Jericho may well have suggested this ultimate victory.

On the other hand, the actual historical circumstances surrounding Jerusalem's destruction by the Babylonians (586 BC) and later by the Romans (AD 70) enable us to appreciate the prophetic stance of Jeremiah and Ezekiel in the earlier case and that of Jesus in the latter.

Literary Criticism

In all forms of literature, literary criticism is wholly taken up with the text itself, rather than with the external factors that influenced it. It examines the various forms of verbal and written expression that a work contains. Clearly if Jeremiah is at one moment uttering an oracle and in another writing a letter, we are involved in two distinct types of literature. If an evangelist is recounting events from Christ's life to deepen faith, then he is not writing a biography. The literary critic goes beyond specific forms and evaluates the development of certain key ideas, as the covenant in both Testaments. He or she is always interested in the author's overall intent and the ways in which his design has been realized. The literary critic looks at a form like apocalyptic and "decodes" the plethora of signs and symbols present.

Again, an example may prove helpful. In the Gospel of John, the apostles make their journey from John the Baptist to Jesus in a way quite different from that of the other evangelists (John 1). There is no mention of their occupation as fishermen. They take very measured steps in responding to Jesus' invitation. There is, at the same time, a gradual recognition of who it is they are following, from rabbi and messiah to Son of God and king of Israel. What was undoubtedly a much longer process historically becomes in John a theological summation of where discipleship leads in terms of recognition. This is wholly in keeping with John's *literary* theme of the passage from darkness to light, from ignorance to true knowledge. It is the work of literary criticism to determine the author's predetermined imprint on his work. *Source criticism* is closely related to literary criticism inasmuch as it sorts out diverse strands or traditions that the author has drawn on in composing his work. In the book of Genesis, for example, there are parallel accounts of events the author has used. There are two accounts of creation (Gen 1–2) and two accounts of the flood (Gen 7–8). The explanation of the use of these duplicates and their significance is the task of the literary critic.

Form Criticism

A subordinate part of literary criticism, but very important in its own right, is form criticism. We are all familiar with different forms of literary expression and upon encountering them our minds quickly adjust. When we read the daily newspaper, we find news articles in the early pages wherein we expect a fairly accurate recount of events. We then meet feature articles, which may be fact or fiction, serious or light, and those are read in a very different light. The editorial page expresses opinion, and we immediately realize that we may agree or disagree. All of this means we are dealing with different *literary forms*. In the Bible, we meet a variety of forms, which because of their oral origins have become fixed and stereotypical. The job of the form critic is to sort these out, investigate their origins, and determine the way in which the author has used them. It is easier for us to recognize the forms of speech or writing that are part of our everyday life. When we say, for example, that a person was born with a silver spoon in his mouth, we know that we are dealing with inherited wealth, not with an unusual form of birth. It is more difficult to determine the forms that were used in antiquity and the role that they played in scriptural composition. *The Song of Songs*, for example, once seen as an allegory expressing Yahweh's love for his people, is today seen as originally a series of Hebrew wedding songs. Many of the psalms betray their origins in the liturgy of the temple.

The New Testament has proved to be a fertile field in its preservation of literary forms. Many identifiable forms can be found in the gospels in recounting events from Jesus life, as miracle stories, pronouncement stories, and logia, as well as the more obvious examples as the parables. These originally existed in oral form in early catechesis and for practical reasons became highly stylized. These were then incorporated in collections in the composition of the gospels. These self-contained units, quite complete in themselves, readily explain why they can be easily excised and understood in our present-day liturgical use. It is for this reason that every Sunday's gospel makes complete sense in itself.

Pericopy

Form criticism flourished in the last half of the twentieth century and has shed broad light not only on the forms themselves but on the communities that used them.

Redaction Criticism

This looks to the final stage of a work's composition. A redactor is an editor and in many instances an author as well. Redaction criticism goes beyond the individual units or forms to ascertain the contribution of the work's final editor. Study shows that most biblical authors were not simply compilers; rather they gave their material a well-determined shape and direction, and in this sense they were authors in a true sense of the word. We may take a very prominent example. The historical books of the Bible, which run from Joshua to 2 Kings, were once seen as a collection of factual data brought together to satisfy historical interest. Today, as a result of redactional studies, they are seen as a collection of books edited with a clear didactic purpose by a theological circle known as the Deuteronomists. They have fashioned the account of the occupation and the monarchy to highlight the blessings that came upon fidelity and the divine displeasure that was subsequent to infidelity. The determination of what that comprehensive vision was is the task of the redaction critic.

Nowhere has redaction criticism played a greater role than in the gospel studies of recent times. When form criticism was front and center, the great emphasis was on the evangelists as compilers of church traditions. Today the emphasis has strongly shifted to a consideration of the evangelists as true authors of their material. The imprint on the material is different for each, and the four give us a multifaceted picture of Jesus of Nazareth. If Matthew is interested in looking at Jesus in the light of Jewish faith and tradition, Luke will present the same Jesus as moving toward Jerusalem and from there, after his resurrection, to the world at large.

At this point, it may well appear that this heavy emphasis on the human component of the scriptures leaves the authorship of God largely overlooked. Such is hardly the case, as the next chapter will be at pains to show. In the past, stress was placed so strongly on divine authorship that scant attention was paid to the role of the human author. If one thing is clear today it is the fact that we would never have the scriptures were it not for the faith community that gave them birth. For some, this can be quite disconcerting because it means divine truth filtered through a weak and often sinful humanity. In the Judeo-Christian tradition, which is as much human as it is divine, the truth was grasped within real limits and transmitted as well as possible, but always in a determined cultural setting. To understand today what that message contains we must use the technical and literary tools that will bring it to light.

BIBLE AND CHURCH

All of what has been said may help us to see the intimate connection that exists between Bible and church. Not only has the Bible come out of a believing community but there it has been preserved, interpreted, and proclaimed. In its teaching the church looks to the scripture for guidance and verification. In its prayer it gives scripture primacy of place. In every Sunday liturgy, especially since the Second Vatican Council, the first part of the Mass is wholly centered on the word of God, and the first duty of the homilist is to explain the word and apply it to the life of the congregation. In preparing for ministry in the church, the importance of biblical studies is strongly underscored.

Even a passing knowledge of church history indicates the extent to which the sacred text and its exposition played a part in the life of the early church fathers. Their reflections, partially preserved in the liturgy of the hours in the postconciliar church, shows the extent to which the Bible nourished their spiritual lives. The beginnings of scholastic theology at a much later date were primarily an exposition of the *sacra pagina* ("the sacred page"). After the Protestant reform, a wary Catholic Church largely discouraged a personal reading of the Bible and unfortunately many generations, even to modern times, remained woefully ignorant of the inspired word of God. Fortunately, much of that has changed since the Vatican Council, but there is still a way to travel in making Catholic knowledge of the Bible a trademark of our life.

Scripture has come from a community, Judeo or Christian, rests in the community, and guides and directs its life and worship. God has never spoken in a vacuum. He has accommodated himself in many ways, preeminently of course in the sending of his Son in human form, although he has also transmitted his thought and direction through human channels. Besides Jesus Christ himself, the scriptures remain the greatest witness to God's condescension.

II.

THE WORD OF GOD

It is a basic tenet of the Judeo-Christian tradition that in the scriptures God speaks to us. This is not simply a reverent or poetic way of speaking but expresses the belief that this book is divinely accredited. In some way God was present in the process of composition. Although human minds were at work in birthing it, the literary work is ultimately attributed to God. This was accomplished by the action of God's Spirit, which is said to have *inspired* or breathed the work to realization. Or in the words of Vatican II: "the books of the Old and New Testament, whole and entire, with all their parts...written under the inspiration of the Holy Spirit, have God as their author" (Const. On Divine Revelation, para. 11).

INSPIRATION

In earlier times the divine activity in inspiration was strongly emphasized; it was a conscious response to a force moving an author to transcribe what God dictated. Of the various illustrations used, one was that of the harp and harpist. In musical terms, the harp is acted upon and largely passive; it is the harpist who makes the sounds; in different terms, the harp is the human author and God the harpist. The consequences of this mode of thinking are obvious. God is wholly responsible for whatever is written; every word committed to writing has an infallible and irrevocable quality. The Bible, then, escapes any shade of error; it is totally inerrant.

In modern biblical scholarship this is a position that is no longer seen as tenable. However divine authorship be defined, it does not mean dictation. A better starting point is the way inspiration is used in common speech today. One is said to be "inspired" by a beautiful panorama, be it a majestic mountain range or ocean waves striking a sandy beach. It is often said that God is "revealed" in the beauty of creation. Works of art are also often said to be "inspired," music and painting, said to give a glimpse of God. When the composer Pietro Mascagni was once received by Pope Pius XII, the pope is said to have remarked: "When you wrote the intermezzo for 'Cavalleria Rusticana,' you were inspired by God." This is a poetic or creative way of speaking. It simply draws attention to the beauty of God that appears in natural and human creation.

Biblical inspiration is analogous to this mode of speech but also distinctive. Not only is the Bible generally reflective of God; in some way he is its proximate cause and its ultimate source. Each book of the Bible, upon its completion, is at some point recognized by the faith community as being authored by God and therefore distinct from other works, as profoundly spiritual as they may be. The question remains, however, as to how this is accomplished. Biblical authorship is not simply to be equated with prophetic revelation. The prophet is fully aware that God speaks through him, and the message he communicates is not his own. No author of any part of the scriptures makes such a claim for what he writes. The authors may well know that what they write contains God's message, but they give no indication that their writing is directed by God.

The prophet Isaiah receives his initial call in a temple setting (c. 6). The entire scene in its majestic sweep leaves no doubt that the Lord is revealing himself to the prophet. Yet in the composition of the book, which may at least in part stem from the prophet himself, there is no indication that the work itself is inspired and destined for posterity. A clear example appears in the letters of Paul. For all their truth and depth of insight, Paul does not give the slightest hint that those letters would have a life coextensive with the church itself and would be read in the liturgy two millennia thence.

How then does inspiration take place? What is its psychological dimension? Some have argued that inspiration is posterior to composition and that it consists in the book's official recognition by the believing community. As far as Christians are concerned, the scriptures are part of the constitution of the church. They are as essential as grace or the sacraments. As constitutive of the church, they share in its divine protection and guidance. Therefore, their truth is divinely guaranteed and in that sense they are said to be inspired. Thus inspiration largely centers on recognition, and because they are thus seen as integral to the saving plan of God, the books in this sense can be said to be "authored" by God.

However, this position raises its own questions. Does this "post factum" recognition do justice to what a long tradition has seen as the antecedent character of inspiration. It has long been held that there was a supernatural quality to the act of writing itself, even if that position became extreme at times. God's use of human authors has a long tradition in both Judaism and Christianity. What is often suggested today is a more subtle, even unconscious action of God on the human subject. The author would have proceeded like any other writer in research and composition, in developing his ideas, and even in making mistakes, although the subtle direction of God in the whole process is assured. The book is destined to be something more than its human author ever intended. This divine authorship from the beginning is realized in the book's final formal acceptance. Not only is the revelation contained therein confirmed but the book as a whole receives definitive approval.

This position is further substantiated when one realizes how many hands were at work in the composition of any biblical book. There was an early formulation of the task in bringing together various sources, which were carefully transmitted; these then were finally edited and fashioned in a final edition. Even stating the procedure thus, we are probably involved in a form of oversimplification. This means that the charism of inspiration must be seen as extending to many people over a considerable period of time. Thus, to preserve the antecedent character of inspiration and allow for its broad reach, a valid and helpful working position today would see the charism as institutional or ecclesial. For Christians this would mean that the supernatural assistance would be given to the church or to the Israelite community, in the case of the Old Testament. Canonicity is a recognition that this divine assistance was present from the work's beginning, whether all those involved were fully conscious of it or not. The key to understanding inspiration and canonicity is to understand the vital importance of preserving the tradition both of Israel and of Jesus in an authentic fashion. If that message is vital to the lives of generations, it is essential that it be transmitted with a fidelity that is divinely assured. The gift is analogous to that of the teaching office of the church. This is nothing other than assurance that the church will not fall into essential error, that, with all its ups and downs, it is faithful to the original message. This is a gift, given antecedently to the church, that is not experienced consciously by all of its human functionaries and certainly does not exclude error in its nonessentials. We are simply assured that in its essence the revealed message is kept intact. The case with the scriptures is no different.

INERRANCY

Closely connected with the questions of inspiration and revelation is that of inerrancy. This rests on the belief that the Bible cannot err without impairing the faith of its adherents. In its basic form, then, inerrancy means that the essentials of faith, whether in the Jewish or Christian tradition, are kept intact with divine assurance. While safeguarding the interests of revelation, however, inerrancy should not be considered as coextensive with inspiration. The reason for this is that the content of the books of the Bible is broader than revealed truth. They contain history, human conjecture, limited insights, poetry, even humor, all of this part of an inspired body of literature. Yet few would argue that all of this is revealed; rather it is part of a human endeavor. If Luke actually believed that at the time of Jesus' birth, Caesar Augustus called for a worldwide census while Quirinius was governor of Syria (Luke 2:1f), he was certainly mistaken. He may have devised this dating for other reasons, such as placing Christ immediately on the world stage of history. However, regardless of his objectives, this in no way damages the essential message of Luke's gospel. Or, the early church lived with the clear expectation of Christ's proximate return. This appears repeatedly in New Testament writings. The timing was off, as later writings themselves indicate, but the basic message remained part of the church's belief that Christ will ultimately bring history to an end.

Today inerrancy, except in fundamentalist circles, is viewed more broadly and looks to the salvific truth of the scriptures. They are safeguarded from error in enunciating those truths that are essential to belief. Vatican II states it in these terms: "...the books of Scripture firmly, faithfully, and without error, teach that truth which God, *for the sake of our salvation*, wished to see confided to the sacred Scriptures" (Const. On Divine Revelation, para. 11). From this it is clear that preservation from error extends to those truths related to God's salvific design.

CANONICITY

One final question remains unresolved. Inspiration profoundly influenced the composition of scripture, but how was inspiration recognized? When and where was it decided that these books and not others were to serve as the basis of Jewish and Christian belief? This question is treated under the heading of canonicity. The word *canon* (Greek: *kanon*) in its Hebrew use meant a measuring stick or standard. In biblical use, it came to mean those books that are seen as normative in both Jewish and Christian belief. It clearly distinguished this writing or body of writings from other books of sacred history or piety and makes a unique claim in their favor, that is, they have God himself as their ultimate source.

As we have mentioned, the Catholic canon contains seventy-three books, forty-six in the Old Testament, and twenty-seven in the New. It matches exactly the number accepted in Eastern Christianity. The Jewish and Protestant Bibles, however, limit themselves to those thirty-nine books of the Hebrew tradition, with the seven added books accepted by Catholics, seen as apocryphal. This difference in enumeration obliquely points up the difficulty that obtained in determining which books were sacred and normative and which were not. At what point did discussion cease and formal recognition take place?

The question is not easily answered. There were two collections of accepted books within Judaism, one connected with the Jews of the homeland (the Palestinian canon), and the other with the Jews of the Diaspora (the Alexandrian canon), the former in Hebrew, the latter in Greek. Because Christianity grew mainly outside of Palestine, it drew on the Greek Old Testament, which contained seven other books (Tobit, Judith, 1–2 Maccabees, Wisdom, Sirach, and Baruch). The Palestinian canon was officially determined at the end of the first or in the early second century AD and was seen as normative for the Jewish people. It is often connected with a gathering of rabbis in the city of Jamnia sometime after the fall of Jerusalem (AD 70) but this cannot be stated with certainty. The criteria for the selection of sacred books rested on their content and the extent to which they had attained a position of being normative in Jewish life. Literary attribution also played a part. The books are identified, if only by literary attribution, with the important figures in Israel's past, for example, Moses with the Torah, Solomon with the Wisdom literature, David with Psalms, and, of course, the prophets with their respective books.

The situation in Christianity was somewhat more fluid. However, it can be said that the separation of inspired from apocryphal writings took place over a relatively short period of time. Some books of the New Testament were not written until the second century, but it can be safely said that by the end of that century, the canon was fixed, if not officially at least in practice. This is not to say that all discussion ended about one or another book of either Testament. What is certain is that the differences had been narrowed by the end of the second century. No formal list of the canonical books received official sanction until the council of Florence in the fifteenth century, with the council of Trent later repeating the Florence decision.

What were the standards used to determine New Testament canonicity? In general, they can be said to be three in number. The first was *apostolicity*, that is, the book was claimed to have been written by an apostle or an early church figure. Second, *orthodoxy* played a major role. This was reflected in its doctrinal content and its seriousness of approach, with the book reflecting the authentic belief of early Christianity. Finally, *continuity* was important. The book had to have a link with antiquity. It was not a work that suddenly appeared at a later date or had been lost and rediscovered. These criteria served to distinguish biblical books from many and sundry expressions of piety and devotion, not to speak of devious teaching that was not absent from either Jewish or Christian history. It also excludes alterations or additions made at some later date.

The Protestant reform accepted as inspired only the books of the Jewish (Palestinian) canon, thus accounting for the seven fewer books in the Protestant Bible. Protestants see these added books as sacred but not inspired and lists them as the apocrypha. Today many published Bibles are the result of ecumenical endeavor. Because they are used on an interfaith basis, the apocryphal books are included for the benefit of Catholic as well as Protestant readers.

TRANSMISSION AND TRANSLATIONS

The preservation of the Hebrew text of the Old Testament continued well into the Christian era. The Masoretic text, composed by scribes between the seventh and tenth centuries AD, introduced vowels into the earlier consonantal text and has served as the basis for modern translations. With the gradual dispersion of the Jews through the centuries, translations were made from Hebrew to Syriac and Aramaic. The Greek translation known as the Septuagint, dating from the first century BC, is the most celebrated early translation. It had widespread use in the extra-Palestinian Jewish culture and served as the principal source for early Christianity. In modern times, the Hebrew biblical texts found at Qumran in caves along the shore of the Dead Sea, dating from the first century BC, are the earliest manuscripts to date; they predate the Masoretic texts by more than eight hundred years and have shed considerable light on our better understanding of the Hebrew text.

The New Testament was written entirely in Greek, with our earliest complete manuscripts dating from the fourth century. Fragments and sections from an earlier period have shed light on the later manuscripts that serve for modern translations.

The translation of the complete Bible into Latin, known as the Vulgate, was the work of St. Jerome in the fourth century. By that time Latin had obtained widespread use in western Christianity, giving paramount importance to Jerome's work. The significance of the Vulgate can hardly be overestimated. Its author had a good knowledge of Latin and Greek and was, in the main, a cautious translator. There are times when his Christian coloring of the Old Testament is overdone wherein orthodoxy is prized over accuracy, but there is no question about the monumental stature of the work. It served the Catholic Church for centuries both in liturgy and academe.

It was the Vulgate that served as the basis for all vernacular translations of the scriptures in Catholic usage until the early 1940s when Pius XII in his encyclical letter *Divino Afflante Spiritu* insisted that all future vernacular translations be made from the original biblical languages. These same translations were then to be used in the Church's liturgy. This was not meant to disparage the Vulgate or any earlier versions. It was simply a recognition that accuracy is not well served in making a translation from a translation.

The popular use of the Bible in Catholic circles was minimal after the Protestant reform. The Vulgate remained normative for centuries after Latin had ceased to be a spoken or understood language. Translations of the Bible from the original languages were largely the work of Protestants or Protestant sympathizers, with English being the dominant language of translations. Notable among these was the work of William Tyndale, whose New Testament was published in 1525, followed by the Coverdale Bible in 1535. The most significant translation was the King James version in the early seventeenth century. With the continued spread of the vernacular Bible, the first complete Catholic translation into English appeared. Done from the Vulgate, the Douay-Rheims version, named for the two French cities where the work was done, held sway for centuries in the English-speaking world. For Protestants, the King James version in its later revisions, known as the Revised Standard Version (RSV), remains the most celebrated English version and enjoys a wide readership to the present-day. In recent years it has been approved for Catholic use as well.

The main Catholic Bibles on the American scene, now translated entirely from the original languages, are the New American Bible (1952–70) and the English version of the French Jerusalem Bible. These two, together with the Revised Standard Version, serve both liturgical and personal use.

TOOLS

To assist in the study of the Bible, there are important tools to assist the student in his or her work. These include *encyclopedias* and *dictionaries* that contain information on all subjects related to the scriptures. *Commentaries*, which may be single or many volumes, contain a line-by-line interpretation of the biblical books, while at the same time setting each book in its broader historical and literary context. A *concordance* is a word index that can identify the chapter and verse of any word that occurs. *Atlases* contain maps of the Mediterranean and Near Eastern world, together with accompanying information on the people and culture related to a particular biblical location.

THE DEVELOPMENT OF THE BIBLE

We have looked at the factors that comprise the composition of the Bible, but we have done so in a piecemeal fashion. At this point we shall attempt to bring these various pieces together to present the composition of the whole in something of an organic fashion. Here we are admittedly dealing with hypotheses but they are solid working positions that have won a wide measure of acceptance. They contribute to our resolving many of the vexing problems that beset scriptural interpretation.

Old Testament Development

There are three major sections of the Hebrew scriptures: the Torah, the Prophets, and the Writings. Each of these has its own story to tell related to its origins, transmission, and final composition.

The Torah

The Torah makes up the first five books of the Bible (Genesis, Exodus, Leviticus, Numbers, and Deuteronomy). Traditionally these were known as the books of Moses and until comparatively recent times they were believed to have been written by Moses himself. Today this position has been almost universally abandoned. Almost all phases of biblical criticism have become increasingly aware that the Pentateuch was composed over many centuries and is not the composition of any single person. There are laws and customs that postdate Moses by centuries. The content of the Bible's first five books clearly reflect Israelite life over many centuries, something that could never have been captured in the desert experience. Although some features of the Pentateuch may very well stem from Moses, the books can be said to be his inasmuch as it is the cloak of his authority that reinforces its authenticity.

The Torah is generally seen today as containing four major strands or traditions, which have been brought together in the editorial process. The oldest strain, the Yahwist or J, derives its name from its identification of God as Yahweh. It dates from about 1000 BC and appears in Genesis, Exodus, and Numbers. In addition to its name for God, the Yahwist tradition is characterized by a lively and colorful style. A second source in the Torah is the Elohist or E, whose name for God is Elohim. It parallels J in many instances, comes from a slightly later period (after 900 BC), and is identified with the Northern Kingdom of Israel after the division of the country. The Priestly source or P plays the dominant role in compiling and editing the previous traditions. It is seen as emanating from priestly circles with strong cultic and legal interests. Whereas its editing hand is seen in all of the first four books of the Torah, the Book of Leviticus with its detailed laws and prescription reflects the P tradition in its entirety. Centered in Jerusalem, the priestly school gave the first four books their final form at the end of the Babylonian exile in the fifth century BC. It brought together the earlier strands or traditions, fashioned them, and added to them in giving continuity to the work as a whole. The final result of the priestly school's work is often termed the Tetrateuch or four-book series.

The fourth and final source, known as the Deuteronomist or D, is found only in the book that carries its name. Because it contains a very important law code and is closely attached to the figure of Moses, it has been aggregated to the four books that precede it. Actually, it belongs with the historical books that follow it (Joshua, Judges, 1–2 Samuel, 1–2 Kings), wherein its themes and motifs are more than evident. This deuteronomic school had its origins in the eighth and seventh centuries and continued into postexilic times (fifth century). Although its sources are older, it is predominantly a postexilic composition. Its dominant theme is one of reward or punishment in terms of fidelity to the Lord or the lack thereof.

The Prophets

There are four major prophets (Isaiah, Jeremiah, Ezekiel, and Daniel). Daniel, however, is a book of a different genre and, although listed as a prophetic book, it is really pseudoprophetic in building itself around a prophetic figure centuries removed from the time of composition. The minor prophets are twelve in number (Amos, Hosea, Micah, Zephaniah, Habakkuk, Nahum, Haggai, Zechariah, Joel, Obadiah, Jonah, and Malachi). With the exception of Jonah, which is basically a parable, the books contain the oracles of the prophets themselves and offer some biographical data. The distinction between major and minor prophets is not one of superiority but simply based on the length of the books. The prophets range over a period extending from the eighth to the fifth century BC. This embraces their prophetic careers, the collection of the oracles attributed to them, and the final editing of the books attributed to them. Some were prominent in the Northern Kingdom (e.g, Amos), others with the south (e.g., Isaiah and Jeremiah). There is no indication that any prophet was responsible for the final composition of the book that bears his name.

The Writings

This is a "catchall" category of the Hebrew Bible, with special emphasis on the Wisdom literature (Proverbs, Ecclesiastes, Song of Songs, Lamentations, Job). The Psalms are part of the Writings, as well as some history (1–2 Chronicles, Ezra, Nehemiah) and didactic narrative (Ruth, Esther). Even though some of these books may date from late preexilic times, most of them are products of the literary explosion that characterized the period after the exile. Although the name of Solomon is most often connected with the Wisdom literature and David, with the Psalms, this is ascribed more to literary attribution for authoritative purposes than with historical fact. Solomon was renowned for his wisdom and was logically connected with books like Proverbs and Ecclesiastes. There are some sections of Proverbs that may well be dated in the Solomonic era. David's legendary musicianship connected him with the book of Psalms, a number of which may very well be dated in his time. Again, however, it was the broad cloak of their authority that counted for more than actual authorship.

This summary, as brief as it is, calls attention to the oral and literary life span of the Old Testament. It highlights the multiplicity of sources, the many hands at work, and the length of time required to give birth to the biblical books.

New Testament Development

Fortunately for the student, the New Testament has a much shorter history, in fact less than sixty years in terms of composition. Although not commonly seen as such, the writings of Paul predate the gospels. The letters that are considered authentically Pauline (1 Thessalonians, 1–2 Corinthians, Galatians, Romans, Philippians, and Philemon) were completed during the period of Paul's active ministry in the AD 50s or early 60s. The Deutero-Pauline letters, which contain much of Paul's thought but were probably not personally authored by him (2 Thessalonians, Ephesians, Colossians, 1–2 Timothy, Titus), stem from a later period in the first century. Other writings from different authors (Hebrews; 1–2 Peter; 1, 2, 3 John; Jude; and Revelation) are commonly thought to come from the post-Pauline era and have a very distinctive theological approach.

The earliest gospel is Mark, written between AD 65 and 70, followed by Matthew and Luke which are dated after the fall of Jerusalem sometime between AD 80 and 90. Matthew and Luke have used Mark as one of their sources. Finally, there is John, with its highly developed theological perspective, which is commonly identified with the end of the first century.

Like the Old Testament, the New Testament developed in stages. The gospels originated as oral catechesis expounding the deeds and teaching of Jesus of Nazareth. This grew into small written collections and finally written gospels. The letters of Paul circulated in local churches for a period of time, acquired a prominent place in liturgical life, and were finally preserved as permanent expressions of the church's belief.

All of this only underscores the importance of seeing canonical recognition as a gradual process and of seeing biblical inspiration in broader terms than that of a single author. It also shows the significant part that the believing community, Jewish and Christian, played in preserving the sacred text.

III.

LAND AND PEOPLE

GEOGRAPHY OF PALESTINE

The religion of Judaism and Christianity is geographically a Mediterranean reality. The biblical story in its totality extends from Egypt in the south to Rome in the north. If most of the Old Testament narrative can be said to extend from Palestine to the east and south, the New Testament goes from Palestine north through present-day Turkey, Greece, and into Italy. The center point, of course, is Palestine, where Hebrew history was born and developed and Christianity saw the light of day in the person of Jesus of Nazareth. It is a land measured more in terms of culture than extensive territory. In antiquity it was bounded by Phoenicia to the north and Egypt and the Sinai on the south, comprising about 150 miles from north to south and 60 or 70 miles from east to west. This suffers by comparison with the thousands of miles of the empires of Assyria, Persia, and Greece in their time.

That having been said, Palestine, or Canaan as it was first known, had an ideal location. It was part of what has been termed the Fertile Crescent, an area of considerable verdant and fruitful land, arching from the Persian Gulf in the south, to the juncture of the Tigris and Euphrates rivers, and then moving west and south through Palestine to Egypt. Not only did the Crescent have large stretches of arable land, but, even more important, it provided a trade route with caravans making their way from Mesopotamia to Egypt, with stops at inhabited territories along the way. The journey

31

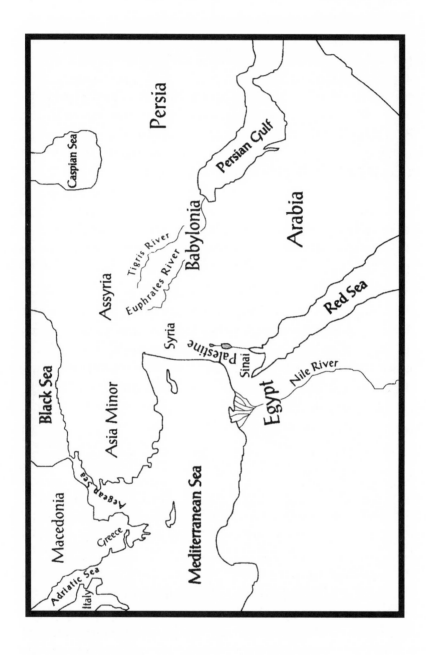

of Abraham from Mesopotamia north to Haran and then south to Canaan followed the route of the Fertile Crescent.

The coastal location of Palestine worked to the Hebrews' advantage for the cultivation of the land and the raising of livestock. It also gave them a broad cultural reach, although the coast gave them nothing in terms of natural harbors or seafaring advantages. For a long period of time, the coast was occupied by the Philistines, and the Phoenicians to the north held the major ports, giving them a decided advantage in trade and travel. However, the location on a major trade route brought international contact and that certainly proved to be a positive factor. The other side of the coin, however, was that the country proved desirable to every major power that arose on the Near Eastern scene over two millennia. Invasion and conquest became the order of the day.

Names

Some initial clarification is needed to explain the various names that have been given to this land historically. *Canaan*, the oldest, is derived from the name of the country's earliest inhabitants. The Canaanites appear as early as 3000 BC and therefore preceded the Hebrews by almost two millennia. *Israel*, an alternate name for the patriarch Jacob, was the term given the land occupied and named by the Hebrews themselves. It designated the entire country until Solomon's death, after which a major schism divided the country in two parts, with only the north retaining the original name. The southern part of the country was known as *Judah*, which had Jerusalem as its capital. In modern times Israel is the official name for the Jewish state. Ironically the name *Palestine* is derived from the perennial enemy of the Hebrews, the Philistines, who occupied the coastal region from the twelfth century BC. The *Holy Land* designates the land as sacred to three world religions—Judaism, Christianity, and Islam.

Today there is a frequent use of the term *Semite* as applied exclusively to the Jewish people. Originally it designated any people that spoke one of the Semitic languages (e.g., Babylonians,

Assyrians, and Canaanites). Today the Semites would include most of the people who inhabit the Arab world.

Topography

The land of Canaan had four major sections. The first and most western was a long *coastal plain* bordering the Mediterranean, a mostly arid land with spotted areas of fertile soil. Proceeding then from west to east, there were the *central highlands* or the *shephelah*, foothills gradually rising to a *central mountain* range. Often reaching two thousand feet in height, this mountainous area served to divide the east and west of the country and had some areas of rich, arable land. On the eastern side of the mountain area was the *Jordan Valley*, one of the lowest areas on earth. The Jordan River traverses this region, originating at the base of Mt. Hermon in the far north, passing through the Sea of Galilee and continuing south until it terminates at the Dead Sea. Considering the very low altitude of the Dead Sea (1,290 feet below sea level), the journey of the Jordan is one of sharp descent, about 700 feet from the Sea of Galilee to the Dead Sea. The Dead Sea is so named because of its high concentration of salt and the resultant absence of living organisms. The three major regions of the country from north to south in Hebrew times were Galilee, Samaria, and Judah. The Negeb region in the southernmost part of the country was a largely desert and arid region. The northern region (Galilee) had much the opposite climate and was proximate to prosperous neighbors (Phoenicia and Syria), and viable trade routes, all of which contributed to a reasonable prosperity.

The Sinai peninsula lies to the south of Israel separating it from the Egyptian mainland. It was through Sinai that Moses led his people after their departure from Egypt at the time of the Exodus. This is essentially a desert area with a large mountain range in the south, often identified with the location of the Sinai covenant made with Israel. Occupying the country to the east of Israel beyond the Jordan were Edom, Moab, and Ammon, countries generally hostile to Israel and subdued during the reign of

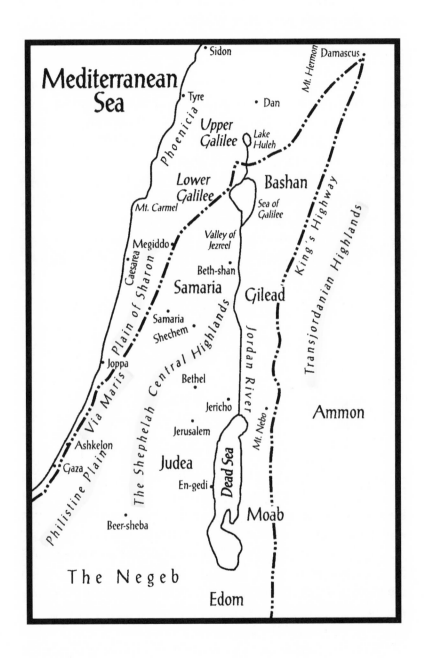

Mediterranean Sea

• Sidon

Damascus •

Mt. Hermon

• Tyre

• Dan

Phoenicia

Upper Galilee

Lake Huleh

Lower Galilee

Bashan

Mt. Carmel

Sea of Galilee

King's Highway

Caesarea

Megiddo •

Valley of Jezreel

Transjordanian Highlands

Plain of Sharon

Beth-shan

Samaria

Gilead

Samaria •
Shechem •

Central Highlands

Jordan River

• Joppa

Via Maris

The Shephelah

Bethel •

Jericho •

Ammon

Jerusalem •

Mt. Nebo

Ashkelon •

Judea

Dead Sea

• Gaza

En-gedi •

Philistine Plain

Beer-sheba •

Moab

The Negeb

Edom

David. The fertile land of Bashan, bordering on the Sea of Galilee, was in northern Transjordan.

Climate

The climate of Palestine is marked by intense heat in the summer, especially in the low-lying regions and a cold and rainy winter, with snow in the mountain regions. There are two rainy seasons, one in the fall (October) and one in the spring (March–April) (cf. Deut 11:14, Hos 6:3, Jer 5:24), both necessary for good crop production. Planting took place at the time of the first rain, and the reaping, at the second. The climate varies according to the topography. The land closest to the sea is characteristically the hottest (averaging 80 degrees in the summer), whereas the mountain range temperature is generally ten degrees cooler. The greatest discomfort in the mountains comes from the hot wind, known as the *sirocco*, which brings dust and uncomfortable heat for periods of the spring and fall.

The rainfall of the country is not abundant, compared with that of other countries, but was sufficient by Near Eastern standards. Heavy rainfalls from the sea do not often penetrate the barrier presented by the mountain regions. The result is a lighter measure of rainfall in the east; in fact it is estimated that in biblical times less than half the country had arable land and much of that was not uniformly fertile. Much of the good farm land lay to the west of the mountains, which produced wheat, grapes, and olives. The limited amount of agriculture resulted in the raising of livestock: sheep, goats, and some cattle. This remained a major source of livelihood through most of Israelite history.

In short, the climate of the country can be described as subtropical, with the marked change in elevation from sea coast to mountain range, in an unusually small country, allowing for considerable variation.

EARLY HISTORY

If we were to identify the neighbors of Israel by the names these countries bear today, our task would be considerably simpler. To the north of Israel is Lebanon; to the east, Jordan; to the northeast, Syria; to points farther east, Iran and Iraq; and to the south, Egypt. In terms of the Bible, the names of Lebanon, Syria, and Egypt remain the same, even with the presence and even domination of various empires in the course of time. However, in identifying the nations that were present to and influenced Israel through its history, it has to be admitted that the picture did not remain constant. Some of the names would be quite foreign to us today. In presenting here a brief overview of the historical picture, we will use the stages of Palestinian history as our point of departure and look at the foreign influences that were prominent in biblical times.

The Patriarchal Period

Two major pre-Israelite cultures that came to play a part in Hebrew history were Mesopotamia and Aram Naharaim. Abraham was a Mesopotamian native, coming from Ur of the Chaldees deep in what is present-day Iraq. However, his family settled in northwest Mesopotamia, the region of Haran, and from there, following the line of the Fertile Crescent, settled in Canaan at the time when the Amorite peoples were moving into Mesopotamia and Palestine. Although many scholars would date this move of Abraham with the early centuries of the second millennium, we cannot claim certainty in the matter. The reason for this is clear and applies as well to affixing dates for many events in the patriarchal period. We have no evidence external to the Bible about any of these events. In the main, we look at the established data and see where the narratives and personalities of the Bible would best fit.

Abraham's settling in Canaan found him in the midst of a semitic population that had probably been settled there since the fourth millennium BC. In the third millennium they were beset by seminomadic invaders. This meant that by Abraham's time, the population was quite mixed and the land had experienced much devastation. It was, however, a basically verdant land that had much to offer any incoming population. From this conjectured point of Abraham's arrival in the mid-nineteenth century BC, we date the beginnings of the Hebrew people with a considerable number of hypotheses about the events that are narrated in the book of Genesis. Many influences came to bear over the years that follow with the presence in the region of the Sumerians, Akkadians, Amorites, Babylonians, and Arameans. We will probably never know how much intermingling with the Hebrews took place but there is no doubt about the cultural influences that came to bear. This is not the concern of the Genesis narrative, which is really a patriarchal family portrait rather than any type of historical document. It is within Canaan itself that most of Genesis 12–36 takes place, centering principally around Abraham and his grandson Jacob, with his son Isaac serving as a link between father and grandson.

Joseph

The latter part of Genesis is wholly concerned with the sojourn of the patriarch Joseph in Egypt. It serves an important function in the biblical narrative, linking two vitally important anchors of Hebrew faith: the promise of Canaan to Israel's ancestors and the departure from Egyptian slavery, known as the Exodus. After Joseph's rise in Egypt to a position of prominence he provides for his brothers in a time of need. Not only is this stay in Egypt difficult to date, but the historicity of the narrative itself is frequently called into question. Attempts to identify the Hebrews with other groups that entered Egypt in the second millennium cannot rise above the level of conjecture. The 'Apiru, known from the Amarna Letters written to an Egyptian Pharaoh in about 1375 BC, have often been identified by scholars with the Hebrews, but again we are not certain. What can be established with certainty is the influx of semitic peoples into Egypt during the second millennium and the presence of people known as

Ramesses II

Hebrews in Canaan in the late thirteenth century, the time generally assigned to the Exodus and conquest.

If we are to assign a date to the arrival of the Hebrews in Egypt, the evidence would point to the mid-second millennium BC during the period when foreigners, known as the Hyksos, ruled the country (1750–1550 BC). The return of Egyptian authority would then eventually bring about the expulsion of the Hebrews at the time of Ramesses II (1290–1224). This would mean an Egyptian sojourn of about three hundred years and would then date the Exodus in the thirteenth century. This hypothesis is admittedly based on evidence that is circumstantial and tangential but it is reconcilable with the recorded accounts from the Bible and secular history.

Moses

The Old Testament has no more monumental figure than Moses; he was the leader of his people from Egypt through the Sinai desert to the Land of Promise and the mediator of the primary covenant of God and people at Sinai. Here we are concerned with the history and circumstances of this landmark event.

The Exodus, as we have seen, is generally assigned to the thirteenth century BC. After their hasty departure from Egypt, the Hebrews first crossed a body of water claimed to be the Red Sea, but more accurately known by its Hebrew name, the *yam suph* or Reed Sea. Whereas the southern Sinai is the main staging area of the book of Exodus, there are strains of another tradition that point to a shorter more direct route into Canaan. The northern tradition would point to a crossing of the water at a marshy area in the area of Suez with an entrance into Canaan from the south. The eastern route would have carried the people east and then south on the Sinai peninsula. This position would have the group avoid the more direct line of the northern route, in accord with the biblical injunction to avoid the "way of the Philistines." It has been posited that we may be dealing with two distinct groups participating in the Exodus at different times.

There is no doubt that the major route of the book is that which carried the people to the east and south to Sinai, perhaps to the mountain known as Jebel Musa, a longtime contender for the mount of God's presence, or at least to the mountain range in that area.

Despite the theologically inflated numbers given in Exodus, the original group would have been small and undistinguished. Again we have no extrabiblical evidence pointing to any of the events connected with the exodus or covenant, but it might well be asked: why should there be? There was nothing historically significant about a group of people wandering nomadically through the desert. Yet, beyond question is the centrality of the Exodus and covenant to the Hebrew tradition. Without them, it is hard, if not impossible to explain the faith of Israel.

The desert experience of the Israelites is said to have lasted forty years. Unsuccessful (Num 14:39–45) and partially successful (Num 21:1–3) attempts to enter Canaan were offset by the major entry that took place from Transjordan through or near the lands occupied by Edom, Moab, and Ammon. Moses died at Mt. Nebo

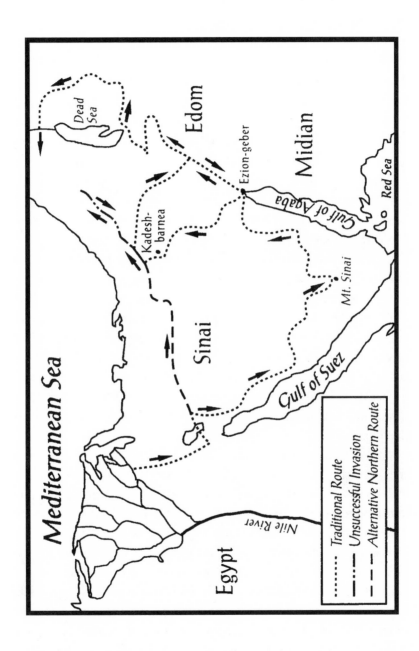

on the plains of Moab without being able to enter the land with his people.

Joshua

If we are correct in dating the Hebrew entrance into Canaan in the thirteenth century, the timing was certainly propitious. Egypt had lost a great deal of its control over the country; the Hittite empire was largely spent; smaller national forces were establishing themselves in Edom, Moab, and Ammon. The Sea People from the west coming by way of the Mediterranean were the only major threat. In Canaan they settled on the coast and established five cities in the twelfth century. Known as the Philistines, they were key players in the early history of Israel.

The biblical account of the occupation of Israel will be treated later with the book of Joshua. For our purposes here, it must be noted that the account of a "blitzkrieg" attack of Canaan by the invading Hebrews is more a statement of Yahweh's ultimate deliverance of the country into the hands of his people than a historical replay of events as they occurred. The three-pronged biblical account (central, south, and north) has left no historical traces and, in fact, is at odds with archaeological evidence. For example, it is now clear that the cities of Ai and Jericho were not only not subdued but were actually unoccupied at the time of the conquest.

What, then, was the status of the land and how did it become the possession of the Hebrews? There are three major theories that address the question. One is that of *invasion*, which argues for a limited conquest of parts of Canaan by small forces of Hebrew invaders. The second is *assimilation*, which sees other foreign populations in Canaan gradually assimilated into the religion and culture of the Hebrews as they gradually and slowly became more extended in the land. By the same process, other Hebrews who had never left Canaan or been part of the Egyptian experience were incorporated as well. The third proposal is *revolt* against the existing city states within the country by the excluded peasant population. This would have included the invading Hebrews who eventually became the dominant force in a restructured society.

The truth may well lie in a convergence of the three theories. What history does show is a country made up of feudal-like city states. The Canaanites were largely a people of land and livestock who practiced a religion centering on fertility deities in sanctuaries where sacred prostitution was practiced. The Hebrews eventually replaced them but not before their enemy's cultural and religious relics had taken their toll. Originally the Hebrews were socially grouped along tribal lines, only gradually to be identified with the twelve sons of Jacob. They were loosely joined together around a common faith and local sanctuaries. In short, it was a much more gradual occupation than that which the deuteronomistic editor has set forth for purposes that will be discussed later when the book of Joshua is viewed from its own perspective.

Judges

The story of early Israelite life in the promised Land is recounted in the book of Judges. The historical period extends roughly from 1200 to 1050 BC. Although not comprehensive or detailed, Judges gives us a picture of the tribal life that prevailed before the monarchy. Geographical isolation contributed partially to the largely individualistic pattern of the way of life. There was no sense of national unity; people were bonded in a common religion that found expression in local sanctuaries. The north was separated from the central region by the broad Esdraelon Valley. Tribes in the mountain area were separated by peaks and valleys, whereas the Jordan Valley effectively reduced contact between east and west.

The heroic character of the Judges' narrative reflects certain historical realities, as the syncretistic dangers inherent in contact with the prevailing fertility cult, the threat from neighboring peoples as the Canaanites (c. 4) and Moabites (c. 5), the foreshadowing of the future monarchy in the Abimelech story (c. 9), and the ascendancy of Ephraim as a harbinger of a future divided country.

The advantages of tribal autonomy meant a great deal of freedom in acting and making regional decisions. "States rights" were in possession in a simple, nonbureaucratic life. Drawbacks lay in military vulnerability and the absence of national unity and collective decision making. Despite the occasional incursion of hostile forces, this was something of an idyllic picture wherein allegiance was owed only to Yahweh. However, it was soon to be superseded by the rise of kingship.

THE MONARCHY

The history of the Israelite monarchy is traced by the deuteronomistic author in 1–2 Samuel and 1–2 Kings. Here we shall deal only with the historical picture that prevailed from the time of the first king, Saul, to the end of the Babylonian exile (1020–539 BC). Before the selection of Saul, the only major threat to the country came from the coastal Philistines. These were the occupying Sea People, located on the Mediterranean, with their five major cities, Ashkelon, Ashdod, Gaza, Gath, and Ekron. Life in the greater part of the ancient Near Eastern world was relatively tranquil. The Hittites to the north had lost their power and the hegemony of Egypt over Canaan was weak and practically nonexistent. The major problems of the region still remained in the future.

Saul (ca. 1020 BC)

There is evidence in the text of Samuel of a clear division of thought regarding the establishment of kingship, the opponents seeing it as a probable threat to the singular sovereignty of Yahweh. Ultimately Saul was selected, and from a military perspective, his reign witnessed skirmishes with the Philistines (1 Sam 14) and the Ammonites (1 Sam 11). There is no list of major accomplishments during his reign, which was largely marked by his own psychological problems. His was a troubled life that contributed in no small measure to his downfall and rejection.

David (1000–962 BC)

The consolidation of Israel as a country was largely the work of its second king and renowned figure, David. He brought about national unity, and after taking Jerusalem from the Jebusites, established it as the religious and political center of the country. He handily defeated foreign invaders and either conquered or diminished hostile forces—Philistia, Edom, Moab, and Ammon. He extended the borders of his country to Aram in the north and as far as the confluence of the Tigris and Euphrates rivers. Although the boundaries of Israel were certainly more modest than other first-millennium powers, its expansion reached a level never again equaled in its history, reaching from the Gulf of Aqaba in the south to Aram and Phoenicia in the north and from the Mediterranean to the Euphrates river in the east.

The only revolt during David's reign came from his son Absalom (2 Sam 15–18) and from Sheba (2 Sam 20). In the main it was a reign of considerable stability and tranquility, as well as prosperity, for the young nation. Although secessionist elements may have been present during David's reign, they did not emerge until the death of Solomon.

Solomon (961–922 BC)

In many ways Solomon built on the accomplishments of David. If David's reign was largely characterized by military exploits, that of Solomon was marked by diplomacy. The unity of the country was reassured by his construction of the temple in Jerusalem, a grandiose undertaking that underscored the priority of Yahwistic faith as well as focusing the attention of the country as a whole. Solomon constructed the Jerusalem city wall and fortified other military centers at Megiddo, Gezer, and Hazor.

Relations with neighboring countries were strengthened both by treaty and by marriage, even though the latter violated the law forbidding marriage with non-Israelite women. Realizing the importance of trade, Solomon cultivated strong ties with the Phoenicians, who controlled important maritime routes and who assisted Solomon in the construction of his own port on the Gulf of Aqaba. He imposed taxes on countries using Israel as a trade route. With his borders secure, Solomon could dedicate himself to strengthening the infrastructure of the country. He enjoyed good relations with his neighbors from Egypt in the south to Phoenicia in the north and Aram and Arabia to the east.

Yet like his father, Solomon too had his "Achilles' heel," which became more evident with the passage of time. His taxation was seen by the people as excessive, with the taxes serving to support a burgeoning government bureaucracy. He used forced labor in his building projects. He repeatedly infringed on the "states rights" of the individual tribes in realigning province boundaries and increased centralized political power; however, his greatest failure lay in compromising his religious faith. His court was peopled by wives and concubines from foreign countries, as he catered to their religious and cultic interests. With the construction of pagan places of worship, there was increased idolatry throughout the country.

In all of this, Solomon sowed the seeds of insurrection. He was strong enough to prevent secession during his reign; Jeroboam's revolt did not succeed but was revived again at Solomon's death. This led to the subsequent division of Israel into two countries. There is much to admire in the accomplishments of David and his son Solomon. The transition from tribal life to a national empire was no small feat. At the same time, there is much to lament. There was an internal moral and political upheaval about which Solomon seemed to be oblivious. It was only a question of time until the results would be evident. From a purely historical perspective, Israel would never be the same again.

A DIVIDED KINGDOM

The North

Although there were signs of division in the Davidic-Solomonic era, it is still rather surprising that the split came as quickly as it did. Unity did not outlive the reign of Solomon. His son Rehoboam entered upon the succession at Shechem, standing strongly on the success of his father's policies. That alone was enough to stoke the fires of rebellion, and Jeroboam, the opposition leader, succeeded in leading all the tribes to secede, leaving only Judah and a part of Simeon for Rehoboam. The Southern Kingdom (Judah) remained isolated but retained Jerusalem. The Northern Kingdom (Israel) enjoyed a much larger population, a more fertile territory, and access to commerce and trade. What it lacked was Davidic legitimacy and political stability. The Northern Kingdom lasted for two hundred years (922–722) and had nineteen kings; the Southern Kingdom lasted over three hundred years (922–587) and had twenty kings. To maintain his hegemony over the tribes, Jeroboam refurbished the important shrines at Bethel and Dan. He installed the golden bull, a footstool for Yahweh, which in the course of time lent itself to idolatrous practice.

From the viewpoint of secular history, the most important king of Israel was *Omri* (876–864). Although the deuteronomist totally discredits him for his lifestyle and idolatrous practices, he had a high profile in the Near Eastern world. The Assyrians at one point (ca. 700) designated Israel as "the land of Omri." He was on peaceful terms with Judah and cemented relations with Phoenicia by marrying his son, Ahab, to the princess Jezebel. It was during Omri's reign that Samaria became the capital of Israel.

The reign of *Ahab* (869–850) was anything but felicitous. Through the influence of his wife Jezebel, he admitted many pagan practices and gave the worship of Baal official recognition in the country. It was popular in Samaria, which had citizens retained from the former Canaanite population. Perhaps the most disfavored ruler of the North was *Jehu* (842–815). His coming to power resulted in the death of two kings in Israel and Judah. He was responsible for the death of the infamous Jezebel and slaughtered Baal prophets in Samaria. He warded off the Assyrian threat, at least provisionally, by paying tribute to Shalmaneser III in 841. During his reign Transjordan was lost to Syria. It was during the reign of *Jeroboam II* (786–746) that Israel gained a measure of political prominence. He fortified Samaria and secured the borders from the entrance to Hamath in the north to the Dead Sea in the south. He prepared the way for an era of prosperity and commercial development.

Yet, as important as these kings might have been, they are cited as having done "evil in the sight of the Lord" and are quickly dismissed in the deuteronomistic history.

Assyria

The eighth century BC is important for a number of reasons. It was the century in which classical prophecy made its appearance in the persons of Amos, Hosea, and Isaiah. Most important historically, however, was the emergence of the Assyrian empire as a major political force in the ancient Near East. Situated in northern Mesopotamia on the Tigris river, Assyria's hegemony extended to the Mediterranean in the west, to the Persian Gulf in the south, and into modern Turkey in the northwest. It was the sole major power in the Near East from 900 to 600 BC. It conquered Israel and a great part of Judah as well.

Relations between Assyria and Judah began with the so-called Syro-Ephraimite coalition in the eighth century. Invited by Israel and its neighbor Syria to join in opposition to Assyria, Judah declined and turned to Assyria for protection. Ahaz was then king of Judah. When Israel and Syria moved against Judah, Assyria responded by destroying Syria and reducing Israel to vassal status. In view of its military dependency on Assyria, Judah remained a political subordinate.

Assyria was headed sequentially by Tiglath-Pileser III, Shalmaneser V, and Sargon II and was noted for its ruthless cruelty as an occupying force. When Israel failed to pay its established tribute, Shalmaneser moved against it and his successor Sargon II effectively destroyed the Northern Kingdom in 722 BC. The number of Israelite deportees is cited as being 27,290. In keeping with Assyrian custom, the Hebrews were mixed with the Mesopotamian population, whereas other imported foreigners were settled in Israel. Judah's relations with Assyria were tenuous at best and became strained when King Hezekiah tried to eliminate the Assyrian cult from his country. When he later joined an anti-Assyrian coalition, the fury of the major empire was unleashed and by 701 Judah was largely subdued. It was later spared total destruction only because Assyria unexpectedly withdrew its troops. Only Jerusalem was left untouched; Assyrian annals speak of Hezekiah being trapped "like a bird in a cage." Assyria gradually lost its power and was soon overshadowed by a new threat, the rise of Babylon in the seventh century.

The South

The book of Kings shows no more deference toward the Southern Kingdom than it did toward the North. Most of its kings are described as having "done evil in the sight of the Lord," with little more said about their reign. For example, *Ahaz* (735–715) is noted for his lengthy reign and his association with the prophet Isaiah. He made Judah a vassal of Assyria and even showed a certain fondness for Assyrian religious practices. He is largely written off as an appeaser and apostate. The good that kings did was indeed often "interred within their bones"; they were clearly not monarchs of strong Yahwistic faith.

There are, however, two notable exceptions. They were *Hezekiah* (715–687) and *Josiah* (640–609). The son of Ahaz, Hezekiah initiated a bold religious reform in Judah by eradicating pagan cult that had been introduced in the country. The deuteronomist thinks well of him for both religious and political reasons. Assyria was always seen as an unwelcome menace, and when smaller countries moved toward any type of revolt, they had at least the sympathy of Hezekiah. He increased his military strength and fortified Judean cities. He is best remembered historically for the construction of the Siloam tunnel to provide a conduit for fresh water into Jerusalem in the event of a foreign siege. He was attacked by Assyria and, as has been noted previously, only Jerusalem was left intact. In his final days, he could see only national tragedy on the horizon.

Josiah

In the course of Temple renovations in Jerusalem, a "book of the law" was recovered and presented to king Josiah (2 Kgs 22). The book is alleged to have inaugurated one of the strongest religious reforms that the country, north or south, had ever experienced. It is commonly thought that the book was an early short version of the book of Deuteronomy. On the basis of its teaching, Josiah inaugurated his reform, thereby earning him the praises of the deuteronomistic editors of Kings.

What were the major features of Josiah's reform? Primarily, there was the concerted effort to eliminate all elements of foreign cult in Judah and what was left of Israel. To avoid further abuse, Israelite cult was centralized in Jerusalem; all major feasts were to be celebrated there. This was not only in pursuit of a religious ideal but also a means of distancing the population from Assyrian influence.

Fortunately for Judah, Assyria was by then in a state of decline. The Babylonians and the Medes were already in the ascendancy. The result was that Josiah was able to pursue his objectives in an atmosphere of relative calm. Assyria fell to Babylon at Nineveh in 612. Babylon continued its march as far as Haran where the Assyrians had fled. Egypt made the mistake of moving to support Assyria, its former enemy. Judean forces opposed Egypt on its way north, during which campaign Josiah lost his life at Megiddo in 609. He was remembered as a hero, a faithful Yahwist, and an intrepid reformer.

BABYLON AND THE EXILE

The reforms initiated by Josiah were soon overshadowed by Judah's political concerns. It was a country where geography could easily work to its advantage; in other ways it could also spell disaster. Judah found itself caught in a wedge between Egypt and the growing threat from the east, the newly re-created kingdom of Babylon. Under their leader Nebuchadnezzar, the Babylonians first turned their attention east and moved against the threat from another major power, the Medes. They then turned to the north and west to deal with the already weakening force of Assyria. Both pro-Egyptian and pro-Babylonian elements within the country weakened Judah's resolve as it tried to wrest itself free of Babylonian incursion. When it failed to pay tribute, Judah was attacked by Babylon. In 597 the country was plundered and many of its citizens were deported. The final revolt under the last Judean king, Zedekiah, lasted two years and came to an end in 587 with Jerusalem completely overrun and a large part of its population deported. This introduced the fifty-year Babylonian Exile of the Jewish people.

The Jews were allowed considerable freedom of movement in Babylon, with opportunity to pursue their own interests. It was a period of remarkable theological growth for a people now removed from homeland and temple. This is evident from the fact that they retained their religious identity. They became now the "people of the book" as Torah became codified and given a central importance. It was a time of pronounced literary productivity. The major schools responsible for editing the books of the Bible were busily engaged during this period. This included the work of the deuteronomistic school (commonly referred to as D), which was responsible for Deuteronomy and the historical books that follow it—Joshua, Judges, 1–2 Samuel, and 1–2 Kings. In addition, there was the work of the Priestly school (P) responsible for the final editing of Genesis, Exodus, Leviticus, and Numbers. It was a period of pronounced prophetic activity in the persons of Jeremiah, Ezekiel, and Second Isaiah (the author responsible for chapters 40–55 of the book of Isaiah). Finally with the rise of the Persian empire, southeast of Babylon, in the last half of the sixth century, the Jews were permitted to return to their homeland.

Persia

The end of Babylonian rule coincided with the rise of Persia as a major power. Its major leader, Cyrus, presided over an empire that was eventually to embrace a geographical region extending from Greece to India and from Asia Minor to North Africa. Upon becoming king in 559 BC, Cyrus first conquered the Medes whose empire included modern northern Iran, much of Turkey, and southern Russia. His later military conquests broadened his hegemony to modern Afghanistan and Pakistan to the east. All of this was accomplished by 540 BC.

The rule of Persia was firm but gentle, respecting local values and even a certain measure of independence for conquered populations. After taking Babylon, Cyrus issued a decree in 538 permitting the deported Jews to return to Palestine and rebuild their city and temple. The first wave of repatriation was under Sheshbazar, probably a son of Jehoiachin. The work of restoration was slow and arduous. The reasons were varied: the limited number of returnees, a shortage of funds, and difficulties arising from the mixed population that then inhabited Judea and Samaria. The prophets Haggai and Zechariah were strong proponents of a rebuilt temple. Finally, the work was completed in 515 under Zerubbabel the governor and Joshua the high priest. Cyrus's edict of reconstruction was reconfirmed by the later Persian king, Darius II (522–486). By the mid-sixth century the Jewish community may have been twenty thousand people.

Some Jews had preferred to remain in Babylon. Many of those who did return had become accustomed to a pagan culture and had merged with foreign influences, wandering far from their Yahwistic faith. This situation paved the way for the rise of two important Jewish figures: *Nehemiah*, the governor, and *Ezra*, the high priest, in about 445. Major religious reforms were introduced, which among other things excluded marriage with a foreign wife. Conflicting data make it difficult to determine the temporal sequence of their rule, but it seems likely that Ezra followed Nehemiah. This would place the beginning of Nehemiah's rule in 445 and that of Ezra in 428. With the resumption of secular and religious leadership, there was no continuation of the line of David. Again, the main thrust of postexilic rule was to distance the Jews from foreign influences, to insist on the primacy of the Jewish Torah, including a renewal of the covenant, Sabbath observance, and the payment of temple tithes.

No secular ruler in the Bible receives the praise and recognition that is accorded Cyrus. He is seen as an instrument of Yahweh in the liberation of the Jewish people. The Jews enjoyed not only religious liberty but commercial freedom as well. There is archeological evidence showing that they minted their own coins. Much of this was attributed to the size of the Persian empire, which hardly allowed for much "micromanagement," although a supervisory contact was always maintained. The vast construction of roads by the Persians facilitated development on many fronts. Although subjugation to a foreign power was never something to be desired, the Persian period proved beneficial to the Jewish people on several fronts.

THE LATER POSTEXILIC PERIOD

Greece

The Greek empire, certainly one of the most celebrated and extensive in world history, lasted from 333 to 75 BC to be superseded by the Romans in the mid-first century BC. The Greek hegemony in Palestine has three main phases: Alexander the Great, the Seleucids, and the Hasmoneans.

Alexander the Great

The main architect of the Greek empire, Alexander brought the Persians to their knees. He was the son of Philip of Macedonia (a region in the northeastern part of the Greek peninsula), who first moved against the Persians in 336 BC. Philip had only partial success before he was assassinated; he was followed by his son Alexander III, better known as "the Great." Warrior, statesman, and politician, he not only conquered the Persians but lived to see an empire that included not only Greece and Macedonia but Asia Minor, Palestine, and part of Egypt. In the latter country he founded the city of Alexandria, which became renowned as a center of learning and Greek culture. His later conquests carried him through present-day Afghanistan as far as the border of India. All of this was accomplished before his death in 323 at the age of thirty-three.

The accomplishments of Alexander go beyond military prowess and geographical extension. He brought Greek culture to the world he conquered and installed the Greek language as the *lingua franca* of the empire. It must be remembered that Greek culture was then at its apogee—the philosophy of Plato and Aristotle, the drama of Sophocles, the moral philosophy of Epicurus—and through conquest it made its way through the far-flung empire. There was an ongoing construction of theaters, gymnasiums, and stadiums; there was a common currency and extensive trade. Much of this proved positive but it had its negative side as well, uprooting other, even more ancient cultures in its wake. It resulted in the Greek translation of the Old Testament, the Septuagint, for the benefit of Diaspora Jews. Paradoxically, some books, such as Maccabees and Wisdom written originally in Greek, witness to the dire effects Greek culture had on Jewish believers.

It was during the Greek period in Palestine that the breach between the Jews and Samaritans became definitive.

The Seleucids

After the death of Alexander, the government of the empire was divided among four generals, only two of whom interest us here: Ptolemy and Seleucus. Ptolemy claimed Egypt and Seleucus, Syria, with Palestine once again sandwiched between superior powers. Although the Ptolemaic rule was not aggressive, Hellenization continued apace. In 198 BC, the Ptolemaic control of Palestine ended with the rise to power of Antiochus III, a Seleucid. The rule of the Seleucids was ruthless and godless, vividly captured in the book of Daniel and the history and narrative of 1 and 2 Maccabees. The major "villain" was Antiochus IV Epiphanes, who set about to destroy every vestige of Jewish belief and culture. Not only did he outlaw Jewish cult but also forbade circumcision, Temple sacrifice, and the possession of sacred books. He profaned the Temple with pagan idols, even installing a statue of Zeus Olympios. Persecution and murder were widespread. This period, which lasted from 175 to 164 BC, proved to be one of the darkest moments in Jewish history.

The Hasmoneans

The revolt against the Seleucids was led by the orthodox Jewish family, the Maccabees. Initiated by Mattathias, an elderly priest, the insurrection found its most notable hero in the figure of his son, Judas Maccabee, whose successful overthrow of the Seleucids brought freedom to the Jews and who has been immortalized in Handel's oratorio named after the hero. Judas routed the Seleucids and the Syrian army. He regained control of Jerusalem and in 164 rededicated the Jerusalem Temple in a feast still celebrated today as *Hanukkah*. Judas' forces were joined by a segment of pious Jews, known as the *Hasidim*, known for their exclusivist and conservative mentality. The Maccabees, it should be remembered, were both a military and priestly family.

However, Judas wanted more than religious freedom; he wanted political independence as well but met with only partial success. After his death, the struggle for freedom was continued by his brothers, Jonathan and Simon. The final solution proved to be more political than military, with Palestine accorded a certain measured autonomy by the Syrians. To the Maccabees' lasting credit, however, they proved to be the final champions of religious freedom for a people that had been repeatedly vanquished.

The term *Hasmoneans* is used of the Maccabeean line of rulers who governed Palestine from the time of the Seleucids to the time of the Roman conquest. The term's origin is uncertain but it is often related to one Hasmon, identified by Josephus as the great grandfather of Mattathias, the father of Judas. The Hasmonean period in Jewish history is seen as beginning with the reign of *Simon*, the brother of Judas. His reign was largely tranquil and free of Syrian interference. His military exploits were largely successful; he was recognized as High Priest and ruler and his heirs accorded the right of succession. He was eventually murdered by his son-in-law and succeeded by his son, *John Hyrcanus*, who solidified Jewish independence and extended the country's borders to include Samaria, Idumea, and part of Transjordan. It was during this period that two important religious groups emerged, the Pharisees and the Sadducees, to be discussed later in reference to their New Testament influence. This was also a period of considerable unrest within Palestine itself. The priestly rulers were seen as illegitimate because they did not spring from the Levitical line. In addition, there were threats from the Seleucid kings, the Nabateans, and even from Roman forces in the west.

Jewish independence finally ended when the Roman general Pompey, to silence political aspirations among the Jews, moved on Jerusalem and placed it under the Roman-installed Syrian government. Palestine became a Roman province in 36 BC.

ROMAN RULE

As the vast reaches of the Roman empire became ever more embracing, the Hasmonean rule in Palestine came to an end.

Pompey made the region a Roman province. There was little change in this status, as the series of conquerors and rulers—Julius Caesar, Cassius, Brutus, and Mark Anthony—came to the fore. This all led to the period of the Pax Romana under Octavius, known best as Caesar Augustus, who ruled his vast empire for forty years.

Whereas all Palestinian leadership was controlled by Rome, religious authority was invested in the Roman-appointed High Priest, with actual power invested in the governor of the region. *Antipater*, an Idumean, was named governor of Judea. In the face of political opposition, his son *Herod* fled to Rome and was subsequently installed as king of Judea with strong Roman support. After thwarting his opponent, Herod, known as "the Great," governed Judea from 37 to 4 BC. He was king at the dawn of the Christian era. He ruled well and was allotted extensive territory, Judea becoming equal in size to what it was in Solomonic times. His building accomplishments included the city of Sebaste (former Samaria), the harbor city of Caesarea (named in honor of Caesar), and the noted fortress of Massada. He reconstructed the Temple of Jerusalem and gave it a renowned splendor, for reasons that were more political than they were religious. Herod's opponents, who were not few in number, took offense at his lack of a totally Jewish lineage and his fondness for Hellenistic culture. He had a dark side to his nature, not hesitating to kill a wife, three sons, a brother-in-law, and mother-in-law.

After Herod's death in 4 BC, his kingdom was divided among his sons, *Archaelaus*, *Herod Antipas*, and *Philip*. Archaelaus, ruler of Samaria, Judea, and Idumea, was eventually removed by Rome and substituted by a Roman governor or procurator, the most celebrated being *Pontius Pilate*, who ruled during the public ministry of Jesus. Herod Antipas was responsible for Galilee from 4 BC to AD 39. Also a contemporary of Jesus, he lives in history as the beheader of John the Baptist. Philip ruled north of the Sea of Galilee until his death in AD 34.

The Herodean line continued in the rule of *Herod Agrippa*, a grandson of Herod the Great, known to us also from the "Acts of the Apostles." He ruled the region formerly held by Philip, with

Samaria and Judea joined at a later date. After his reign (AD 37–44), his son *Agrippa II* had a restricted authority, but by that time the country was effectively ruled solely by Rome.

The Jewish people revolted against Rome in AD 66; they were roundly defeated and their country and Temple, destroyed in AD 70 by the Roman army under Titus. The Temple was never rebuilt; sacrifice, never more offered; the city, left in ruins. The Jews were thenceforth "the people of the Book," wholly given to the study and interpretation of the Torah. Another attempted and fated insurrection occurred under one Bar Cochba in AD 132. Whatever Jewish authority remained in the country was then brought to an end. By this time, Christianity was growing in much of the ancient world.

RELIGIOUS DEVELOPMENTS IN LATER JUDAISM

The Jewish historian Josephus highlights three groups in the intertestamental period, all of which played a part directly or indirectly in the life of Jesus of Nazareth. Judaism was certainly broader than these three groups, and in the lives of many Jews they played little or no part. However, their overall influence is undeniable, and they merit consideration in any historical survey. These are the *Sadducees*, the *Essenes*, and the *Pharisees*.

The Sadducees were conservative in their attitude toward the Law and worship and were strongly opposed to innovations such as those proposed by the Pharisees. They accepted literally the teaching of the Pentateuch and nothing more, thus excluding categorically any belief in the afterlife, the existence of angels, or resurrection from the dead. On the other hand, they were liberal in their approach to daily life and customs, their acceptance of foreign rulers, and the privileges of the aristocracy.

The Essenes, who are not mentioned in the New Testament, were a desert-oriented, exclusivist group who lived in strong opposition to the Jerusalem Temple and its priestly personnel. They may have sprung from the *Hasidim* or "pious people," who attained prominence in Maccabeean times. Living somewhat like a monastic group, the Essenes espoused celibacy for at least some members and lived in expectation of an imminent arrival of the end time. They lived in mortal opposition to the Jerusalem and Temple clergy, accounting for the fact that they withdrew completely from the religious circles of the time and lived a life of Messianic expectation in the desert wilderness. They are best known in modern times from the Dead Sea Scrolls, found in caves near the Dead Sea in 1947. The community was founded in about 140 BC by one known as the Teacher of Righteousness and was destroyed by the Romans about AD 68. Some eight hundred manuscripts found at the site of Qumran are considered by many authorities to be part of a concealed Essene library. There are similarities between Essene tenets and those of John the Baptist, who preached in the same region. As an isolated group, the Essenes played little part in the religious and social life of the times. After the second Jewish revolt in the mid-second century, they fade from the historical scene. As a religious sect, they continued into early Christian times. The impact of their thinking on Jesus and the early Christians is disputed, but there are distinct similarities in thought and practice. Their way of life at Qumran and their library, concealed in the caves above the Dead Sea, were lost to sight with the Jewish revolt under Bar Cochba in the mid-second century AD.

The Pharisees were dominantly a lay group with little interest in the Jerusalem hierarchy or its legitimacy. They strongly upheld that the Law of Moses was in need of interpretation and so admitted a second "oral law," which mitigated and explained various features of the original Law. They accepted postexilic beliefs, such as the resurrection and angels. While admitting an oral law based on tradition and other sources, the Pharisees believed that they were forcefully safeguarding the validity of the Law itself. However, while drawing on other sources and seemingly arguing for greater flexibility, they proved equally conservative, and even fundamentalist in their approach to the Law. In building a body of laws, prescriptions, and statutes, they contributed to a legalistic mentality.

THE OLD TESTAMENT

IV.

PREHISTORY AND EARLY HISTORY

Having completed our historical survey, we are in a position to look at the text of the Bible in the light of its setting in history. The truth of the matter is, however, we actually begin before the dawn of any recorded history. Genesis 1–11 is called prehistory because it predates any period of Israelite history; it is actually a theological preface to the whole of salvation history. After these early chapters of the Bible, we shall examine the period of the patriarchs—Abraham, Isaac, Jacob, and Joseph—who lived in the second millennium. We shall then continue with the Old Testament high point, the Exodus and covenant at Mount Sinai, followed by the occupation of Canaan. This is the period of Moses, Joshua, and the judges. The period of the monarchy in Israel extends from the twelfth century to the fall of Judah and the Babylonian captivity in 587 BC. In this chapter, then, our primary focus will be centered on the book of Genesis, and in subsequent chapters, the other four books of the Pentateuch and the deuteronomistic history (Joshua, Judges, 1–2 Samuel, and 1–2 Kings).

THE STORY OF CREATION
AND THE EPIC OF SIN

Genesis 1–11

The story of creation and the first sin stands at the beginning of the Bible, but in the order of composition it is one of the last sections to be written. It actually represents a long process of refinement and was written to deal with important theological questions. How is the universe to be explained? What is the position of man and woman in the hierarchy of the universe and what is their relationship to God? How is the presence of evil to be explained?

When later biblical authors saw the necessity of responding to these questions in giving final form to their history of salvation, they drew on documents and sources that had long been in circulation. In the first three chapters of Genesis, biblical scholars have detected two of these sources that have been combined in the narrative. The first is termed the Yahwist, so called because it consistently uses Yahweh as the name for God. For practical purpose this is known as the J document. It develops its own themes, uses its own vocabulary, and is characterized by a very vivid and lively style. The second source found in Genesis 1–3 is the Priestly document (or P), so called because of its concern with matters of priestly concern, for example, genealogies, the blessings of God, and religious ritual. It is the P school that finalizes not only the book of Genesis but the three books that follow it. In the Genesis creation account, P has taken the J document and edited it according to this school's distinctive purpose.

It is important to remember that the stories of Genesis 1–11 are viewed through the prism of a much later history. The highpoint of Hebrew history is centered in the thirteenth century Exodus and covenant on Sinai. It was the covenant that gave the Hebrews an identity as a people and gave meaning to their past experiences. In short, had there been no covenant, the patriarchs and their stories would have been irrelevant, as would have been issues surrounding primitive origins. They might have been the object of casual interest or speculation, but they would not have been part of a sacred history.

In Genesis 1–11, we can trace the presence of the J source in the creation account (c. 2), the primeval sin (c. 3), the giants (c. 6), the flood story (cc. 6–9), the table of nations (c. 10), and the tower

64

of Babel (c. 11). In the creation and fall narrative (cc. 2–3), the author passes quickly over the lower stages of creation to reach the apex in the forming of man and woman. Yahweh's activity is described in very human or anthropomorphic terms. The *dramatis personae* are God, Adam, Eve, and the serpent. A single command is given the favored couple, not to eat of a specific tree in the garden, a precept they violate with consequent punishment and exclusion from the garden.

This serves as an explanation of how sin and evil came to be present in the world. It was not the work of God but that of humans. In all of this, the authors had no more knowledge of the specifics of human origins than we do. In fact, in knowing today that the years of the universe should be placed in the billions, and the origin of humans, at least two million years, we have a distinct advantage over people in antiquity, although these were not the concerns of the biblical authors. Everything came from the hand of God as good—man, woman, and the universe, and at some point human insurrection introduced sin and evil. This is the point that Genesis would make. This is presented in story form, which, whatever it may lack in historical fact, affirms its own truth nonetheless.

Punishment follows upon disregard for Yahweh's law, a hard lesson that Israel had to learn repeatedly in its history. The penalties are linked with daily experience: a land difficult to till, hard labor, pain in childbirth, and a slithering snake; if not causally connected with personal moral failure, these are always a reminder of its seriousness. The peace and harmony of the beginning will be restored only in a final era—in a unique way and on a distinctly different plane.

The Priestly account of creation (c. 1) is solemn, almost hymnic. God's work proceeds in an orderly fashion in presenting at every stage an interdependence—land, water, light, the firmament, vegetation, birds, sea life, and animals—all capped finally with man and woman as the crowning point. There is a pause at every stage as God sees "that it is good." There is no shade of the sinister or the unseemly as everything proceeds from the hand of

God. All of the created order is then made subject to the human pair whose responsibility it is to use and reverence. It is this Priestly chapter that encases the subsequent J account (cc. 2–3) in presenting in unmatched terms the sublimity of creation.

In presenting their account of the beginnings, the biblical authors have drawn on myth and legend, casting them in a wholly original framework. The tree of life, for example, appears repeatedly in Babylonian myths. The earth itself rests on pillars and has a dome covering or firmament. This protects the earth from the waters above and the waters below. It is a primitive cosmogony, but one common to ancient cultures. The story of the sin has interesting legendary features. One hypothesis sees the account of the sin along the lines of the idolatrous fertility cult of the Canaanites. The serpent is an ancient symbol of fertility, the "knowledge of good and evil" is a euphemism for sexual awareness; there is, in addition, guilt and shame connected with nakedness after the sin. All of this gives the primordial sin a sexual connotation. This is probably related to the Canaanite cultic practices that, even with their cult prostitutes, stood more for idolatry than sexual license. This may well have served the biblical interests of describing the specifically unknown original sin along lines popularly understood. All of this is but to say that we will understand the creation narrative best if we see it as a story, but one that has a significant and lasting truth of its own.

Genesis 4–11

Sin once unleashed takes on a life of its own. This is the sense of the stories that follow in Genesis 4–11. In the presentation of the prehistoric saga of sin, popular legend continues to play a part. The story of Cain and Abel pits brother against brother (c. 4); it also mirrors the antipathy between agricultural life (Cain) and its pastoral or shepherding counterpart (Abel), with the original seminomadic Israelites favoring the latter. Sin continues to abound with the coupling of heavenly beings and human females resulting in a breed of mythological giants who are said to have roamed the earth (c. 6).

The ancient legend of a universal flood, found in various forms in Near Eastern literature, lent itself well to the Genesis saga of sin. It derives from both the Priestly and Yahwistic sources (cc. 6–8) woven together in a less than seamless fashion, with the flood in one source lasting forty days (7:12, 8:6) and one hundred and fifty days in the other (8:24).

Although the flood destroys the human population of the earth, God's continued fidelity to his own is reflected in the preservation of Noah and his children (c. 9). It is a salvation sealed with a covenant (reflective of Sinai) in which Yahweh forswears further annihilation of the world. The promise is as overarching as the rainbow, which stands as its lasting assurance of well being and heavenly fidelity. In the ongoing deluge of sin, the ridicule of his father's drunken nakedness by Noah's son closes the flood story (9:20–24).

The tower of Babel story brings the epic of sin to its close (c. 11). The key to understanding the story lies in a familiarity with the Babylonian ziggurat or step temple, which towered over all sur-rounding structures. In its "reach for the heavens," it was seen as a manifestation of human pride and arrogance. The account derives from the J source and is expressive of the human desire to reach the divine, not unlike the desire of Adam and Eve to become like God. The punishment that ensues is one of division and separation, the diversity of languages that inhibits human communication.

Genealogies serve as important links throughout the Bible, and notably so in these chapters of Genesis (cc. 5, 11). In general, genealogies were popular rather than historically accurate and serve to join later Hebrews with their forebears.

In Genesis 1–11 we have passed from the heights to the depths, from glory to misery, from grace to sin. It is this spread of sin throughout the world that lies at the heart of this literary mélange, but through it all Yahweh's fidelity is assured. The unfolding story of a better future begins in chapter 12. With the call of Abraham from far-off Ur of the Chaldees, the light of dawn appears on the horizon. The history of salvation has begun.

THE MESSAGE OF PREHISTORY

In these early chapters of Genesis we have met two of our major sources: the Yahwist (J) and the Priestly (P). Because the P source brings the whole of the narrative together and edits it, the author is fully aware of what the J source contains. In the narratives of the Fall, the first homicide, sexual commerce between angels and humans, the flood, and the tower of Babel, J is at pains to show that human disobedience to God's will does not go unpunished. Throughout the narrative, God's concern and compassion are present as he sets his human creatures on the correct path. When they fail, they pay the price of their waywardness, although in the last analysis, Yahweh always extends the possibility of a new beginning. The narrative, of course, is the product of centuries of reflection as it uses ancient tales to make its point. It is also interesting to note that for J, the name for God is Yahweh from the very beginning. In the P and the E traditions, to be discussed later, that name is revealed only to Moses at the burning bush (Exod 3).

The P tradition is not keen on an overly human God but rather a God of grandeur and an overarching otherness. This is clearly seen in Genesis 1 where God creates with an effortless Word and stands over and above all creation, including the first couple. Although P recognizes the authority given humans to preside over and use creation, the author steers clear of any human imperialism. Human likeness to God does not consist primarily in control or domination but rather in mirroring God's conduct. By the time the P source edits Genesis in the postexilic period (after 546 BC), there is a realization that historically things have not gone that well for Israel. There has been repeated conquest, domination, and exile. This does not mean abandonment by the God of their fathers. P's genealogies, for which the source has a particular fondness, clearly link later generations with the beginnings. When he extends the age of the patriarchal figures to an incredible number of years, the author is only showing people, held to an earthbound, time-limited vision, that God's goodness to their ancestors is unquestionable. Long life proves it. God has not abandoned his people, but by the same token, he is not a God to be manipulated; the world is his and all that it contains. Future blessings are assured where there is a willingness to accept the divine will.

Genesis 1–11

THE PATRIARCHS (GEN 12–50)

The ancestral figures playing a prominent role in Genesis are Abraham, Isaac, Jacob, and Joseph. The events of their lives are seen as both ancient and revered, underscoring primarily the hand of God in their lives. They are not biographical in the modern sense of the word; they may best be described as *family memoirs*, highlighting heroic features of people from a distant past. On the other hand, they are not imaginary tales spun out of whole cloth. They are certainly elaborated, but they remain accounts of people who were seen as having a true flesh and blood existence. The events and customs described are not incongruous in terms of a second-millennium provenance. The life of the ancient Near East is today known to us from many discovered sources, and in many ways, the events of Genesis are a good fit. This is not to deny that the accounts have taken on legendary features with the passage of time. They are the stuff of saga. If a historical counterpart were to be sought it would be more in terms of the type of history found in Homer or Virgil than that of David McCullough. The people of the patriarchal period resemble the relatives found in photographs from dusty old albums whose deeds are recounted by our grandparents in ways that are sometimes larger than life.

These were God-fearing people who made some dreadful blunders, but through it all, in thick or thin, Yahweh was with them. Abraham and Sarah (Gen 12–25) stand at the head of the

69

list. Dated in the early nineteenth century BC, and called from a Mesopotamian culture, they mark the beginning of salvation history. Their son Isaac is a transitional figure to whom little attention is given. He is the husband of Rebekah and the father of Jacob, and the stories related about him center primarily on his relationship to father and son (Gen 21–27). Jacob takes a center-stage position as the father of the twelve sons, who give ancestral identification to the twelve tribes of Israel (Gen 27–36).

A large part of the patriarchal narrative is dedicated to Joseph (Gen 37–50). He is intimately linked with Jacob, whose life is coextensive with his own, which takes something away from his patriarchal position. Joseph, however, even without a totally independent existence, is the centerpiece of one of Scripture's most engaging and carefully crafted narratives. His humanity brings him as close to the modern reader as any biblical personality.

How, then, are we to read Genesis 12–50? One of the most important keys is to be found in a single word, *eponym*. When a single person embodies the characteristics of a group, much as Columbia or Uncle Sam do on the American scene, the individual is an eponym. Thus Jacob embodies Israel; he is upright but also cunning and shrewd in his dealings with his brother Esau, the progenitor of the Edomites, seen in later centuries as despised, dull-witted, and inferior relatives. Hence, in reading Genesis and later books as well, this notion of a figure vested in the clothing of a people, seen as his descendants, is an important feature to keep in mind.

THE ELOHIST SOURCE

The Elohist (E) is the third source of the Pentateuch. In our treatment of Genesis 1–11, we spoke of the Yahwist (J) and Priestly (P) sources. The Elohist appears frequently in the remaining chapters of Genesis and is so named because its characteristic name for God is Elohim, just as the Yahwist used Yahweh. However, this distinguishing characteristic tends to fade after God's name is formally revealed as Yahweh in Exodus, a name that then becomes common to all three sources.

The Elohist dates from about 900 BC and comes from the Northern Kingdom, which was formed after Solomon's death. The source shows little concern for or interest in human leaders. Its emphasis falls on the divine authority governing all creation. The suitable human response is obedience to God under all circumstances and an unwavering trust in God's fidelity. In looking at human conduct, the Elohist has stronger moral nuances and avoids the Yahwist's "folksy" or down-to-earth pattern of speaking of God in emphasizing divine transcendence or otherness. Its northern provenance explains a marked interest in Jacob, who had a strong contact with the north, and a determined rejection of foreign gods, a constant threat to the northern population.

Evidence points to E's being added to the earlier J as complementing this earlier source, as happens in the covenant account in Genesis 15, as well as adding duplicates, such as Genesis 12:10–20 (J) and 20:1–17 (E). At times, the two traditions are so closely intertwined that it becomes impossible to separate them.

ABRAHAM (GEN 12–25)

As the father of his people, the ancestral figure of Abraham, or Abram as he was first known, enjoys a certain biblical primacy; his character in Genesis is viewed from various angles. The centerpiece is the covenant of promise between God and the patriarch, retained in all three traditions (Gen 15, 17). The initiative is God's who promises Abraham both descendants and land. The event as recorded is being viewed through the lens of the much later Sinai covenant. In c. 15 from J and E, there is the promise of both offspring and land in a version that retains features of ancient covenant making. The ritual called for the slaying of an animal and the contracting parties walking between the two parts, underscoring bilateral solidarity. In the Genesis account, only God passes between the parts (15:17), Abraham remaining in a trance-like state. In this version there is no covenant obligation placed on the patriarch other than trust and confidence.

In the Priestly (P) account (c. 17), the primitive ritual is missing. There is again the promise of land and descendants, concretized in announcing the forthcoming birth of Isaac. In this version, there is an obligation placed on Abraham, that of circumcision, which is to be the sign of a covenanted people. It is an event the importance of which in the faith life of Israel cannot be overestimated.

The narratives regarding Abraham are traditional pieces that originally had a life of their own. It is only the person of the patriarch that serves as the point of convergence as various events from his life are recounted. There are, of course, frequent references to land and descendants. The birth of Isaac seals the promise (21:1–21). Abraham's foibles are not overlooked, as, for instance, when he poses his wife as his sister to avoid Egyptian displeasure (12:10–20) or as he allows the dismissal of Hagar, a slave girl, who is pregnant with his child (16:1–16). In the main, though, he is seen against a background of great fidelity and trust. Nowhere is this captured more poignantly than in his willingness to sacrifice Isaac, the son of promise, to a God who was asking of him the incomprehensible (22:1–24).

In a promise fulfilled, Abraham acquires land in Canaan where he is finally laid to rest (c. 23). He dies but not before seeing to Isaac's marriage to Rebekah, his kinswoman (c. 24).

Genesis 12, 15, 17, 21–22

ISAAC AND JACOB

The story of Isaac is told in a very few chapters (24–27). He bridges the gap between Abraham and Jacob, but it was important that the line of succession be kept in full view, thus making of Isaac an important conduit of the promise made to Abraham. When the time comes for his son to marry, Abraham sends a messenger to his home country, Aram Naharaim in northern

Mesopotamia. Marriage with a Canaanite woman is out of the question, just as there is no doubt about where the couple is to live (24:1–7). The wife is to be from the home country; the home, the land of promise. In these chapters it is the interesting figure of Rebekah who emerges with great clarity. As the story of Isaac unfolds, she plays a key role. The narrative wherein Abraham asks the hand of Rebekah for his son is thoroughly engaging as well as reflective of ancient marriage customs (c. 24). Once the marriage is secured the narrative quickly passes to the birth of Jacob.

Jacob and Esau are the twins born of Isaac and Rebekah and are eponymous ancestors *par excellence*. Representing Israel itself, the younger Jacob contrasts sharply with the senior Esau, who embodies a long time enemy, Edom. The Edomites were characterized as slow-witted and ill-bred, and Esau embodies these ugly traits and more. He is the elder son who sells his birthright to Isaac for a meal to satisfy his hunger (25:27–34). He seldom reflects on the incongruity of his actions. Jacob, on the other hand, is clever and cunning, gifts that were not lost on his posterity. The two are at odds as they grow and mature: Esau, the wild hunter; Jacob, the more cultivated sheepherder. Rebekah provides for them both but leaves little doubt that her preference lies with her younger son.

Genesis 24–26

The story of Jacob wresting the final blessing from his sight-impaired father is a classic example of an eponymous story (c. 27). God's promise was to be realized through Jacob, not his unlettered brother. In the order of preference, between Israel and Edom there is no comparison. The obtaining of the paternal blessing from Isaac, through the machinations of Rebekah, by the younger son Jacob, is definitive; once given it can never be retracted. Future generations can clearly see the results. Esau will stand forever on the periphery while Jacob's continuous ascendancy is assured.

The events and influences of Jacob's life are a blend of tales that originally existed separately and were eventually brought together, principally through the editing work of J and E, and then given final form with the editing of P in the postexilic period. It is difficult to find coherence and unity in this disparate collection of stories and events, but when one considers the overall view of the biblical authors, it is possible to determine the reason why many of the accounts have been preserved. In reading the Jacob narrative, three key themes come to the fore.

The Israelite and Edomite Rivalry

This appears clearly in the persons of Jacob and Esau. It appears in the struggle in the womb, and the obtaining of the birthright (25:19–34), Jacob's grasp on the final blessing (27:1–45), and the peace overture and reconciliation (32:3–21, 33:1–17).

Conflict between Israel and Aram

Aram was the place of Abrahamitic origin. The record of early contacts had a special importance. Jacob marries two of his uncle Laban's daughters, Rachel and Leah, who with the help of two of their maidservants become the parents of the twelve sons (tribes) (27:46—28:9; 29–30; 35:22–26). In a match of wits with Laban, Jacob is initially disadvantaged but ultimately succeeds in outwitting his uncle. These are stories of legendary heroism that were cherished in Israelite circles (cf. 29:1—32:3). In all of them the hand of God rests heavily on Jacob, the heir of the promise and the father of the twelve tribes.

Sacred Places

Another important term in understanding the Bible is *etiology*. Etiologies are basically a means of explaining names or customs, in a way that is popular, not scientific. For example, the name Bethel means "house of God" and the story of Jacob's dream (28:10–19) popularly explains its name; the same is true of Peniel, "the face of God" (32:23–31).

Some of Israel's noted shrines make their appearance in Genesis. Their origins, more popular than historical, are recounted in a series of shrine stories in the Jacob narrative. Bethel's origins are presented in a dream of Jacob wherein a stairway links heaven and earth, with heavenly messengers ascending and descending. It is a place where the patriarchal promise is again renewed (35:1–15). As Jacob wrestles with the heavenly messenger, his hip socket is injured, occasioning another etiology as to why the Hebrews do not eat that animal muscle.

In all the contests of the Jacob narrative, he clearly bests his opponents and is thus evidently a worthy forebear. He is variously linked with places and noted people or is simply seen as a heroic person. There are four women who mother his children (35:21–25), not all of them of equal stature. By the same token, the eponymous sons they bore (and the tribes they sired) were of unequal status. The two sons of Rachel, Joseph and Benjamin, have a primacy of honor. Jacob ultimately returns to his father Isaac at Hebron, where Abraham had also stayed, and there Isaac dies and is laid to rest. Jacob will then live through the lifetime of his son Joseph. The narratives of his life are as colorful as they are varied, but his status as a worthy ancestor is assured.

Genesis 27–29, 32:23–32

JOSEPH (GEN 37–50)

The book of Genesis closes with an account that links the early settlement of the patriarchs in Canaan with their later sojourn in Egypt. The story is that of Joseph, a favored son of Jacob, who arouses the jealousy of his brothers, is badly mistreated by them, and is sold into slavery. Taken to Egypt, he suffers imprisonment there but eventually wins the Pharaoh's favor by dream interpretation. In one interpretation, he foresees seven years of plenty to be followed by seven years of famine. This insight earns him the position of the country's chief overseer and procurator during the years of abundance and scarcity. When his brothers in Canaan come to seek help in Egypt, they no longer recognize Joseph as they make their plea before him. After testing their good will, Joseph forgives them their past injustice and installs them and his father Jacob in Egypt. This sets the stage for the Exodus, which will take place centuries later under Moses.

Authors have long noted the literary quality of the Joseph story, with its thematic flow and dramatic buildup. It bears resemblance to a modern short story with a plot that unfolds in a well-developed way. Yet, as elsewhere in Genesis, different traditions are present; both J and E can be detected. In chapter 37, for example, both the names Jacob and Israel are used, both Reuben and Judah are said to speak on his behalf, and his captors are at one point called Ishmaelites and at another, Midianites. This points to two separate accounts of his brothers against Joseph. This diversity, however, does not detract from the overall unity of a narrative that has been carefully crafted. Joseph's captivity serves as the basis for his dramatic rise to power; the authority then invested in him sets the stage for his providing safekeeping for his family and their subsequent settlement in Egypt.

This has all the features of the heroic saga. Yet we are left with no key as to how much of this is based on historical fact. We shall probably never know. Scholars have long pointed out the situations in the story that correspond to what we know of second-millennium Near Eastern life. The evidence is circumstantial but it lends a note of authenticity. There is a period story, similar to the Genesis account, of a young man who rejects the advances of his brother's wife and is subsequently accused of seduction by the rejected woman (cf. Gen 39). There is also the fifteenth-century story of king Idri-mi of Syria, exiled after his father's dethronement, who succeeds in regaining his kingdom with no help from his brothers. He forgives them and restores them as well. This is a striking parallel to Joseph's lot. Yet none of these accounts is a direct counterpart of the Genesis narrative and may be nothing more than coincidence. They do show, however, that elements of the Joseph story would not have been unheard of in a second-millennium setting. On a historical level, the period of Israel's Egyptian sojourn is probably to be identified with the period of the Hyksos rulers, invaders who held control of the country from the eighteenth to the sixteenth centuries.

The overarching theme of the Joseph story is clear enough. Unusual twists of fate notwithstanding, Yahweh was with Jacob's sons in their trials and misfortunes, their sins, and their triumphs. The path of their destiny may have been obscured but never obliterated. It moves inexorably toward a predetermined future.

Genesis 37, 39–50

V.

EXODUS AND COVENANT

No book of the Old Testament is accorded more importance in the life of Israel than that given to Exodus. Its centerpiece is the Sinai covenant that stands at the heart of the Jewish faith. This is preceded by the account of deliverance from Egyptian bondage, embracing the conflict between Moses and the Pharaoh, the ten plagues, the Passover, the Red Sea crossing, and the journey toward Sinai. These are events that go beyond historical recall; they were constantly relived in the life and cult of the people. The law of Sinai became the norm of moral rectitude for the Israelites, although from the start it must be said that Exodus is not an uncomplicated book. When one considers the long and involved evolution it has gone through, this comes as no surprise. It is to this question that we must now direct our attention.

The plot line of Exodus is clear enough. At some point in the thirteenth century BC, a Pharaoh came to power in Egypt "who did not know Joseph" (Exod 1:8). The Pharaoh is commonly identified as Ramesses II, during whose reign the two cities of Pithom and Raamses were built (Exod 1:11). Moses, who bears an Egyptian name, was of Hebrew birth but raised in the Egyptian court by Pharaoh's daughter. Strongly reacting to the Hebrew plight in Egypt, Moses first made his way to live among Midianite nomads and there had his first encounter with the God of the Hebrews, who gave him the mission of liberating his people. With the help of his brother Aaron, Moses succeeded in overcoming the Pharaoh's repeated denial of permission to leave by invoking a series of plagues on his opponents. When the last plague brought death to the Egyptian children, he was granted permission to lead his people away.

When the Pharaoh had second thoughts, he went in pursuit of the Hebrews with his military forces. Upon coming to the Red Sea (more appropriately known by its Hebrew name: the Sea of Reeds), the Hebrews crossed unscathed as the waters parted, whereas the Egyptians were killed as the waters receded. As they made their way through the desert of Sinai, the people had a totally unique meeting with Yahweh, when at Mount Sinai, with Moses as their mediator, they formed a covenant with the Lord. It was this that gives them their identity and future unity, as a disparate group of refugees became the people of God. It is impossible to determine their number because the biblical figure of 600,000 (Exod 12:37) is certainly inflated; the actual figure would have been much more modest. The people then continued their journey to Canaan, the land of promise, as the ongoing narrative presents their successes and failures.

It is this narrative, as simple as it is in its basic lines, that gained ever greater importance in the life and worship of the people. The text before us today, retained in the traditions of J, E, and P, has overlays of ritual, tradition, and law that make it difficult to ferret out the "basic facts." The account of the plagues has become highly stylized to underscore Moses' superiority to Pharaoh and his wizards. The ritual of the later celebration of Passover and Unleavened Bread gives a liturgical coloring to the people's departure. The covenant at Sinai is a composite of cultic norms, priestly legislation, and laws that come from a later period than the desert experience. Many of the laws in the covenant code reflect a settled life, not a nomadic one. In addition, in the desert narrative, we can see the influence of ritual coming from a period of fixed liturgical norms at the time of the Jerusalem Temple.

Although these factors make literary dissection very difficult, and at times, impossible, they underscore the historical and religious importance of the central event, the bond that united God and people. What we read today in its final form is the result of a lengthy, centuries-long tradition, preserved for us by the Yahwist and Elohist and given final form by the Priestly authors. The number of accretions, then, is not surprising. Our attention will now be directed to the major moments in the Exodus tradition.

OUT OF EGYPT

The Name of God

Like Joseph before him, Moses rose to an unexpected level of importance in Egypt, ascribed to the decision of the Pharaoh's daughter. However, his fortune proved to be short lived. Incurring the Pharaoh's displeasure, he flees to Midian and a non-Hebrew nomadic population. It is there that the name of God is revealed to him (Exod 3). The revelation of the name, however, may well have been the *explanation* of a name already known. An early Egyptian inscription speaks of the Midianite god YHW, long worshiped in the Sinai desert. Regardless of the background of the name, its revelatory value is not diminished.

The voice from the burning bush first establishes continuity with the past; this is the God of the patriarchs—Abraham, Isaac, and Jacob (Exod 3:5f). Pressed further on the question of identity, the Lord responds: I AM WHO I AM. "Thus you shall say to the Israelites 'I AM has sent me to you'." Much discussion centers around the translation and meaning of this self-identification. "I am who am"; "I am who I am"; "I am who I shall be"; "I am the one who causes to be." Partial explanation can be found in the text itself: "I shall be with you" (3:12). "I AM sent me to you (3:14). In short, God is identified with the verb "to be" because *he is the God who is as opposed to the gods who are not.* His being is active and dynamic, as was clearly evident in the events that are to follow. In other words, this is the God *who really is.*

As problematic as the name may be for commentators, its sacredness within Israel was unquestioned. Originally spoken only in a reverent context, it eventually was not pronounced at all. To the present-day, devout Jews will use only a substitute for YHWH like Lord (Adonai) or some other appellation. The divine name itself is not spoken.

Exodus 3

The Plagues (Exod 7–11)

The contest between Moses and the Pharaoh is actually between Yahweh and Egyptian gods. It must be remembered that Israel's monotheism was practical and not theoretical. For centuries, there was no categorical denial of other gods. Whatever status they had was ineffective and rendered them less than real deities. Other people had recourse to them and thus they were not figments of the imagination, but for the Israelites, in practical terms, they simply did not exist. There was only one real God and to him total allegiance was due.

The plagues listed in Exodus were not misfortunes unknown in Egypt. They were inconveniences to which Egypt was and still is subjected. Of the ten plagues, eight are identified with the J and E tradition and two, gnats and boils, with P (with Aaron's prowess to the fore). There was a long history of problems with frogs, gnats, fleas, locusts, and the ruddy color of the Nile. It is not the events themselves but their timing and the circumstances that give them relevance in Exodus. The trial between the opponents is dramatic and highly competitive, thus underscoring Yahweh's supremacy. The climax comes in the tenth plague with the death of the Egyptian firstborn.

Our modern sensibilities make us shrink from a divinely directed killing of infants, but the fact is that we must leave to Christianity something of its novelty. Humanity did not arrive at a finely tuned moral sense in a short time, and it certainly was not that well developed in the second millennium BC. The dealings of God were with people as they were, as he patiently brought them along. The plagues were a contest between the true God and his opponents as his people were wrested from slavery. It is in that context that the plague accounts must be read.

Passover (c. 12)

The importance of the tenth plague lies in its connection with the most significant of Jewish feasts, Passover. In the spring of each year the Jewish household commemorates solemnly the deliverance of the Hebrew people at the time of the last plague. It was at that historic moment that the Lord "passed over" the houses of the Hebrews and spared their children from the avenging death. Thus, what we read in Exodus 12 is a rather detailed presentation of the Passover ritual as it was celebrated in the Jewish community at a period later than the event being described. The eating of the lamb, the other foods to be eaten, the location, the seven-day observance are features that are carefully spelled out. In this chapter the Passover is connected with the feast of Unleavened Bread because in the course of time they were celebrated conjunctively.

Actually we are dealing here with two feasts that actually predated the Hebrews, arising in ancient pagan settings. With the intention of placating the gods of flock and field, an unblemished lamb was offered by a nomadic pastoral people and unleavened bread by agrarian groups. These feasts were taken over by the Hebrews and given a meaning appropriate to their own history. This is similar to what happened in Christian circles when pagan midwinter and spring feasts became Christmas and Easter, respectively.

When reading the Exodus narrative it is important to keep this liturgical imprint in mind because we are not used to reading a story that unexpectedly becomes a detailed ritual. The deliverance of the first born at the time of the Egyptian captivity is also connected with the later custom of dedicating every first-born male to the Lord.

Exodus 7–12

The Red (Reed) Sea (cc. 13–14)

This event became identified with the Red Sea only with the Greek translation of the Hebrew Bible. Originally it was the Sea of Reeds. This passage through the waters has significance not only for the Jewish people but, as a symbol of the saving waters of baptism, for Christians as well. The prose account appears in cc. 13–14 and in poetic form in chapter 15.

Those who remember a Hollywood version of one of the Red Sea's numerous reincarnations will recall the walls of water that held back the surging sea to let Hebrews pass dry-shod. This was followed by the devastating return of the water, which spelled death for the pursuing Egyptians. The coloring and overstatement is actually a part of the Exodus narrative as well. The actual passage in whatever form it took made an indelible impression on the Hebrew psyche. About that there can be no doubt. However, the account has become embellished to underscore the saving hand of God. This juncture of an actual event and an act of faith makes it difficult if not impossible to determine the historical circumstances. A possible clue lies in the statement that "the LORD drove the sea back by a strong east wind all night" (14:21). This may have been a more shallow marshy area, north of the Red Sea, in the region of the present-day Suez Canal. This region near Lake Sirbonis is often cited as a locale where shifting winds result in dry areas where an easy passage can be made before the waters return to their normal level.

What is undeniable is the fact that in Israelite tradition this became a providential act of divine intervention; and thus, it lived in faith and worship. The poetic form of the account (c. 15) is one of the oldest pieces of Hebrew poetry and no doubt found its proper setting in the prayer life of Israel. It actually goes beyond the actual event in citing the occupation of Canaan, even arriving at Jerusalem, "the mountain of your own possession" (v. 17).

Exodus 13:17—15:21

SINAI

Nothing is more central to the faith of Israel than the covenant. It speaks of God's love for a poor and rejected people and his willingness to become part of their life and to give them laws that were to serve as the suitable response for his goodness. Any covenant was two-sided and usually represented responsibilities for both parties. The idea of a covenant or *berith* covered a broad variety of bilateral agreements. It might mean a contract between two persons regarding land, personal holdings, or livestock, and thus was a matter of everyday life. It could also include treaties between countries of equal strength (parity treaties) or unequal status (vassal treaties).

The bond between Yahweh and Israel was unique; it did not fit any of the accepted categories. However, it was designated a *berith*, and the Sinai event, as difficult as it may have been to describe, can, in general lines, be seen against the background of the second-millennium treaty form.

The Covenant (Exod 19–24)

What must be recognized from the start is our inability to determine the actual details of this historic encounter. The event has become encased in literary, theological, and rubrical accretions as it was transmitted through the centuries. These additions have become part of the J and E sources and then given final form by the Priestly school (P). Not all the laws found in these chapters were part of the original agreement but were added according to necessity in the course of time. All of this contributed to the gradual expansion of the narrative. Yet it can be said that the basic features of the account can still be ascertained.

Chapter 19 is a preface to the actual covenant. God makes the proposal and Moses is given the task of determining the willingness of the people. The people then express their intention of espousing the relationship. In chapter 20, Yahweh presents himself and recalls briefly his past favor on behalf of the people (20:2). This is followed by the first body of laws, known as the Decalogue (20:3–17). At this point, we pass over the subsequent laws that postdate the earliest form of the narrative (cc. 21–23) and pick up the narrative in chapter 24. Here the people give their consent to the earlier form of legislation (24:3). The arrangement is then made concrete in the writing of the law and the erection of memorial pillars, thus giving the transaction a visible and permanent character (24:4). Blood rites formed a symbolic highpoint to the proceedings. Life was seen by the ancients as being in the blood. In sprinkling blood on the altar, signifying Yahweh, and on the people, the bond was effected (24:5–8). With this single act, Israel would never be the same again. Its identity had been definitively established.

In the complexity that this narrative reflects, the influence of the vassal treaty (i.e., the international treaty between nations of different status) is present. Although not duplicating it in every sense, the general outline seems clear enough. The vassal treaty had a self-presentation, a recalling of past benefits, the terms of the agreement, and some concrete expression of the commitment. Although some features of the treaty form are absent, as for example, the curses and blessings and the invocation of deities, and therefore this is not an ironclad reproduction, it still seems probable that this common convention served as the broad backdrop for the way the covenant in Exodus has been expressed. The account also has rubrical norms, reflecting its later life in Israelite liturgy. As in the Temple precincts, physical limits are clearly set, with the people kept at a distance, and ritual purity, required (19:9–13). In approaching the Lord, lines of demarcation are established. The people do not ascend the mountain; limited ascent is allowed Aaron (the priest) and his companions, whereas Moses alone has immediate access to the Lord (24:9–18).

Exodus 19:1–25, 24:1–18

COVENANT SIGNIFICANCE

Before leaving the covenant narrative it is important to clarify the relationship between law and the covenant. As presented in the Exodus covenant tradition, law is seen as an expression of gratitude for God's goodness and favor. It regulated personal conduct in such fashion that the otherness or holiness of the Lord might be reflected on the human scene. The Law was never intended as an end in itself.

This understanding was not always to the fore in later Israelite life, and the same can be said to be true in the life of institutional religion in general. Laws are seen as stepping stones to holiness and often become multiple and detached from their basic purpose. Given that this is a concrete path to holiness, law wins acceptance and gives assurance that the right path is being followed. Law can easily become a form of human control, spelling out the ways in which divine favor is assured. What it leads to is what Paul of Tarsus saw as the great obstacle, the belief that divine approval is obtained through observance. It soon overlooks the fact that the whole religious experience begins with God's favor. Love and salvation are not ends to be attained. They are already present; they are lost only with rejection.

Jesus moved strongly against the legalism of his day. Law observance in its multiple forms had obscured the more important values, and the position of Christ, as controversial as it was, was really a corrective. Paul went on to claim freedom from the law in making the law of love the singular commandment.

Law is necessary. We cannot live without it, but it must be moderate and always seen as an expression of love, the most authentic way of giving thanks to the God who has first loved us.

AFTER SINAI

The following chapters of Exodus (cc. 25–40) find the people continuing their journey toward Canaan, the land that had been promised. The journey is a slow one, however, with the addition of more laws, many of them from a later date, regulating largely the life of an already settled population. Much of it looks to the liturgical appurtenances and practices of a Temple-centered first-millennium life. The *ark of the covenant* long remained a centerpiece of life and worship. It is described in detail (c. 25) and was

Carving of the Ark of the Covenant

basically a portable shrine, not unknown to other Near Eastern cultures. It served to localize the invisible deity; in Israel it was a seat or footstool for Yahweh. It was carried with the people on their journey and even after settlement in Canaan was carried into battle to ensure victory over an enemy (1 Sam 4). It consisted of a large box, made of costly wood, gold-plated inside and out, and carried on poles attached to the sides. It was used for discerning God's will for the people and at a later date housed the tablets of the law. David brought the ark to Jerusalem soon after he took the city (2 Sam 6); there it was housed in the *Tent of Meeting.* Eventually it was housed in the Temple until its disappearance with the destruction of the Temple in 586.

The Tent of Meeting has a tradition that runs parallel to that of the Ark. Its construction and appurtenances are given in detail (c. 40). Upon its completion the Lord took possession in the form of a descending cloud and there Moses went to consult with the Lord. The Tent and Ark traditions eventually merged and with the construction of the Temple the Tent ceased to have meaning. In fact, its description in the Pentateuch is reflective of the

Temple substitution. For example, the priests who attend it in the Pentateuch are clearly Temple personnel.

The remainder of the Pentateuchal narrative deals with the continuation of the journey. In many ways it is a disappointing account. Yahweh remains faithful, but, despite their protestations of fidelity, the Israelites fail repeatedly, and their grumbling is seemingly endless. The account is aptly summarized in the forging of the *calf of gold* under Aaron's direction (Exod 32). The calf was an image of Yahweh himself, in clear violation of the law prohibiting any images of Yahweh (Exod 20:4). It is an archetype of the idolatry to which Israel would be prone for centuries. In fact, the Exodus incident is probably a retrojection of Jeroboam's two calves of gold constructed to represent Yahweh at the sanctuary in Bethel (1 Kgs 12:28).

The journey continues in the book of Numbers. The grumbling takes different forms: dissatisfaction with desert life, leadership, or even, food. There are seven instances of rebellion, sometimes directed against God himself (Num 11:1,4; 21), but most frequently against Moses and Aaron (Num 14, 16, 20). Although the people are punished, they are never abandoned. Although their generation was denied entry into Canaan (Num 32:6–15), as was Moses himself, their progeny is given assurance of future occupation. As the Pentateuch comes to a close, Joshua is designated Moses' successor and the Hebrews are poised to enter the land of promise (Deut 34:9).

Exodus 25–26, Numbers 11, 14, 21

MAJOR LAW CODES

It has already been stated that many of the laws found in the covenant account (Exod 19–24) were not part of the original covenant form; however, it is generally recognized that they represent an early body of laws. There are three basic law codes in the Pentateuch. The first is the *Law of the Covenant* (Exod 21–23). Its origins lie in the period of early settlement in Canaan. There

Sinai Peninsula

are laws regarding slaves, personal damage, property rights, and boundary transactions—matters that would have had little meaning in a desert life. They are early laws, however, probably dating from the twelfth or eleventh centuries, and were probably incorporated into the covenant legislation at an early date.

The second major law code is the *Holiness Code* (Lev 17–26). It comes from the Priestly school and deals with such questions as the major feast days, the sabbatical year, as well as sundry features of ordinary human conduct. It is generally seen as becoming part of the Leviticus legislation in the sixth century BC. The third major code forms the bulk of the book of Deuteronomy and is termed the *Deuteronomic code* (cc. 12–26). This code strongly emphasizes the law of love as undergirding all legislation. It emphasizes the single and central sanctuary (identified with Jerusalem), ritual purity, feast day observance, and priestly duties; it contains judicial decisions regulating various aspects of community conduct. In its earliest form it is identified with the law code discovered by Josiah at the time of Temple renovations in the seventh century; it was later expanded upon by the deuteronomistic school until finally becoming part of the Pentateuch.

The *Decalogue* stands apart from all subsequent legislation. Its main features stand up well with what we know of all ancient legislation and is generally situated in the late second millennium. Its laws are apodictic, that is, general statements of right and wrong not conditioned by circumstances. It is a remarkable compendium of the basic requirements of a moral life in society, and although later times have expanded on its primitive meaning, its original features remain remarkably intact. In its covenantal form (Exod 20:1–17), its directives are ten in number. The first three look to human conduct in relation to God (prohibition of icons, reverence for the name, Sabbath observance) (vv. 2–11). The remaining seven deal with human relations. Priority is given to parents (v. 12), then, in a sequence of values, the right to life (v. 13), marital rights (v. 14), the right to freedom (the authentic meaning is "you shall not steal *a person*") (v. 15), the right to a good name (v. 16), the right of ownership (v. 16). Violations against these "freedoms" are seen as seriously reprehensible. It is important to note that after three thousand years it remains a fundamental moral guide for individuals and society as a whole.

Exodus 20:1–17; 21–23

VI.

OCCUPATION AND SETTLEMENT

With the arrival of the Hebrews in the land of promise, a new chapter begins in their history. This starts with the crossing of the Jordan river under Joshua's leadership and will continue until the time of the country's destruction by the Babylonians in 587 BC. This is contained in what is termed the deuteronomistic history, embracing the books of Joshua, Judges, 1 and 2 Samuel, and 1 and 2 Kings. It is so named because this series of books was composed and edited by the school responsible for the book of Deuteronomy. This group of authors and editors has taken the early accounts of the settlement (Joshua), early tribal life (Judges), and the later monarchy (Samuel, Kings) and fashioned and edited this material, giving it a very distinctive stamp. This editorial imprint is expressed succinctly in Deuteronomy: "You must therefore be careful to do as the LORD your God has commanded you; you shall not turn to the right or to the left. You must follow exactly the path that the LORD your God has commanded you, so that you may live, and that it may go well with you, and that you may live long in the land that you are to possess" (Deut 5:32–33). It is a message as clear as it is brief. Obedience to the Lord will bring life and prosperity; disobedience brings only devastation and death.

As part of the Pentateuch or the books of Moses, Deuteronomy belongs with the four books that precede it. As the moral barometer pointing to Israel's subsequent history, it belongs with the books that follow it. The historical books clearly bear the stamp of Deuteronomy, a fact evident both in content and style. It should be noted that there are other books that record periods of the history of the Old Testament, which are not connected with the deuteronomistic school. These are 1–2 Chronicles, Ezra, Nehemiah, and 1–2 Maccabees.

JOSHUA

When it comes to recounting the actual occupation of Canaan, we encounter remarkable accomplishments as well as some rather bewildering complications. The book of Joshua is simple and direct in its account of what occurs. The heroic centerpiece is a "new Moses" figure; even Joshua's entrance into Canaan in crossing the Jordan is patterned on the Red Sea experience at the time of the Exodus. The appearance of dry land facilitates the crossing (c. 3).

The conquest of the country (cc. 4–11) is carried out in three separate campaigns: one in the central part of the country, followed by one to the south and then one to the north. This is followed by a detailed list of all the kings conquered (c. 12). The major part of the book's second half deals with the allotment of the land to the Israelite tribes (cc. 13–21). If the reader's credibility is rather strained at this remarkable turn of events, with many cities and regions not even mentioned in the conquest, such is perfectly understandable. Everything seems to have occurred in record time and with little opposition.

This brings us face to face with some of the historical problems in Joshua. In fact, the idea of a complete elimination of the Canaanite population from north to south is opposed to what the book of Judges states in its first three chapters. After Joshua's death, there were numerous Canaanite town and cities still intact and there were regular forays against this native population. To understand Joshua then, we have to stand back and take a broad look. Did the Hebrews eventually make the land their own? About that, there is no doubt, although traditions retained by various tribes show that this happened over a considerable period of time in a long series of military exploits. Moreover, some cities were left intact and were eventually aggregated to the Hebrew community by treaty, intermarriage, or other means.

However, there are further problems in determining the accuracy of some of the conquests that Joshua is said to have made. Some of the cities that are allotted to the tribes (cc. 13–22) were not made subject to the Hebrews at this early period. Joshua had conquered none of the cities on the coast or in the central hill country, or even an important city like Shechem. The Jebusites were not expelled from Jerusalem until the time of David. In short, the biblical evidence itself indicates that at the time of Joshua's death, there was still much to be done.

There is the further question of some of the sites indicated as occupied by Joshua's troops. Even there, archeological findings present some difficult questions. The fabled walls of Jericho that fell at the sound of Israelite horns were not in existence nor was Jericho itself standing from 1400 to 1200 BC (cc. 7–8). There is no record of a standing city at the time of the Hebrew settlement in the late thirteenth century. It may well be that the impressive ruins of Jericho suggested the destruction that became part of the record. That there was turmoil in Canaan during this period is amply attested; both Hazor and Lachish were violently destroyed. There is no reason to doubt that Israel entered Canaan in the late thirteenth century and had successful military exploits. Their acquisition of the land evidently came about in different ways, as has been previously suggested, and in the course of a century the country to a great extent became theirs. The account of how this occurred has been idealized in the Joshua narrative, which presents a very rapid conquest. What is being underscored in this *religious* history is the power and fidelity of Yahweh, who had promised the land and ultimately fulfilled the promise. That the facts are made to bend in the telling is not done to deceive but to highlight the power and commitment of a God who is above all others.

In this gradual takeover, some groups moved in one direction while others followed a different course. In Joshua, separate traditions and sources have been joined. Some impressive military victories were part of that tradition. At the same time, there was a gradual assimilation of segments of the local population. Some of these may well have been people related to the Hebrews who had never taken part in the Egypt experience. In other instances there may well have been local revolts against wealthy landowners, which found common cause in the efforts of the Hebrews. What is clear is that the history of the occupation was not unilinear but multifaceted. Nonetheless in the last analysis it became the land of God's people.

Joshua 5–6, 20–21. Compare this with **Judges 1**

This same idealization is present in the chapters that deal with land distribution (cc. 13–21). It is an allocation that best fits the time of the monarchy (ca. 1000 BC). In Joshua, the tribes are presented as unified and coherent, with the respective territories carefully cordoned off. The reality was not that neat. The social demography from early times was broken down into families, clans, and tribes; people were seen as related by blood or by simple assimilation. They became identified with an eponymous ancestor, identified with one of the twelve sons of Jacob. The same would obtain if it happened that Pennsylvanians were identified in some way ancestrally with William Penn. For Israelites, this form of tribal identity with the patriarchs strengthened ties with the broader country and was undoubtedly a form of recognition. The same obtains today as people identify strongly with a country or a region that is seen as part of their patrimony, but it was even stronger for the ancients for whom relationships to people and land were a vital part of life. Eventually there were fixed boundaries for the Israelite tribes, even though most of the inhabitants may have had no direct link with the eponymous namesake.

In reading the book of Joshua we also realize that the notion of *herem*, or total destruction in waging war, is distant from our way of thinking. In taking a city, the Israelites were often enjoined to destroy an entire population, often including material holdings. Our sensitivities find abhorrent the destruction of noncombatants in war, although modern warfare has been guilty of the same in more than one instance. It is necessary to realize that the ancients saw evil as an infectious reality; it had to be rooted out and destroyed in its totality. To do so indicated the superiority of one deity over others. If Yahweh was author of all good, distinguished from any form of evil, and powerful as well, then malice had to be eradicated completely. It is unlikely that *herem* was ever carried out as ruthlessly and completely as described, but its very expression is a theological statement more than anything else.

Joshua 8

The best summary of Joshua is found in the book's final chapters (cc. 23–24), In Moses-like fashion, Joshua enunciates the deuteronomistic teaching (c. 23). God had given the people the land. Enemies had been vanquished. There must now be a response of unwavering fidelity. No false gods. No false worship. No intermarriage or intermingling with other peoples. Fidelity would spell success and infidelity, disaster. It is a speech that Joshua could not have made if the victory had not been complete, at least in a theological and literary sense.

In the final chapter of the book (c. 24), there is the ceremony of covenant renewal at Shechem. Elements of the treaty form, discussed previously, are seen in the account. There is a lengthy recall of past history and benefits (vv. 2–12). The people are asked to make their choice (vv. 14f) and three times they opt in favor of the covenant (vv. 18–24). After consigning the agreement to writing, a memorial stone commemorates the event (vv. 25–28).

As the past is recalled, there is no mention of the Sinai covenant. Perhaps this is because the covenant was viewed not as something of the past but a formal act taking place *today*. This was a new generation; many of those present had been in no way connected with Sinai. If the conjecture is true that inhabitants of Canaan were brought into the covenant relationship for the first time, then Sinai was clearly *now*. If the Sinai generation was then dead, then there was the question of new stock, united at that moment with those who either had not gone into Egypt or were being assimilated into the community for the first time. It is this chapter more than any other in Joshua that casts a strong light on the deuteronomist's intention in underscoring the importance of covenant fidelity in explaining the conquest, as well as the setbacks, so central to the book as a whole.

Joshua 24

JUDGES

The book of Judges is the record of Hebrew life from the late thirteenth to the late eleventh century. It portrays a very distinctive type of settled life centered around the different tribes; although there were stirrings in the direction of centralization, the individual tribes were much to the fore. Leadership sprang from charismatic personalities who were known as judges and twelve of whom are cited in the book that bears their title. Six of these have tales recounted of their exploits, accounts that were largely retained in tribal circles. Six other are little more than mentioned; they remain practically unknown.

The judges, with few exceptions, did not exercise the role of judicial magistrates, as the word would be understood today. They executed justice in a different way. They were instruments of God's fidelity to his people in difficult circumstances and "judged" Israel in the sense that they brought Yahweh's justice to bear in situations where human injustice had taken control in regional or tribal calamity.

The deuteronomists have fashioned these narratives around a single basic theme: sin, punishment, repentance, and deliverance. The people are guilty of some serious separation from Yahweh's will; they are made to suffer for their wrongdoing; they recognize their waywardness and turn to God seeking forgiveness; a judge arises as their deliverer from affliction.

As we have mentioned earlier, the early chapters of the book (cc. 1–3) treat, in what is probably a quite accurate way, the early occupation of Canaan by the Hebrews. There is mention made of the foreign peoples who remained in the country after the conquest. It was a slow process of domination and assimilation until the land was finally theirs. Foreign deities play no small part with the cult of Baal, the principal god of the Canaanite pantheon, much to the fore. He was accompanied by three prominent goddesses, Asherah, Anat, and Astarte. Worship of these deities centered around fertility of family, livestock, and land and took place on the "high places" or hills throughout the country, with a ritual that included sexual relations with cult prostitutes. In this way a person honored the gods and assured fertility for himself and his holdings. The fertility cult proved to be a great temptation to the Hebrews whose moral principles were of a totally different order. There are relics of the problem sprinkled throughout the Old Testament, but it was especially prominent in the early years of occupation.

For our present purposes, we will look at the activities of a few of the judges and must leave to the reader the fascinating exploration of the others. Here we will treat of Deborah and Samson, and in a different context for other reasons, the son of Gideon, Abimelech.

Deborah is the only woman judge, being both a civil magistrate as well as a charismatic leader (cc. 4–5). At one point the Israelites are threatened by the Canaanite king Jabin and his military general Sisera. Deborah lived in the central hill country of Ephraim. The Israelite leader Barak is engaged to fight the Canaanites but prevails on Deborah to accompany him. Deborah agrees after adding the unpleasant footnote: the victorious outcome will mean that "the LORD will sell Sisera into the hand of a woman" (4:9). The forces of Sisera were no match for Barak, who handily overcomes them, with Deborah very much in command. Sisera escapes on foot and flees to the tent of the Kenite Heber. His wife Jael invites the distraught warrior into her tent and then, while he sleeps, drives a tent peg through his head. God had clearly acted on behalf of his people, with the victory obtained through the work of two women.

The prose narrative is followed by a poetic recounting (c. 5) in what is one of the earliest examples of Hebrew poetry. It contains strong cosmic imagery and a citing of many of the tribes of Israel. The prowess of Deborah is sung together with that of Jael in taking vengeance on Sisera. Striking dramatic irony characterizes the final verses as Sisera's mother awaits at the window of her home for the victorious return of her son and cannot understand the reason for his delay (5:28–31).

Judges 4–5

Samson is undoubtedly one of the Bible's most colorful and unprecedented characters (cc. 12–16). His story has reached filmland and the operatic stage. Consecrated to the Lord from birth, he is given the task of liberating his people from the Philistine threat, the people who had settled on the Mediterranean coast close to the time that the Hebrews had entered Canaan. At the time of his consecration, in keeping with the Nazirite tradition, his hair was to remain uncut. His strength was the stuff of legend; he was capable of dismembering a young lion. His prowess, however, is attributed to the *"spirit of the LORD"* (14:6), an invisible and invincible force, like the wind, that enabled a person to accomplish feats far beyond his or her native abilities.

Samson marries a Philistine woman, and, when her father gives her to another man, the spurned husband's fury is unleashed and he destroys the man's grain by sending foxes with firebrands on their tails through the fields. When he is taken prisoner, Samson easily breaks the ropes that hold him. Repeatedly he outsmarts and defeats his opponents. It is only the wiles of a beautiful Philistine women, Delilah, that proves his downfall. When he confides to her, after considerable coaxing, that his strength lies in his long hair, she tricks him into being shorn; he is easily taken captive and blinded. Yet Yahweh remains at his side. When the Philistines are celebrating in the temple of their god Dagon, Samson is summoned for the amusement of his enemies. He asks Yahweh for strength and then moves against the temple pillars. The entire structure falls on him and the celebrating Philistines.

Samson is no model of virtue in any sense, Hebrew or otherwise. One scholar has referred to him as "that wenching lout." However, he acted at a critical moment in the interests of his people and vindicated the autonomy of the one God. He is not meant to be a paragon of virtue, but, with all his weaknesses, he remained a witness to the justice of God on behalf of his people.

Judges 13–16

Abimelech, Son of Gideon (8:29—9:56)

This man stands out for a single reason. He was not a judge but a king in a very limited sense. He ruled only at Shechem and for a relatively short period of time, although his story represents the beginnings of a monarchical sentiment among the Israelites, a sentiment that will come to the fore in the subsequent books of Samuel.

Abimelech was one of the seventy sons of Gideon. Not content with being one of a herd, his ambitions soon got the best of him. He eliminated any possible claimant to leadership by killing all of his brothers, save one, Jotham. Abimelech makes an impassioned plea to the citizens of Shechem to name him king, yet is opposed by his single remaining brother. In his address to the citizenry, Jotham speaks of the selection of Abimelech as akin to the choice of a buckthorn bush in a verdant forest. However, Abimelech is selected and rules locally for a three-year period. It was a disastrous reign, marked by ruthless atrocities. He fights off opposition by killing in a merciless fashion. Ironically, he is felled by a falling millstone thrown by a woman, and is mercifully dispatched by his armor bearer.

Nothing about Abimelech augurs well for the future of kingship. This is all part of the deuteronomistic problematic regarding the kings of Israel and Judah. This will appear later in the books of Samuel and Kings. Whatever was to be said in its favor, the move toward monarchy, especially in the early days, represented a serious compromise in the country's basic religious allegiance.

Judges 8:24—9:57

We are left with a picture of relative tranquility at the end of Judges, after a series of God given victories. The autonomy of tribal life is a keynote feature. Again the dominant note through-out is that of fidelity as bringing blessing, whereas waywardness, especially in the case of idolatry, brings disaster. Tribal life worked well for a time. There was no felt desire for a king, even though such a sentiment was to be short lived. There is no evidence of a structured city-state unity as was true in the later Greek empire. The basic point of unity was a common belief in the delivering God of the Exodus, and that evidently sufficed.

The Monarchy

1-2 Samuel
1-2 Kings } Deuteronomistic author

VII.

THE EARLY MONARCHY

The period that preceded the rise of the monarchy was one free of major political concerns. It was largely a period of adaptation to a new form of life and new neighbors. There were no major international threats because foreign powers were either consolidating past gains through the strengthening of infrastructures or watching cautiously for any possible danger from without. Even Israel's immediate neighbors were not in a bellicose mood, with the exception of the Philistines who had occupied the coastal region at about the same time as the Hebrew occupation. More remains to be said about these People of the Sea.

Within the country there was a gradual coexistence between the Hebrews and the earlier citizenry. The latter were either being displaced or assimilated, the result being that there was no felt need for a king. Tribal rights were in the ascendancy, and religious sentiment was high that the sovereignty of Yahweh should not be compromised. However, as we saw in the Abimelech narrative, the stirrings were present, and inevitably in the course of time the desire for a king became more pronounced. Sentiments expressed initially in a whisper gradually became more strident. Before treating the monarchical period, we shall take a closer look at the international and national scenes that contributed to the rise of kingship.

THE PHILISTINES

The state of thirteenth- and twelfth-century Palestine cannot be understood apart from the Sea People. This was an invading non-Semitic people that it is believed originated in southern Russia but ended up dominating the Aegean and the Mediterranean. By this time Egypt was no longer a major power; its control of Palestine was largely nominal. It had very limited force to respond to any major attack. The Philistines were a segment of the Sea People; they were effective warriors who had a marked advantage in their bronze and iron weaponry. Ramesses III succeeded in opposing their attempt to take Egypt, but they settled in five major cities on the Palestinian coast— Ashkelon, Ashdod, Gath, Ekron, and Gaza. In fact the name Palestine is derived from the Philistines.

The presence of the Sea People in the vast Near Eastern world tamed any expansionist fervor that might have been present. They defeated the once-powerful Hittites, who then passed from the scene as a threat. The Assyrians had been a major power until after the reign of Tiglath-Pileser I (1114–1076); for some three centuries they remained largely dormant, rising to power again in the ninth century.

The fact is, then, that from the time of the occupation, the Israelites were not threatened by major external forces. They passed from being a nomadic people to a largely agrarian one. They were cultivators of the soil, owners of livestock, and presided over a gradual development in town and city life. Because they had no maritime holdings or ports, their access to international trade was effectively blocked. It was a period that allowed for a process of growth and consolidation. There was no major danger from north, south, or east; the only "thorn in the side" lay to the west in Philistine territory. It was a problem that did not quickly vanish.

With the Sea People effectively controlling the coast, the Israelites were landlocked, a fact that did not augur well for peaceful coexistence. The Philistines were non-Semitic and worshippers of pagan gods, especially the major deity, Dagon. Their ethical code left much to be desired. On the other hand, the Israelites were monotheistic and noniconic, with an exceptionally high code of ethics. The Philistines were warriors, with a metal weaponry largely unmatched in the Near Eastern world. The military force of Israel, although respectable and capable of maintaining a line of defense, was not equipped as was that of its opponent.

An initial reading of First Samuel makes it clear that Philistia was a superior military force. On two occasions they roundly defeated the Israelites, with the defeat at Aphek leaving four thousand men dead (4:1–3). When the ark of the covenant was brought from Shiloh as a protective measure, it was captured by the enemy (c. 4). Only the "power of Yahweh" reversed this trend, but the Philistines never ceased to be a threat and major concern. They spread their tentacles into Israel as far as the central hill country. They effectively prevented the Israelites from making arms (13:19–22). It was this encroachment and accompanying danger that contributed to Israel's promonarchical sentiment. Ironically, it was an atmosphere of relative peace internationally, with only the danger from Philistia nearby, that promoted the selection of Saul as king.

SAMUEL

If he had no other claim on our attention than the fact that two biblical books bear his name, Samuel would be important enough. However, he commands our attention for a variety of reasons. First, he is the main transitional figure between the era of tribal life and the rise of the monarchy. In addition, he is the last of the judges and the emissary of Yahweh in the selection of both Saul and David. The future importance of biblical figures is frequently signaled in the circumstances of their birth, and Samuel is no exception. His ageing parents were childless, but the woman Hannah was resolute and relentless in her prayerful request for a child, especially at the shrine of Shiloh. The couple's prayer is heard with the birth of Samuel, who is dedicated to the Lord and put in priestly care at the sanctuary. He is privileged with divine communication at an early age and emerges again, later in life, as a judge, a man of upright conduct in every respect.

Samuel is also a prophet and a priest. In the latter role he officiates at worship and offers sacrifice for his often beleaguered and troubled citizenry. It is in his role as a prophet, however, that he plays a decisive role in the life of Israel. When the notion of kingship arises, he takes an opposing stand in Yahweh's name, his words forming part of the antimonarchical tradition (1 Sam 8:6–18). He (and Yahweh) acquiesce in the light of the people's persistence but not without sounding important caveats (12:13–25), but his role in the monarchy had just begun. His selection of Saul as king appears in three different accounts or separate traditions, all centering on Saul's rise to prominence (9:1—10:16, 10:17–27, cc. 11–12).

On the occasion of Saul's later misconduct, the prophet is again pressed into service, as he is sent to Bethlehem to designate David as the future king (c. 16). As David rises to prominence, Samuel tends to fade from sight. His death occurs at Ramah, with an outpouring of grief from the country as a whole. He appears only once more, from beyond the grave, when the witch of Endor summons him at Saul's request (c. 28), but he offers little consolation to the aggrieved king.

Samuel stands in the book that bears his name as a steady and stabilizing force. In the face of the Philistine threat, his countrymen were concerned about the lack of stronger centralization. His personal character commanded wide respect as he steered his country through largely uncharted waters. For him the interests of the Lord were always paramount; his wisdom and wise direction resulted in the institutionalization of the monarchy on a solid theological basis. There was to be no absolute monarchy in Israel. Samuel became the literary focal point of both the promonarchical (9:1–10, 16; 11:1–15) and antimonarchical (8:1–22, 10:17–26, 12:1–25) sources. His final support for Saul served as a leaven in the face of considerable opposition. His religious and political contribution in the course of his life was significant. The great irony of Samuel's life is that the kingship that he initially opposed and later supported and Saul whom he designated as God's choice was the king to whom he later brought the message of divine rejection. It was an unusual twist of fate, though as for the prophet himself he lived and died as a faithful representative of his God.

1 Samuel 1, 3, 8, 12

SAUL

Saul's selection as king was as divinely designed as any vocation could be. He was the son of a Benjaminite herdsman to whom Samuel is sent as God's emissary. His ascendancy to power has three plateaus: anointed by Samuel (1 Sam 9:2f), acclaimed at Mizpah (1 Sam 10:17–27), and fully accepted at Gilgal (1 Sam 11:12–14).

His military successes were limited; his troops at one point number six hundred (1 Sam 13:15), but the spirit of the Lord was upon him forcefully (1 Sam 11:6). He succeeded in defeating the Ammonites at Jabesh-gilead (1 Sam 11) and had a major victory against the Philistines at Michmash (1 Sam 13:5—14:6). He regained the hill country from them but never succeeded in completely eliminating the Philistine threat. He also waged war successfully against the Moabites, Edomites, and Amalekites.

Even though he was a dedicated Yahwist and never abandoned his duties as a military leader, it is clear that he is not favored by the deuteronomistic editors. His early rejection by Yahweh is surprising, as are the reasons for it. In one account he offers sacrifice illicitly (1 Sam 13); in the other, he fails to slay completely the Amalekites (1 Sam 15) and is denied forgiveness. All of this is read in the light of David's far more egregious crime for which he is readily forgiven (2 Sam 11–12).

The latter half of the Saul narrative is almost wholly taken up with his hatred and jealousy of David. When this state of mind forces David to become an outlaw, the king spends a disproportionate amount of time tracking him down to kill him. The youth's popularity in the realm was seen as a genuine threat to Saul's position. On the other hand, fighting the Philistines was a matter of far greater importance; yet it was left aside in the interests of Saul's manhunt. All perspective was lost in this unjustified war against a youth who had shown only loyalty to the crown.

David's deep friendship with Saul's son, Jonathan, did not ameliorate the situation. Rather, Saul's fury was turned on his son, with the father unable to comprehend his son's posture of friendship toward a person who endangered his right of succession. Saul died fighting the Philistines; he was beheaded and impaled at Beth-Shan. Only the citizens of Jabesh-gilead, mindful of how Saul had fought on their behalf, claimed his body and provided for a proper burial.

Saul remains always an enigma, the first chosen and the first rejected. Not even David's apotheosis, Saul, the "glory" of Israel (2 Sam 1:19), can erase Yahweh's earlier dictum: "I regret that I made Saul king" (1 Sam 15:11).

1 Samuel 9, 15, 19, 26, 31

DAVID

> "Now these are the last words of David:
> …'Is not my house like this with God?
>> For he has made with me an everlasting covenant,
>> ordered in all things and secure.
> Will he not cause to prosper
>> all my help and my desire?'" (2 Sam 23:1, 5)

In the eyes of the deuteronomist, David is the unsurpassed hero. If Saul's character was cast in shadows, that of David basks in the light of God's favor. So translucent is the presentation that even the failings of David, and they are not insignificant, are presented in the full light of day. The rise of David was as humanly unexpected as it was divinely foreseen. There are three accounts of his ascendancy: Samuel's designation from among the sons of

Jesse of Bethlehem (1 Sam 16:1–13), his selection as a musician to calm Saul's disturbed mental state (16:14–18), and finally his victory over the Philistine warrior Goliath (c. 17). These are diverse traditions that, interestingly enough, highlight David's traditional gifts: divine choice, musician, and warrior. As Saul begins to pass from the scene and David emerges as the favored leader, he quickly exhibits his political skill. Even when an outlaw in his own country, he wages war on behalf of the South when the Negeb was attacked by the Amalekites. When they are defeated, he generously shares the booty with the people of Judah (1 Sam 30).

David was first installed as king of Judah at Hebron (2 Sam 2:2–4). Then turning his attention north, he fought Ishbosheth, Saul's son, overcomes him, and is proclaimed king by the northern tribes. Thus he began a forty-year reign as king of Judah and Israel. The dual allegiance is important; these were separate entities held together only until the end of Solomon's reign. This was never a "seamless garment"; there was division even before David became king, a division that would later reemerge.

The new king's political skill moved in two major directions. First, he kept attention riveted on the Philistines, as he continued to deal with the threat militarily. Second, he wrested the city of Jerusalem from the Jebusites and made it the seat of his government (2 Sam 5). He further consolidated his position by bringing the ark of the covenant to Jerusalem and solemnly installing it there. Jerusalem became both the religious and political center of the country. David would have gone farther in constructing the Temple as well had he not been obstructed by divine intervention. For all of his authentic piety, David was also a skilled political person. He has a strong noble side as well, seen, for example, in his care for Jonathan's son, Meribbaal, whom he installed at court.

The expansion of Israel brought Moab, Edom, and Ammon under his control. He fought the Arameans and quartered his troops in Damascus (2 Sam 8). Never again would Israel see such extension, from the Red Sea in the south to the Euphrates in the north, including all of Transjordan. He had no great bureaucratic concerns; these would come later under Solomon. It is small wonder that David became identified with his country's "finest hour" and sketched broadly the lines of what a future kingdom would be.

One would only have hoped that David would have been as adept at handling his personal and family life. It is the deuteronomist who gives us the account of his adulterous affair with Bathsheba, the wife of Uriah the Hittite, one of his soldiers. What is most unconscionable about this sordid matter was David's decision to kill Uriah after he made his wife pregnant (2 Sam 11). He is severely punished for his malice, having exhibited a serious character flaw. There were other moral blunders along the way, most of them family related. Perhaps because of his own weakness, he is strangely silent in the face of serious problems. His son Amnon rapes his own half sister, and David remains silent. He does nothing, with the result that his son Absalom takes justice into his own hands to avenge the crime. He kills Amnon and again David does nothing. Absalom flees the country, seething with anger against his father. Determined to unseat the king, he plans a revolt—the only one David had to face in his long career. Absalom's forces were no match for the superior army of David. He goes down in defeat and is himself killed in battle. Having failed to mend fences over many years of withdrawal and silence, David is finally touched by tragedy as he gives expression to his sorrow unrestrainedly: "O my son Absalom, my son, my son Absalom! Would I had died instead of you, O Absalom, my son, my son!" (2 Sam 18:33).

David died at an advanced age but not without first conferring succession on his son Solomon, a child by Bathsheba, whose maternal intervention made the succession secure (1 Kgs 2). With all of his failings, his figure is as impressive as Michelangelo's sculpture of the young warrior. In a most impressive chapter of Samuel, Nathan the prophet tells him that he will not built a house (temple) for Yahweh but rather God will build a house (dynasty) for him (2 Sam 7). It is this oracle that is seen as launching the messianic hope in Israel. The name of David will never be lost in history. The Christ to appear centuries later will bear the title "son of David."

1 Samuel 17, 24
2 Samuel 5, 7 -12, 15, 18

THE BOOK OF RUTH

Ruth was the mother of David's grandfather, his own great-grandmother. She lived in the time of the judges, which accounts for the book's ordinary location after the Book of Judges. This short book of four chapters merits our attention because it recounts one of the Bible's most touching stories. A Moabite woman, Ruth married the son of Naomi, a pious Israelite woman, who looked forward anxiously to the birth of a grandchild and the continuation of the family line. Both of her sons died, leaving the daughters-in-law widowed. Fully cognizant of their foreign background, Naomi pleaded with the two young women to return to their home country where their future could be assured. While one woman returns, Ruth does not but rather pledges loyalty and fidelity to her widowed mother-in-law. Ruth then takes up permanent residence with Naomi in Bethlehem.

In the course of time, Ruth meets one of her kinsman, Boaz, who shows exceptional kindness to her as she gleans in his field. Encouraged by Naomi, she presents herself to him as a possible spouse. Their love deepens, and Boaz eventually takes her as his wife. Realizing that Naomi is now left without offspring, Ruth looks forward to her first child, with her mother-in-law's plight much in her mind. When the child Obed is born, the news spreads quickly that a grandson has been born to Naomi.

The story lives as part of the David legend, but it has a domestic beauty all its own. Its strong sense of family, faith, and loyalty give it a warm and lasting quality. It does more than point to David's non-Israelite background. In shedding the positive light that it does on Ruth, it is a story of God's embrace of all people in a love that knows no boundaries. She lived much of her life outside the land and the faith of Israel, yet she exhibits some of its finest qualities.

Ruth 1–4

SOLOMON

David's son by Bathsheba, Solomon, like his father, ruled Israel for forty years. He was renowned for his wisdom, which is understandable only up to a point. He requested the gift from God and his desire was fulfilled. An interesting example of this wisdom is cited in the story of the child claimed by two women. Solomon resolved the issue by deciding to divide the child in two parts. The true mother opposes the solution; the case is solved; and the wisdom of Solomon amply attested (1 Kgs 3). As is more than evident, however, many features of Solomon's long reign were short on wisdom.

Solomon's major accomplishment was to consolidate the gains made by his father. He divided the north into provinces with their own administration and levied an annual tax on each for the support of the court. In addition, he introduced military conscription and recruited laborers for public works. His defensive posture was improved by strengthening the charioteers and he greatly increased the number of chariots and horses. Trade and commerce had not been a dominant feature of Israel's economy; they improved greatly under Solomon, who saw the wealth attached to being situated on a major trade route, with Egypt to the south and Phoenicia and Aram to the north. In this way he built up mineral resources and other commodities not manufactured at home. For trade afar, he built a seaport on the Gulf of Aqaba with the help of the seafaring Phoenicians.

From a biblical perspective, Solomon's major contribution was the construction of the Temple in Jerusalem. It was impressive by every standard, a worthy dwelling place of the invisible God. Not to be overlooked is the construction of his own palace, considerably larger and more grandiose than the Temple. It took

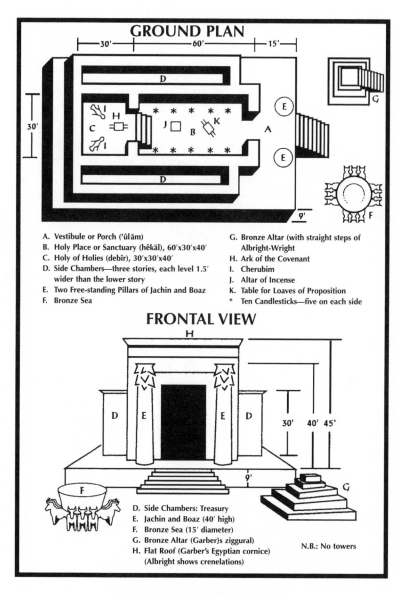

GROUND PLAN

30'   60'   15'

30'

D

C   H   J   B   K   A

D

E

E

G

9'

F

A. Vestibule or Porch ('ûlām)
B. Holy Place or Sanctuary (hêkāl), 60'x30'x40'
C. Holy of Holies (debîr), 30'x30'x40'
D. Side Chambers—three stories, each level 1.5' wider than the lower story
E. Two Free-standing Pillars of Jachin and Boaz
F. Bronze Sea

G. Bronze Altar (with straight steps of Albright-Wright
H. Ark of the Covenant
I. Cherubim
J. Altar of Incense
K. Table for Loaves of Proposition
* Ten Candlesticks—five on each side

FRONTAL VIEW

H

D   E   E   D

30' 40' 45'

9'

F

G

D. Side Chambers: Treasury
E. Jachin and Boaz (40' high)
F. Bronze Sea (15' diameter)
G. Bronze Altar (Garber}s ziggural)
H. Flat Roof (Garber's Egyptian cornice)
   (Albright shows crenelations)

N.B.: No towers

Floor Plan of the Jerusalem Temple

111

thirteen years to build, to the Temple's seven (1 Kgs 7). The palace was adorned with the finest Lebanon cedar and imported luxurious appointments. For the people as a whole, nothing matched the Temple in importance; it served as a national focal point and a source of cohesion. Its dedication stood out as one of the country's most historic moments (1 Kgs 8). The actual layout of the Temple will be discussed in the next chapter.

Had we only to consider the first 10 chapters of 1 Kings, the evaluation of Solomon's reign would be very positive, but the deuteronomists—always forced to honesty at a given moment—close their treatment of Solomon with a ponderous listing of his failures (1 Kgs 11). Serious enough was the fact that he had "seven hundred wives and three hundred concubines," but they had been selected from foreign realms. This violated the Hebrew law against mixed marriages; in Solomon's case it could only be considered flagrant abuse. He then catered to the religious tastes of his foreign household by building shrines to the idols Chemosh and Molek and involving himself in their worship as well. Much of this occurred as Solomon's reign drew to a close. What had begun so impressively ended on a decidedly negative note. Dissatisfaction within the country made it ripe for division, which in fact occurred with Solomon's death. Despite his failures, his place in history was assured, especially with the building of the Temple, giving him a special place of revered remembrance.

1 Kings 3, 5–7, 11

VIII.

THE WORSHIP OF ISRAEL

"Hear, O Israel: The LORD is our God, the LORD alone.
You shall love the LORD your God with all your heart,
and with all your soul, and with all your might." (Deut 6:4–5)

"O LORD, I love the house in which you dwell,
  and the place where your glory abides." (Ps 26:8)

Nothing was to take priority in Israel over recognition of the God who had brought his people from bondage to freedom. It was a recognition found principally in worship. No discussion of the history and life of the Hebrew people is complete without turning to their life of prayer. As the Old Testament makes clear, cult evolved over a period of many years. Here we can give only an overview. Sequentially we shall look at the Temple, the central place of worship, and the major Israelite feasts. Then we shall turn to sacrifice and religious personnel. Finally, attention will be directed to the psalms, the cultic prayer book, still viewed as a major source of prayer in Judaism and Christianity.

THE TEMPLE

Solomon's Temple was not exceptionally large by modern standards. By the standards of the time, however, it was larger than equivalent sanctuaries in other countries and was particularly impressive for its exquisite and costly furnishings. The Temple was located on Mt. Zion (Sion), the center of Jerusalem. Before its construction, worship was decentralized and held in sanctuaries located in various parts of the country, where sacrifice could be offered and priests were in attendance. The danger of syncretism arose from contact with pagan worship offered by the earlier inhabitants of Canaan. This autonomy of the local sanctuaries became a threat to authentic Yahwistic faith and continued until the cultic reform of king Josiah in the seventh century. At that time Jerusalem became the center of worship, and all major feasts were to be celebrated there.

The Temple was roughly a little over one hundred feet in length and thirty-five feet in width. It was made up of three major areas: a *porch* at the front entrance, which led through an elaborate entrance way into a large chamber known as the *Holy Place*, a room about sixty feet in length, which contained an incense altar, ten golden lampstands, and a table where the unleavened bread offering, known as the "showbread" was kept. This room in turn led to the *Most Holy Place* (Holy of Holies), a perfect cube—30x30x30 feet with no windows for light or ventilation. Here it was believed Yahweh dwelt above the ark of the covenant, which was presided over by two winged figures or cherubim, with wings extended. This span served as a throne, or perhaps more accurately, a footstool for the invisible Lord. Only the high priest entered the Most Holy Place on the annual Day of Atonement (Yom Kippur) to offer sacrifice in expiation for the sins of the people.

Outside the Temple was a courtyard with a large bronze tub of water, called The Sea, which provided the water needed for temple ritual. Nearby was the large altar of holocausts where the ordinary animal sacrifices were offered. The Temple entrance was flanked by two large pillars with bowls on top for fire or incense. It is against the background of this Temple layout that much of the priestly legislation of Leviticus is to be understood, such as the sacrifices of Leviticus 1–7.

1 Kings 5–6

THE MAJOR FEASTS

There were numerous feasts observed in Israel over the centuries but the most important of these was the *hag* or *pilgrimage feast*, which originally meant celebration around local sanctuaries but, with the centralization of cult, came to mean celebration in Jerusalem (Deut 16:16). The first of these was *Passover*, which was joined with *Unleavened Bread*, in commemoration of the deliverance from Egypt at the time of the Exodus. It was celebrated in the spring at the time of the barley harvest. The second was *Pentecost* or *Weeks*, celebrated fifty days after Passover in commemoration of the giving of the law on Sinai. Pentecost occurred at the time of the wheat harvest. The third pilgrimage feast was *Booths* or *Tabernacles*, which recalled the period of the desert wandering of the Israelites. It came at the time of the fall harvest and early planting. It was a joyful feast of thanksgiving for the Lord's benefits. *Yom Kippur* or the *Day of Atonement* was an annual feast of mortification and cessation of all work. It was dedicated to the atonement of personal and community sin. The High Priest entered the Most Holy Place at that time and sprinkled the propitiatory or locus of the sacred presence with animal blood.

Leviticus 16, 23

SACRIFICES

There is a detailed list of sacrifices given in Leviticus. The spirit underlying sacrifices was self-deprivation and a certain unity with God.

The *holocaust* (Lev 1:3–17) required the total destruction of calf, sheep, goat, or bird. The animal was to be a male without blemish, completely burned in recognition of divine supremacy, as well as in atonement for sin.

The *grain offering* (Lev 2:1–16) or cereal offering was connected with the harvest at which the first and the best from the fields was offered to Yahweh. This was a popular offering because it was within the means of the poor. The part of the offering not consumed by burning was given to the priest for his support.

The *peace offering* (Lev 3:1–17) was an animal offering (exclusive of birds), which was eaten by the offerers and their families after the offering took place; only a fraction was burned. The eating symbolized unity between God and the offerers. The unblemished animal could be either male or female. The *sin offering* (Lev 4:1—5:13) was offered for some form of inadvertent wrongdoing. It could, for example, be a sacred object tainted in some way by a personal act. An animal was killed and its blood sprinkled on the altar of sacrifice, or if it was a collective sin, on the altar of incense. Inadvertent sin meant that the act in the objective order had set things awry, quite independent of any intentional wrongdoing. The wrong had to be righted, the sin atoned for.

The *guilt offering* (Lev 5:14–20) served as a corrective for personal offenses, whether conscious or not. This is an "over-and-above" type of sacrifice of reparation. After the injustice had been righted (e.g., by paying debts or making retribution), this further act repaired the damage done to God's name. For this sacrifice a ram sheep was called for.

In blood sacrifice, death was the only means to obtain the blood. Life was in the blood and life alone was worthy of God. Because God takes no pleasure in death, this was not the heart of the sacrificial action. Death was present in other sacrifices only as an act of abnegation or total self-denial.

Leviticus 6–7

PRIESTS

The origins of priesthood in Israel remains shrouded in mystery. Because priesthood is primarily related to the offering of sacrifice, the manner in which this ritual was carried out in early times should lead us to some understanding. Although there is some evidence of priests, even levitical priests, being connected with sanctuaries (e.g., Judg 17), sacrifice was also offered by kings

(1 Sam 13; 2 Sam 6:13; 1 Kgs 8:62–64) as well as by the father of a family or head of a clan.

When tribal identity was emphasized after the occupation, the tribe of Levi was invested with the responsibility of priestly service. In the course of time that service became exclusive. The Levites did not receive a land allotment as the other tribes but only a certain number of cities for habitation and sustenance (Lev 20–21). What were the duties of the levites? Initially, offering sacrifice on behalf of the people at local sanctuaries was a primary duty. Changes took place with the construction of the Temple. The levites were all related to Temple service but in different degrees. The high priesthood, as well as priesthood in general, was reserved to a descendant of Aaron (Lev 8–10), although other Temple and sanctuary duties were exercised by the broader category of levites, not connected with the line of Aaron. They were temple assistants of a lesser grade (Num 18). Although this neat distinction would appear to have been clear from the beginning, the facts show that factors other than strict lineage determined who would offer sacrifice. Deuteronomy, for example, does not make the distinction between priests and levites. However, it is clear that by the end of the exile the distinction was strictly enforced. Its beginnings are traceable to the centralization of cult in Jerusalem in the seventh century BC; the resident priests were then in control of sacrificial offering, whereas other religious duties were in the hands of levites, many of them transient and connected with sanctuaries beyond Jerusalem.

The period after the exile brought other changes as well. The destruction of the Temple by the Babylonians in 587 brought about many changes in priestly function. With no temple in the early postexilic period, the scriptures increasingly became the focal point of worship. The Jews gradually became the People of the Book. It was at this time, in the late sixth century, that the books of the Bible were either composed or finally edited. The study and teaching of the law was in the forefront with increasing importance given to the *rabbis* and *scribes*. The synagogue, for teaching and interpreting the faith, came into being. Although cultic priests were members of the community and eventually rendered service in the restored Temple, they were not always the leaders. The centering of religious practice in the home and synagogue gave less emphasis to the traditional priesthood, a development that continued into the Christian era.

Leviticus 8–10, Numbers 18

THE PSALMS

There is one book of the Bible that can be properly called a prayer book. That is the book of Psalms, which is sometimes referred to as the Temple book of prayer. In fact there are some psalms that find their natural setting in temple processions and liturgies. An example of this would be Psalm 24 in which there is an antiphonal exchange upon entering the temple (vv. 7–10). There is some conjecture that such psalms were connected with a suggested Enthronement of Yahweh ceremony. Such remains conjecture but there is no doubt that many psalms have a strong liturgical character. Although the psalms clearly reflect the Jewish faith, they are integral to Christian belief as well. One need but think of the Liturgy of the Hours and the Responsorial Psalm in the daily Mass or the many wake services that include Psalm 23.

The psalms, numbered as 150, are divided into five books like the Torah (1–41, 42–72, 73–89, 90–106, 107–150). King David, a gifted musician, was at one time thought to have composed the entire collection, a position that has been abandoned today. It is now realized that the psalms grew out of the worship of Israel over many centuries. Some clearly portray a period of history, such as Psalm 126, wherein the people are returning from exile in the mid- to late-sixth century. However, because of the generic character of much of the psalter, it is difficult, if not impossible, to pinpoint the time of composition with any degree of accuracy. For some time features, the centrality of the temple or developing theological perspectives offer a key to dating.

Types of Psalm

Over the last century biblical commentators identified the genre or type of the psalms and then grouped them into various classified headings. These are hymns of praise and lament and thanksgiving; as well as wisdom, royal, and historical psalms. As a general norm, the various categories are characterized by basic structures that are readily recognizable.

Hymns of Praise

Many psalms fall into this category as they center on the praise of God for his many favors. They begin with an invocation calling for a posture of praise, such as "Praise the Lord" or "Sing to the Lord." This is followed by the body of the psalm explaining the "why" of praise, such as blessings received and the beauty of creation. Finally, there is a conclusion that either repeats the call to praise or contains a blessing. Examples will make the genre clear.

Psalms 8, 29, 33, 149

The Lament

This is the prayer of the sufferer. The distress may be physical, mental, or moral; the cry is one of utter dependency on God's help. Some laments are individual; others, communal or national. Because there was not a strict adherence to structure in every instance, we admit that the classical structure does not fit in every case. It consists of a cry to God for help, followed by a description of the misfortune, a further cry for help and expression of repentance, and finally a note of confidence in God's protective care.

In understanding the lament, it is important to remember that in Israel there was no clear notion of an afterlife, only a shadowy existence in the underworld known as Sheol. The latter bore no resemblance to life as it was known. Thus, a prayer for a restoration to health meant regaining life and avoiding death, which was a total separation from all that was good, including

God himself. The second point to be remembered is that suffering and sin were intimately united. Pain came as a result of wrongdoing, whether conscious or not. Although this belief was contested by the Bible itself (e.g., Job), it remained in possession through most of Hebrew history. It explains the often desperate cry of the lament.

Psalms 5, 35, 51, 61 (individual laments)
Psalms 60, 74, 80 (community laments)

Thanksgiving Hymns

Hymns of thanksgiving have a basically simple structure. There is an opening burst of gratitude to God, followed by the reason for it, such as the description of a past personal or communal misfortune. This may be recovery from an illness or some personal misfortune, the forgiveness of sin, or deliverance after a national calamity. The closing is a repeated expression of thanks.

Psalms 30, 32, 66

Wisdom Psalms

These are clearly related to the didactic character of the Old Testament Wisdom literature. They were probably related originally to a teaching setting rather than to a cultic one and only gradually incorporated into the psalter. They are characterized by the *mashal* or proverb form, that is, "happy are they...." They use the antithetical form or contrast, such as playing off the bad against the good. They are primarily concerned with teaching people how to live in a way that reflects God himself. Their similarity to the teaching found, for example, in the book of Proverbs is clear.

Psalms 37, 49

Further classifications of the psalms are made according to content or setting, pointing to their life situation or *sitz-im-leben*. Some center on the king (Pss 2, 18) or Mt. Zion as the seat of the Temple (Pss 46, 48).

What makes the psalms distinctive is their ability to embrace every human emotion. The modern reader may have difficulty in relating to the Hebrew mindset or the historical situation being described. It is not necessary to allegorize the psalms, giving each feature a contemporary meaning. It is far better to read the psalm in its entirety, grasping the psalmist's underlying sentiment, and then relate that to one's life today. We suffer and rejoice, are grateful and disappointed, just as the ancients were. We have all experienced God's loving care as well as tragedy in the course of our life. Mt. Zion for us has become the church. Our lives give relevance to the multifaceted sentiments of the psalms. This makes of the psalter a timeless prayer book.

IX.

THE DIVIDED KINGDOM
AND THE AGE OF PROPHECY

It was in the time of Rehoboam, Solomon's son, that the kingdom divided into North and South. The rupture was not totally unforeseen, given that the seeds of separation had been present from the earliest days of the monarchy; there were long standing differences capable of erupting at any point. Saul's origins had been in the North. When he was replaced by the South's David, there was already some dissension in the ranks. It was the policies of Solomon, however, that brought everything to a head, a fact attested to in 1 Kings 11. The North had felt badly repressed and unrecognized, and Rehoboam, announcing that he intended to continue his father's policies, did nothing to alleviate the pain. The ten Northern tribes opted for secession and chose Jeroboam as their king. To offset the religious allegiance given Jerusalem, Jeroboam made Bethel and Dan central sanctuaries in the North, adorning them with calves of gold to represent Yahweh (1 Kgs 12:26–32).

The deuteronomist is our principal source for the history of both kingdoms. Although there is an evident bias in D's recording of history, it is matched by the strongly pro-Judah bent of the priestly books of Chronicles. The history of the deuteronomist centers mainly on the kings who ruled the two kingdoms, the criterion of whose success hinged wholly on fidelity to Yahweh and the covenant.

The kingdom of Israel lasted two hundred years and ended with the Assyrian invasion in 722 BC. Judah lasted about 340 years,

THE DIVIDED KINGDOM

PREEXILIC KINGS
922–587 BC

ISRAEL (Northern Kingdom)	JUDAH (Southern Kingdom)
922–722 BC	922–587 BC
Jeroboam	Rehoboam
Nadab	Abijah
Baasha	Asa
Elah	Jehoshaphat
Zimri	Jehoram/Joram
Omri	Ahaziah
	Athaliah
Ahab	Jehoash/Joash
Ahaziah	
Jehoram/Joram	
	Amaziah
Jehu	Azariah/Uzziah
Jehoahaz	
Joash/Jehoash	
	Jotham
Jeroboam II	Ahaz
Zechariah	Hezekiah
Shallom	Manasseh
	Amon
Menahem	Josiah
Pekahiah	Jehoahaz
Hoshea	Jehoiakim
Destruction of Samaria	Jehoiachin
	Zedekiah
	Destruction of Jerusalem

until the time of the Babylonian exile in 586 BC. Israel was much more extensive geographically with its ten tribes and its capital, Samaria. The South had only Judah with Jerusalem its capital. The North had less political stability with nine dynasties in its short history; whereas Judah, with its longer history and more kings, had one dynasty only.

The deuteronomist used a number of sources, which he mentions in Kings, for example, "the Book of the Annals of the Kings of Judah" (2 Kgs 14:19–29). In the editor's eyes the heroes are few indeed. Most kings are written off as failures because of "the evil they had done in God's eyes." Only two kings of Judah receive honorable mention, Hezekiah (715–687) and Josiah (640–609), both of whom were reformers. With a lack of moral leadership from the throne, such had to come from another quarter, and this devolved to a great extent upon the prophets.

PROPHECY

The prophet or *nabi* signified etymologically one called by God. In Greek this became *prophetes* or God's spokesperson. It had its early exponents as far back as the Pentateuch, wherein the pagan prophet Balaam was called on to curse the Israelites (Num 23–24). We have already seen an early proponent in Samuel, who fearlessly addressed king or commoner. Later there was Nathan who served in David's court and delivered God's message in good times and bad. He promised David a lasting dynasty (2 Sam 7) and also condemned him for the seduction of Bathsheba (2 Sam 12).

Early bands of prophets appeared throughout the country in the early years of Israelite occupation. These were generally "ecstatic prophets," characterized by states of frenzy or trances, even stripping off their clothes, while communicating with the deity. Saul himself was at one point found in this ecstatic state, giving rise to the question as to whether he too might be a member of the prophets' band (1 Sam 10:5–12, 19:23–24). Even though these were forerunners of the classical prophets, the latter

Elijah

do not ordinarily manifest these unusual characteristics. The prophet Amos is at pains to distinguish himself from such prophetic groups (Amos 7:14).

THE CONSCIENCE OF ISRAEL

The Preliterary Prophets

The prophets of Israel in the classical sense were people who are presented as receiving a very distinctive call from God. They spoke in God's name in addressing the spiritual needs of the people. They were not primarily predictors of the future but commentators on the present. This is not to say that there was no future component to their oracles; there certainly was, but their primary concern is with the prevailing situation. They did not live in a state of prophetic rapture. From the evidence it can be said that they led normal lives until that moment when they realized that "the Word of the Lord came" to them. The prophetic psychology involved some sort of insight into a revealed truth that then found expression in a personal way, such as figures of speech

125

and symbolic actions. The institution evolved in Israel passing from the nonwriting prophets—as Elijah and Elisha—to those whose oracles were written either by the prophets themselves or later authors. It can be said, however, that the beginnings of classical prophecy are found in the two celebrated prophets of the North, Elijah and Elisha.

Elijah John the baptist

The Elijah stories (1 Kgs 17–21) have all the features of heroism and the exceptional, with the result that many authors today see them as legends. The prophet's existence is not questioned nor is the fact that he was a divine emissary who was seen as a wonder-worker. However, in the course of time the stories of Elijah and Elisha outstrip the personalities in taking on many accretions, and what is clear is that in the midst of compromising conduct on the part of royal officials, the prophets clearly enunciate and uphold the prerogatives of Yahweh.

Elijah lived in the Northern Kingdom during the reign of king Ahab. The king had a pagan wife, Jezebel, a devotee of the god Baal and a powerful antagonist of the Elijah cycle. The central story in the Elijah cycle finds the prophet in deadly contest with the Canaanite prophets of Baal. When Elijah asks his pagan counterparts to invoke their god to ignite the fire for the sacrificial offering, he assures them that he will ask the same of Yahweh. When Baal fails to answer, his prophets are roundly mocked. When Elijah calls upon Yahweh, the sacrifice is consumed together with everything in its environs (1 Kgs 18). The piece is reflective of the ongoing polemic against Baalism in Israel.

At Yahweh's direction, Elijah brings a drought on the country (1 Kgs 17) and then foretells the arrival of rain just as readily (1 Kgs 18). His final charge is to replace the king of Israel (Ahab with Jehu), the king of Damascus (Hazael with Ben-hadad), and to name Elisha as his successor (1 Kgs 19:15–16). When Ahab, with Jezebel's assistance, forcibly takes a man's vineyard, as part of his family inheritance, Elijah moves against the injustice, promising disaster for the king and his wife (1 Kgs 21). After designating Elisha his successor, the prophet is carried heavenward in a flaming chariot, leading to the later belief that he would one day return (2 Kgs 2:11).

1 Kings 18–19, 21

Elisha *woodstock*

The Elisha cycle (2 Kgs 2–9) presents a man of a different type than his predecessor. Even though he inherits the spirit of Elijah (2 Kgs 2:15), he is not as rustic and to a considerable extent takes care of the latter's unfinished business. He sees that Hazael succeeds to Ben-hadad in Damascus (2 Kgs 8:7–15). He then sees that Jehu is anointed king to replace Ahab; Jehu then "out-Ahabs" Ahab in killing all of Ahab's family. To illustrate his opposition to Baal worship, Jehu slaughters a large number of cult worshipers (2 Kgs 10:18–27). All of this totally discredits Jehu in the deuteronomist's eyes.

Through it all, even with some puzzling conduct and wanton political bloodshed, Elisha bore the mantle of Elijah and walked in the path of an uncompromising Yahwism.

2 Kings 2, 4–5, 9

The Classical or Literary Prophets

Thus far the prophets have directed their oracles to royalty or to some specific group. Their words are recorded as part of the prophet's story but not because of their independent value. With the classical prophets the picture changes. They are commonly listed as twelve minor and four major prophets, although this is a listing that needs some qualification, a point that will be discussed later. In most instances we know little or nothing about their individual lives, much less than was the case with the preliterary prophets. They are situated in historical periods when little moral leadership emanated from the royal palace or the priestly sanctuary. For this reason the classical prophets can be termed "the conscience of Israel."

What the later prophets shared with their predecessors was an endowment of the "spirit of the Lord," an empowering invisible force like the wind, which enabled them to speak and act in a way beyond and above any human capability. What they spoke was not their own insight or conjecture but a divinely revealed grasp of the mind of God. These prophets are *literary* in the sense that their oracles were consigned to writing either by them or later followers because of their inherent permanent value. Sometimes, under inspiration, their original teaching was amplified or added to by disciples or followers, who actualized the earlier vision. The prophet's work is twice reinforced: it flows initially from a revealed insight into God's plan and then, in ultimately being consigned to sacred books, it shares in inspiration as well.

In a book of this type it is impossible to treat all of the prophets. However, we shall look at those who are considered as having made a striking contribution, including the major prophets, Isaiah, Jeremiah, and Ezekiel.

Amos

A shepherd and vinedresser from Tekoa in Judah, Amos makes a clear statement that he belongs to no professional group of prophets in the traditional sense (7:14). His prophetic mission took him to Israel where he preached a message more terrifying than consoling in its content. Jeroboam II (786–746) was the Northern king during a period of relative tranquility and economic growth. This had only widened the gap between rich and poor; religious practice, when not idolatrous, had been relegated to a second place. Amos made his appearance at the major sanctuary at Bethel where his prophecies of doom led Amaziah the priest, at the king's behest, to order him off the premises (7:10–13). There is no indication that the threat had any effect on the prophet.

Amos is a rustic type, more accustomed to rural ways than the "high life" of the city. His images are colorful and earthy, as he delivers oracles that are full of violence and bloodshed. He

128

spares no one on any level of society (7:7–9, 8:1–3, 9:1–4). He does not speak explicitly of covenant and law, but they are concepts that underlie everything he says. He is particularly concerned with the wealthy class who disregard and even maltreat their less-fortunate coreligionists. They sell people into slavery for a pittance (2:6). Rich women wallow in their luxury while their husbands oppress the disadvantaged (4:1–3). Merchants cannot wait for religious celebrations to end so they can return to their cheating and dishonest ways (8:5f). Religious practice has lost its meaning; it is but a veneer, an attempt to bribe the Lord. How can worship have meaning in the midst of injustice? (5:21–26).

For Amos the end is only a question of time. This is true for Israel as well as neighboring nations because Yahweh is the God of all peoples. His wrath is directed against Aram, Philistea, Tyre, Edom, Ammon, and Moab. As this litany unfolds, Israel and Judah can take no delight that they appear last on the list (cc. 1–2). Clearly, Israel is the focal point here because of its multiple sins: social injustice, pagan cultic prostitution, and its attempt to silence those who speak God's word.

As Amos preaches, the threat of Assyrian invasion looms large on the horizon. Within twenty years Israel would be no more. The images are graphic: panic with no place to run for escape (2:14f), property destroyed (3:12), finding an escape route is to face an even greater danger (5:19). It is useless to pray for the Day of the Lord because it will be one of darkness, not of light (5:18). The language of Amos is dire almost to an extreme, which may explain why a later editor felt it necessary to add a final note of hope (9:8b–15). The book has a permanent relevance, in that many of its problems have a very contemporary ring. As the "prophet of social justice," Amos merits the title today more than ever.

Amos 1–2, 7–9

Hosea

A contemporary of Amos, Hosea lived in the North and carried out his calling in that region. His dates range roughly from

745 to 722 BC. This means that he witnessed much the same scene as Amos during the reign of Jeroboam II: prosperity, moral laxity, social injustice—but he also lived through the reign of the remaining kings before the collapse of the North, four of whom were assassinated.

If Amos's oracles betray a rustic, even "hard-shell" personality, Hosea is much the opposite. Although he was not the final editor of the book that bears his name, with its oracles from different periods interspersed with prose sections, there is nonetheless a certain consistency in his prophecies that betray a tender and compassionate person. He was a man of deep emotions, which find expression in his concern for Israel as well as his oracles of punishment.

The book has a very basic structure: the experience of the prophet (cc. 1–3), the consequences of sinful conduct (cc. 4–13), and a call to conversion (c. 14). Whereas Amos says little about a hoped for future, Hosea assures his people of Yahweh's lasting covenant love (hesed) and sees conversion as the key to a brighter future.

The early chapters speak of Hosea's personal marriage experience. He is told to take Gomer, a prostitute, for his wife. Complying with the divine directive, he marries and has three offspring, all bearing symbolic names. The first, Jezreel, recalls the valley where Jehu's revolt against the house of Ahab resulted in widespread bloodshed (2 Kgs 9); the second, Lo-ruhamah ("not pitied"); and the third, Lo-ammi ("not my people"). All three names were fateful omens, pointing to the people's rejection and suffering. What cannot be determined with certainty is whether Hosea's marriage and family is simply symbolic or actually occurred. Or if it did occur, was Gomer a prostitute antecedently or is this a retrojection pointing to what she later became (1:1–3, 3:1)? Regardless of the historical answers, the symbolism is clear enough. In adopting the worship of foreign gods, Israel had prostituted her marriage to Yahweh in a sacred covenant, and the three children of the marriage point to the country's approaching doom, as becomes clear in the subsequent oracles (cf. 2:4–7, 13:1–6). The priests and leaders had failed to provide moral guidance, indeed had sinned as much as the people (4:4—5:7). Not only was there idolatry and cultic abuse but also a wanton disregard for the commandments. "There is no faithfulness or loyalty, and no knowledge of God in the land. Swearing, lying, and murder, and stealing and adultery break out; bloodshed follows bloodshed" (Hos 4:1b, 2).

The *judgment of God* for this infidelity looms large on the horizon. This is clear from the names given the children, as well as the allusions to a return to Egyptian bondage, a code name for Assyrian subjection (8:13f, 9:3). However, it is the strong note of *hope* and *forgiveness*, rooted in Yahweh's undying covenant love, for which Hosea is most remembered. This is best reflected in the celebrated eleventh chapter. In striking maternal imagery, the child Israel is drawn to its mother with fond caresses and loving support. Even though punishment is in the offing, it is not definitive, simply because the mother cannot reject her child. Even if a human decision might want to terminate the relationship, it is not so with Israel's God. "I am God and no mortal" (11:9). With a true sense of conversion, all that was lost will be restored (14:2–9).

Hosea 1–4, 10, 11, 14

Isaiah

The three major prophets of the Old Testament—Isaiah, Jeremiah, and Ezekiel—are so designated because of the length of the books attributed to them. The book of Daniel is often joined with them, even though it is a book of a distinctly different type. Like *Jonah*, it is a book about a prophet, presented as living during the Babylonian exile, the greater part of whose teaching is presented in symbolic or apocalyptic form.

Identified with the kingdom of Judah, Isaiah is probably the best known of the Old Testament prophets. During his life (740–701), he witnessed some of the major events in the history of Israel and Judah. Israel was overrun by the Assyrians in 722 with a significant part of its population deported. Judah narrowly escaped total destruction by Sennacherib of Assyria in 701; only Jerusalem was left intact. If Isaiah had a long life, the book attributed to him had an even longer one. His own oracles were saved and compiled by disciples, who over time constituted an Isaian school and applied the teaching and mind of the prophet to new situations. This led to the composition of new books over the centuries. Today we speak of First Isaiah (cc. 1–39), mostly dating from the time of the prophet himself. Second Isaiah (cc. 40–55) stems from the time of the Babylonian exile in the sixth century, a book that in style and historical references (e.g., Cyrus the Great), postdates the prophet by two centuries. Third Isaiah (cc. 56–66) deals with the period after the exile and a whole new set of problems. At this point, we shall deal only with First Isaiah, recognizing that some parts (e.g., cc. 24–27) come from a later period.

The Political Scene

When Isaiah came on the scene, the future of both the North and South was in jeopardy. In the face of the threat from Assyria, Israel formed an alliance with Syria and wanted Judah to join them. When Ahaz of Judah refused, the two kings planned to move against him. Isaiah informs Ahaz that their move is futile and their days limited. The symbolic name that Isaiah gave his son—"the spoil speeds, the prey hastens"—meant that the end of the northern coalition was in sight (8:1–4). The king is urged to stand tall and trust in Yahweh, but political interests hold sway and he allies himself with Assyria. Judah then became a vassal state. Both Israel and Syria were then conquered by Assyria. Israel fell in 722.

Both Ahaz and his Assyrian counterpart, Tiglath-Pileser, passed from the scene and were followed by Hezekiah of Judah and Sennacherib of Assyria. In 713 Hezekiah formed his own coalition to be rid of the Assyrian threat. He wanted to include Egypt in the coalition but again Isaiah advised against it (c. 30). With trust in the Lord, Jerusalem will be saved. With the arrival of Sennacherib, Jerusalem was in fact saved but the rest of Judah was lost (cc. 36–37). This is spoken of also in the extrabiblical Annals of Sennacherib, wherein Hezekiah is said to have been boxed in "like a bird in a cage."

Teaching

These major events were the parentheses around Isaiah's full and diversified career. He received his calling during Temple worship. Once his lips were purified for a prophetic vocation, he responded with willingness and alacrity, unlike Jeremiah who shrank from the task (6:1–8). He is assured, however, that his task will be difficult as he brings a message of conversion to a deaf people. His preaching will continue until destruction has run its course, but, because of the Lord's fidelity, a remnant will be saved (6:9–13), symbolically foretold in the name of another of his sons, Shear-yashub, "a remnant shall return" (7:3f).

His career was marked by disappointment. An unfaithful people that called evil, good and good, evil (5:19–22). Social injustice was rampant as the rights of the poor and disadvantaged were repeatedly disregarded (10:1–4).

The holiness of God is the centerpiece of Isaiah's moral call. As the elect of Yahweh, the people should reflect that holiness or "otherness" (6:3; 5:16, 19, 24). This they do by observing his law, which results in a distinctiveness setting them apart from all nations. Thus the eventual future leader, spoken of by the prophet, will walk in a path worthy of his calling as he brings forth justice upon the earth (9:1–6). In this way the true nature of their transcendent God will become evident.

As Isaiah speaks of the punishment to come, it is directed not only to Israel and Judah but all of the surrounding nations. Yahweh is the only sovereign to whom all peoples are subject, but Isaiah is never without hope. Destruction is never total or definitive. The remnant is always there (Isa 4:3). Zion will once again cry out in joy (12:1–6).

Messianism

Closely connected with Isaiah's belief in the future is his view of the Messiah. The belief that Israel would one day have its ideal king, steeped in faith and uprightness, was launched by Nathan in his promise to David of a lasting dynasty and a kingship of honesty and integrity (2 Sam 7). Isaiah returns to this theme of the future kingship in several oracles. In the face of the Syrian-Israelite threat, he promises Ahaz deliverance in the sign of a child's birth. Before the child comes of age, says the prophet, the threat will pass (7:14). The intended child may well have been Hezekiah, the son of Ahaz, whose name Immanuel (God with us) will be symbolic of the Lord's saving hand. This was a prophecy, however, that had a life of its own. The prophecy of a special child born of a young woman was seen as uniquely fulfilled in Christ born of the Virgin Mary by Christians as early as the New Testament itself (Matt 1:23). This would be a meaning that went beyond that originally intended by the prophet centuries before. There was, however, the ongoing belief within Israel in the ideal monarch, especially when particular kings fell short of this expectation.

The thought on the heir to the Davidic throne continues to unfold in Isaiah. This king is to be endowed with exceptional gifts and is to preside over a kingdom that is both vast and everlasting (9:1–6). This descendant of David will possess the gift of wisdom, the ability to execute justice, and will preside over a land marked by a peace and harmony reflective of Eden itself (11:1–9).

These hopes were obviously directed toward a king whose reign was proximate. That failing, these prophecies continued to inspire hope, always looking to the day when the divine plan would be realized. This would be a kingdom marked by justice and fidelity, presided over by one who was heir to the promise. The disappointments brought by the kings of Israel and Judah only made the hope stronger.

Interestingly enough, one of the kings who was possibly envisioned in these eighth-century prophecies was Hezekiah, who was Isaiah's contemporary. He is viewed positively by the deuteronomist and inaugurated a religious reform during his reign (2 Kgs 18–20). However, he met only limited success because of the severe political problems of the time, and his son Manasseh (687–642) managed to undo most of his father's work.

The era of Isaiah and Hezekiah was one of political turmoil but also one of great spiritual insight.

Isaiah 2–3, 6–7, 9, 11, 30, 36–37

Micah

Micah was a contemporary of Isaiah in the eighth century. His preaching career extended from Samaria's fall (722) to the siege of Jerusalem by Sennacherib (701). He is listed as a minor prophet with this book of seven chapters attributed to him. His message varies little from the other prophets of his time: judgment for widespread sinfulness (1:1—3:13) and the promise of restoration (4:1—5:14). We know nothing of his life, except the place of origin, Moresheth, in the Judean foothills.

We sometimes wonder what effect a prophet's word had on his contemporaries. In the case of Micah we learn from Jeremiah, an independent source, that his message had a profound effect on king Hezekiah; it brought about a spirit of repentance and no doubt contributed to the religious reform that the king initiated (Jer 26:18f). There is also a strong davidic messianism in Micah. He contrasts the besieged Jerusalem with the small town of Bethlehem, the town of David's birth. From there the ruler will come destined to preside over a restored Judah and reunited country (5:1–4).

Micah is perhaps best known for a single verse, often seen as a synthesis of moral truth.

> "He has told you, O mortal, what is good;
>   and what does the LORD require of you
> but to do justice, and to love kindness,
>   and to walk humbly with your God?" (Mic 6:8)

In doing the right, one adheres to the law of the Lord. Yet this is done out of a love for goodness, the basic motive for authentic moral conduct. Then, always conscious of one's fragility, there is the realization of an utter and complete dependency as one walks humbly with God.

Micah 2, 5, 6

Jeremiah

In terms of the length of prophetic books connected with one author, Jeremiah has primacy of place with fifty-two chapters. His career was marked by longevity as well. Born in about 625, he preached during the reign of Josiah (628), until the king's death in the battle at Megiddo (609). He continued during the reign of Josiah's two sons, Jehoiakim (609–598) and, most notably, Zedekiah (597–587). He witnessed the fall of Jerusalem and the deportation of its people. This was a career, then, that extended from Josiah's reform to the Babylonian exile, probably the most crucial period in Israelite history.

The book that bears his name was compiled and edited after the prophet's death and after the exile had ended. A variety of sources makes the outline of the book complex, although along broad lines, there are oracles centering mainly on Judah's last days (1:1—33:26), Jerusalem's fall (34:1—45:5), the lot of other nations (46:1—51:64), and a historical appendix (c. 52).

Jeremiah was born of a priestly family, although he did not exercise priestly functions, in the village of Anathoth, near Jerusalem. That he was a reluctant prophet (1:4–10) may be partly retrojection after a life of intense struggle and bitter disappointment. The fact that he was predestined for this task before birth in no way ameliorates his basic sentiments. His prophecies of doom will be mixed with those of hope as he is sent "to destroy and to overthrow" as well as "to build and to plant."

When Josiah began his reform, Jeremiah was evidently an enthusiastic supporter. It was an enthusiasm that waned, however, when he saw the reform as lacking depth and staying power. This was compounded by the early death of the king in 609 at Megiddo as he attempted to break the Egyptian assault against Babylon. At that time all the former moral ills returned and were strongly opposed by Jeremiah. During Jehoiakim's reign, the prophet was bitterly opposed and his life, threatened (c. 26). He was later imprisoned under Zedekiah for favoring capitulation to the enemy (c. 37). It was then, during the reign of Zedekiah, that Judah lived through its final days. The prophet called for nonresistance to Babylon, the Lord's scourge for sinful conduct, although this was seen by many as traitorous. Ignoring the prophet's advice, the king organized forces to resist Babylon. This only served to hasten the destruction of Jerusalem in the prophet's final days. Faced with the choice of going into exile or remaining in a scorched land, Jeremiah decided on the latter. Later he was forced to go to Egypt, the probable place of his death.

Message

Infidelity in the form of idolatry is strongly decried by Jeremiah as he speaks of the impending doom coming from Babylon. The image is one of the unfaithful wife pursuing other suitors (2:1–6). Rather than trust in the Lord, Judah had forged alliances with foreign powers (2:17ff). Now the invasion from the north, the full impact of Babylon, is inevitable (4:1–31). It is like a boiling cauldron ready to pour forth its scalding contents (1:13f). The rich wallow in their wealth with no concern for the poor (5:27f). The desire for other gods makes them like "lusty stallions" panting after their mare (5:7f).

The days of Jehoiakim presented an even darker picture as Josiah's reform was disregarded. This is the period of the "Temple sermon" (c. 7). As the prophet litanies the evils of his time, he reminds his hearers that the formalities of religion are worth nothing. "Do not trust in these deceptive words: 'This is the temple of the LORD, the temple of the LORD, the temple of the LORD'" (Jer 7:4). What meaning has the worship of Yahweh when it is matched by an idolatrous attention accorded false gods

(7:16–23)? So imminent is the disaster that the prophet is advised by the Lord not to marry or have children in the face of the impending disaster (16:1–4).

It was during the reign of Zedekiah that Jeremiah's final prophecies were uttered before the demise of the country (21:1—33:26). To the wishful thought that Jerusalem might still be spared, Jeremiah responds that the king, his government, and people have reached their end. There is no turning back (21:1–10). Seventy years will have to pass before the era of Babylon will come to an end (25:1–14). Will the good be destroyed with the bad? No, says the prophet, like two baskets of figs, one ripe and tasty, the other rotten, so too the exiles; the ripe fruit, the faithful ones, will be ultimately delivered, whereas the king, his government, and their sympathizers, the rotten figs, will perish (24:1–10).

During this period, there is an unusual letter written to the deported Jewish population (c. 29). Jeremiah urges them to settle down, marry, and dedicate themselves to a truly domestic life. They are told to pray for Babylon because its welfare will largely determine their own. With the end of the seventy years of exile, they will return to their homeland. It is remarkable to find such an amicable description of a foreign power, captors who have deprived the Jews of land and center of worship. This contrasts sharply with the sorrowful situation of the exiles elsewhere described (cf. Ps 137). Yet here we see that broadening of vision that will ultimately make Israel less bound to the staples of the past: insights that grew out of the exile experience. It will be complemented by Ezekiel's inaugural vision of a highly mobile God, not hampered by the narrow limits of an earlier belief. The God of the nations will not be restricted to the land of Israel; he will be found wherever the heart turns to him in love.

The New Covenant

The days are surely coming, says the LORD, when I will make a new covenant with the house of Israel and the

138

house of Judah. It will not be like the covenant that I made with their ancestors when I took them by the hand to bring them out of the land of Egypt—a covenant that they broke, though I was their husband, says the LORD. But this is the covenant that I will make with the house of Israel after those days, says the LORD: I will put my law within them, and I will write it on their hearts; and I will be their God, and they shall be my people. No longer shall they teach one another, or say to each other, "Know the LORD," for they shall all know me, from the least of them to the greatest, says the LORD; for I will forgive their iniquity, and remember their sin no more. (Jer 31:31–34)

Jeremiah is the prophet of pathos and hope. He agonizes over the sinfulness and distress of his people, just as he assures them of a better future. Nowhere is that hope given finer expression than in chapter 31, with its brilliant poetry and groundbreaking theology. The deported people from north and south are called to resettle in their homeland. There is joy and exaltation as Zion rejoices over her children's return. Then at a given point in this chapter the authentic spirit of religion, which is to characterize the future, emerges with great clarity. It will be an era of *individual responsibility* (27–30). The former emphasis on corporate or collective guilt will be tempered by a strong emphasis on a personal response to God. The sins of the fathers will no longer be visited on their children. Each person will pay his or her own debt. It will also be the era of a new and *personal covenant*, a covenant of the heart. What was formerly a law written on stone calling for compliance, will be replaced by a deeply internal spirit of faith. The response to God will come from a grateful heart; it will not be marked by a sense of conforming to external norms but by a new spirit wherein humans speak to God and God to them.

There is no passage in the Hebrew scriptures that so clearly speaks to the Christian heart. If there is any prophecy that foretells the teaching of Jesus of Nazareth, it is this. Against this background, the words of Jesus at the Last Supper centering on the "new covenant in my blood" (Luke 22:20) take on a true depth of meaning.

The Confessions

Certain passages of Jeremiah have long been singled out as deeply emotional expressions of his lot in life, spoken of as Confessions (11:18—12:6, 15:10–21, 17:14–18, 18:18–23, 20:7–18). His dissatisfaction covers a wide spectrum. In the first place, the wickedness of the people overwhelms him as they go their own way saying God "is blind to our ways" (12:1–6). The prophet is disappointed with his God, whom he has defended only to be left desolate and disconsolate. He regrets the day of his birth, even as he sees that there are more difficult days ahead (15:10–21). His persecutors assail and mock him, while Yahweh remains strangely silent (17:14–18). If God's cause is not defended and action taken against his enemies, then evil will have prevailed over good.

In the language of sexual seduction (20:7), the prophet says that he has been overcome by Yahweh. His mission has brought him nothing but derision, rejection, and pain. If he could suffocate God's word within him, he would, but he cannot. Friends have been lost; enemies, emboldened; and Yahweh, the assuring avenger, slow to act. Again he regrets the very day of his birth. Whatever consolation he may have provided others, there has been nothing but pain for him (20:7–18).

Never has a prophet spoken in such bold and daring language. Yet his faith is undying, for he knows the cause of the Lord is right. It is his faith that enables him to challenge the Lord himself. Nothing illustrated the truth of the prophet's word more than the exile itself.

The final editor of the book of Jeremiah has added a final chapter on the final days of Jerusalem (c. 52; cf. 2 Kgs 24:18). It is a sad and tragic moment. A king blinded and imprisoned and his family slaughtered. A people who once joyfully took possession of the land now leave it desolate and destroyed. Nebuchadnezzar burned the temple, the palace complex, and much of Jerusalem itself. The invaders took from the temple what they did not destroy, including vessels or furnishings that appeared to be of value. The high priest himself was deported. What was left of a once impressive city was now little more than rubble. It was a bitter turning point, long in the making, for a people that had begun so well.

Jeremiah 1, 4, 7, 16, 21, 29, 31, 37, 52
Confessions: 11:18—12:6, 15:10–21,
17:14–18, 18:18–23, 20:7–18

X.

THE EXILE

From one point of view the exile was a tragic experience. Many of the anchors of Israelite belief were gone: the country, the Temple, the capital city. The people of God had experienced a stunning defeat at the hands of ruthless unbelievers. This had to be explained in one of two ways. The foreign gods, in this case Marduk of the Babylonians, had vanquished the God of the Hebrews, an inadmissible thesis, or the true God was punishing his sinful people, the position that prevailed.

The exile also had its positive side, however. It broadened Israel's vision in seeing the universal sovereignty of Yahweh. This God was in Babylon no less than in Jerusalem and was as much present to his people there as within the precincts of a promised land. In addition, personal responsibility came more to the fore. Solidarity in guilt never vanished completely among a people with a long history of the collective sense, but it was now balanced by a growing awareness of personal accountability. It is the individual who would answer for his or her own wrongdoing. In addition, in the absence of the traditional staples of Temple and priesthood, there was now a stronger emphasis on the sacred word. The exile was the beginning of a literary period, which was to continue well into the postexilic era. The traditions of the Yahwist and Elohist were completed and added to by the Priestly school. The deuteronomistic authors compiled and critiqued the historical traditions from the time of the occupation down to the exile. All of this emphasis on the written traditions led to the designation of the Jews as "people of the book." This is important in centering faith around a religious adherence rather than on God-centered places and times. Even the term *Jew*, which then came to the fore, looked to a religious posture rather than citizenship within a country.

In the two successive deportations (597 and 587), there were probably not more than five thousand deportees. This is roughly the number cited in Jeremiah c. 52. The exiles were evidently treated well in Babylon, settling in their own neighborhoods and pursuing a normal way of life. They married, worked, and were largely undisturbed, only prohibited a return to their own country. In fact, when the exile ended in 546, not all of the Jewish exiles returned to their own country; some remained in the land of their captivity.

We will consider here two of the most important compositions of the exilic period: Ezekiel and Second Isaiah.

EZEKIEL

The only prophet to receive his call outside of Palestine, Ezekiel exercised his ministry in Babylon, being among the first wave of deportees in 597. Of a priestly family, Ezekiel is both innovative in turning new ground and steeped in the traditions of cult and worship so clearly evidenced in his oracles. He lived in the Jewish colony on the Chobar river in Babylon; it was there he received his inaugural vision (c. 1).

It was an awesome moment. Four winged creatures were overshadowed by a firmament and throne upon which God was seated in human form. There were, in addition, four accompanying wheels, which moved with the living creatures. The vision points to two important features of the prophet's later teaching: the majesty and holiness of God and a mobile capability pointing to God's universal presence. Like Isaiah and Jeremiah before him, Ezekiel is assigned his task but here in symbolic form. He is handed a scroll with a three-word inscription: "Lamentation, Mourning, Woe." In eating it, the scroll becomes part of him and his destiny is fixed; he will proclaim final destruction for Jerusalem (c. 2). To point up the distance between his humanity and the otherness of God, he is repeatedly referred to as "son of man."

The structure of the book follows to a great extent the career of the prophet and is divided into four parts:

- Before the final siege of Jerusalem (4:1—24:27)
- Prophecies against foreign nations (25:1—32:32
- Salvation for Israel (33:1—39:29)
- The restored Israel (40:1—48:35)

Message

The judgment against Israel is not unlike that found in the earlier prophets. However, it is Ezekiel's images that are most striking. Idolatry, for example, is described in allegory (c. 16). Israel is a lovely girl, seriously neglected until Yahweh, her suitor, passes by, cleanses and adorns her elegantly. Then, taken up with her own attractiveness, she pursues other men and becomes nothing more than a prostitute. In her lust she takes off after other gods and turns to Egypt, Philistia, and Assyria. Now she must pay the price of her infidelity. It is a graphic picture, an allegory readily understood. In fact, for Ezekiel, Israel never had a period of uninterrupted fidelity. She wandered from the start; even her desert experience was marked by infidelity (c. 20). The punishment for sin is often acted out dramatically by the prophet, sometimes in ways that seem bizarre. He draws pictures, bakes bread, shaves his head, and packs his bags (cc. 4, 5, 12), all illustrations of the approaching disaster.

Perhaps influenced by Jeremiah, Ezekiel too emphasizes *individual responsibility*. The idea of children suffering for the sins of their fathers was a hallowed Israelite tradition (Exod 20:5), yet it is a position from which Ezekiel clearly separates himself in speaking of the future (18:2–4). Each one will pay the price of his or her own wrongdoing in an era of strong personalism. The bitter distaste of sour grapes eaten by one's forebears will not be the offspring's lot.

After the final deportation of 587, the prophet takes a decidedly different direction in his teaching. He speaks at great length about the dawn of a new era and a future full of promise. These are the prophecies of *restoration*, which are replete with Ezekiel's imagery. Yahweh becomes the good shepherd, who, unlike the negligent priests of the past, cares tenderly for his flock (c. 34). Turning aside from the human shepherds, Yahweh himself will assume the role, directing his sheep away from the countries on which they depended and leading them to their homeland once again. In another setting, the dry bones come to life. They were strewn on the desert floor, a lifeless people decimated and destroyed. Imparting a new spirit, Yahweh calls them back to life. They reassemble as a new people, a restored Israel (c. 37). This is not a prophecy of personal resurrection, a concept that will emerge only later, but rather speaks to a national rebirth. Like Jeremiah, Ezekiel speaks of the deeply internal spirit of faith. This involves a cleansing and imparting a new heart. External conformity, which is meaningless, will be replaced by a new spirit, an internal attachment to the Lord and his designs (36:26–28).

Clearly portraying his priestly background, Ezekiel concludes his vision of the future with a grandiose description of a new Temple, part of a new Israel, standing on the mountain top. It is the center of all Jewish life and from it water streams forth to the north, south, east, and west (cc. 40–47). This is clearly a God-centered society that finds the source of its life in the living waters of the spirit. At the same time, however, he is mindful of the traditional institutions of the country. He speaks of the renewed Israel comprised of the union of both North and South and presided over by the descendant of David (37:15–28).

Ezekiel had a profound influence on postexilic Judaism. He was traditional in some ways; innovative in others; and exotic as well. He was strong in hope and vivid in his depiction of the days to come. He combines a morality of daily life with a worship of God, which carries him beyond some of his forebears. He

The Cyrus cylinder

strongly emphasizes the interiority of religion that will come more to the fore after the exile.

Ezekiel 1–3, 16, 20, 36–37, 40, 47

SECOND ISAIAH (Isaiah 40–55)

We have already discussed the divisions of the book of Isaiah. There is no doubt that a study of Second Isaiah shows a marked difference in style, theology, and history from that of the earlier part of the book. In a series of splendid poems, the author of the second section of the book, a member of what may have been an Isaian school, continues the mission of the earlier prophet in a very different setting. Unlike the severity of judgment found in the earlier oracles, the work of Second Isaiah is justly called a Book of Consolation. Harsh words are absent; the era of recrimination is past. The emphasis falls on the future characterized by return, reconstruction, and fidelity. In the sixth century, the Babylonians are passing from the scene, and the Persians, after their defeat of Media and Lydia, are poised to extend their sovereignty westward. It is at this time, about 540 BC, that Second Isaiah appears. In this book, the overarching sovereignty of the one and only God is much to the fore. His power is most evident in leading the Hebrews homeward in what is described as a new exodus. The Persian ruler Cyrus, praised with unmatched affirmation as an instrument of Yahweh, permits and facilitates this return to Jerusalem. This is much more than a moment of historical liberation; it is seen by the author as a new creation similar to that enshrined in Genesis 1. Zion, the mount of God's dwelling, so ruthlessly destroyed some forty years earlier, is hailed as sacred once again as reconstruction is foreseen. Woven into the fabric of this soaring poetry is the story of the life and mission of an unknown prophet, who is identified simply as the Servant of the Lord.

The Notion of God

The first chapter (40:1–31) encapsulates the message of the prophet and portrays the God of the Hebrews in a new light: "The LORD is the everlasting God, the Creator of the ends of the earth" (40:28). This God has no competitors; other gods are nothing but empty idols, the work of human hands. God's power (40:10) and wisdom (40:12) are unmatched; if any doubt remains, his glory is about to be revealed (40:5). He is a mighty warrior (40:12), but is now best portrayed as a shepherd tenderly leading his flock home (40:11).

The New Exodus

Repeatedly there is a hearkening back to that most noted event, the original Exodus. Now as Yahweh brings his people home, there is an underlying Exodus leitmotif to the event. Just as bumpy roads were made level and smooth for a traveling dignitary, so too for the returning exiles (40:1–4). Zion is told to stand on the heights like a sentinel and proclaim to Judah that over the desert floor the people are returning (40:9–11). As at the Red Sea water became dry land, so now the land is watered and made verdant with wondrous irrigation (43:15–21). The new Exodus is a moment of repatriation in unmatched rejoicing (48:20–22, 51:10–11).

The New Creation

The return is also reflective of the creative action of God as portrayed in Genesis. It is unthinkable to compare man-made idols with the God who created the heavens and the earth

(48:12f). In a series of questions, like those asked of Job by God (Job 38), the incomparable might of the Lord is highlighted (40:12–15); he is the Lord, there is no other (45:6–9). It is the word of the Lord that accomplishes all, and like the rain from heaven inevitably rendering the earth fertile, the word of God moves inexorably toward its determined end (55:10–11).

Cyrus

With nothing said about the kings of Israel and their future, Second Isaiah highlights a royal figure from another nation and culture. Cyrus, recognized historically as a benign ruler, is here given exceptional accolades. He is the shepherd of God's people (44:28) and even a messiah or anointed one (45:1). For the sake of Israel he has been chosen that the nations may recognize and acknowledge the only God (45:1–6, 41:1–4). This spotlight on Cyrus is another important indicator of the breadth of vision that the exile had produced. There is no longer a match of force between Baal and Yahweh to see who will have the upper hand (1 Kgs 18). No mention is made of any god but Yahweh; indeed, the thought would be considered ludicrous. As all geographical borders fall, the God of Israel calls to his service those who do not even acknowledge his existence.

The Servant of the Lord

The existence of four songs that have been woven into the fabric of Isaiah's message has long been recognized by scholars. They are found in various sections of the work (42:1–4, 49:1–6, 50:4–11, 52:13—53:12), and although readily recognizable, they present unsolved mysteries of their own. The most pressing question has long been the identity of this servant and emissary of the Lord. In the earlier songs it would seem that Israel itself is the servant; in fact, in the second song, he is called Israel (49:3). However, there is still no consensus around the question of identity, and before offering any opinion here, it is helpful to walk briefly through the songs and see their unfolding message.

In the first song (42:1–4), the servant receives his vocation and, like the other prophets, his mission as well. He is to bring forth justice and, at least implicitly, a knowledge of God in foreign lands. His character is that of a gentle, soft-spoken person, one whose message is that of peace and the justice of God.

In the second song (49:1–6), the mission embraces both Israel and the nations, but there is little said about his mission, except its being a call to conversion; however, there is now a note of anxiety. The Servant has faced a spirit of nonacceptance, a sentiment of opposition. Storm clouds gather on the horizon.

The third song (50:4–11) presents an even more negative picture. The situation has become more difficult. The servant has persevered, but the reaction is now even more severe. He is not heard and is now suffering physical abuse. Despite this growing opposition, the servant remains steadfast in his trust.

Finally, as the final and longest song unfolds (52:13—53:12), the servant has died. His fate is addressed in the tones of a Greek chorus. He is spoken of as an ordinary person, without notable traits, who suffered at the hands of others, a man with a controversial message. He was mercilessly killed and assigned a grave among the wicked. Innocent though he was, he suffered unjust treatment and rejection. However, the great insight of the fourth song, important to the whole Hebrew tradition, is that of vicarious suffering. The servant had given his life for others. "Surely he has borne our infirmities and carried our diseases" (53:4). He was not a victim of circumstances, least of all one rejected by God. He was "wounded for our transgressions, crushed for our iniquities." Because he died for others, he will at some future time be given recognition and a place of honor.

Who then is the servant? The collective interpretation is valid, especially in the earlier songs, although in the last two songs, the figure of the servant is much too concrete; in his suffering and death some individual is seemingly described. The two positions are not irreconcilable for a culture that was not unaccustomed to an individual representing the community. No individual immediately comes to mind, but that has less importance than the teaching of the songs. It is now possible for one to suffer for others. That is the dominant theme. The servant suffers not because of personal wrongdoing. Nor is he being tested. He suffers on behalf of the guilty and atones for them. This is the central teaching of the songs. He does not accomplish his mission in teaching or preaching. We know nothing of his oracles. His is a prophetic action. He is a prophet in what he endures, not in what he says.

The authors of the New Testament were not hesitant in seeing Jesus as the Servant. We may never know whom the original author intended in his writing of the Servant, although the New Testament supports us in the undeniable fact that his mission is clearly reflected in that of Jesus of Nazareth.

Isaiah 40; 48:12–13; 55
Servant Songs: 42:14, 49:1–6, 50:4–12, 52:13—53:12

XI.

THE POSTEXILIC PERIOD

"Thus says King Cyrus of Persia: The LORD, the God of heaven, has given me all the kingdoms of the earth, and he has charged me to build him a house at Jerusalem in Judah. Any of those among you who are of his people—may their God be with them!—are now permitted to go up to Jerusalem in Judah, and rebuild the house of the LORD, the God of Israel." (Ezra 1:2f)

The decree of emancipation, issued by Cyrus and probably adapted by Ezra, represents the historical moment that ended the exile and permitted the Jews to return home. Although a broad-minded Cyrus was not averse to seeing the hand of a foreign deity in his major decisions and was certainly not himself an avowed Yahwist, he is seen favorably on all sides for endorsing the Hebrews' return from the late sixth to the mid-fifth centuries BC.

The books of *Ezra* and *Nehemiah*, which recount the return to Jerusalem, give the impression that Ezra preceded Nehemiah. There is still discussion on this point but logic would favor Nehemiah's presence in Jerusalem before Ezra, in about 445 BC. As the civil ruler or governor appointed by the Persians, Nehemiah was responsible for rebuilding the wall of the city and repopulating the country. Not all of the exiles in Babylon decided to return; a good number remained behind. The priest Ezra, who probably followed Nehemiah, had little concern for administrative duties and saw his task as building up the religious life of his people, especially in seeing that they were isolated from their pagan contemporaries.

The books of Ezra and Nehemiah are part of a corpus that includes the two books of Chronicles and that reflects a distinctly priestly point of view. Although the authors may well have used the deuteronomistic history as a source, the priestly school left an even stronger imprint. In many ways the work of the priests in postexilic Jerusalem represent a retrenchment. Ezra worked to eliminate foreign influences by prohibiting marriage between Jews and non-Jews and by promoting a type of isolation, which in time became identified with the Jewish "ghetto."

One of the reasons for this enclosed mentality was the presence of the *Samaritans* in the central part of the country. This was a decidedly mixed population, a Hebrew base laced with Mesopotamian settlers, some dating from the Assyrians times. In short, they were "half Jews" at best and probably reacted to the return of the exiled population in a negative fashion. The Jews considered them heterodox, and a spirit of hostility between the two peoples continued for centuries.

THE LITERATURE OF THE RESTORATION

In addition to the books already cited, this was the period of five of the minor prophets (Joel, Obadiah, Haggai, Zechariah, and Malachi). Stemming from this same period are the books of Esther, Judith, the Book of Jonah, and Third Isaiah. Esther and Judith are considered pseudohistorical by most authorities and are important as reflecting the postexilic emphasis on the singularity of Israel's call.

Esther has a shorter Hebrew form and a longer Greek edition, the former considered canonical for the Jews and Protestants, the latter by Catholics. It is the story of a Jewish queen Esther who champions the cause of her people in late Persian times and, with God's assistance, succeeds in interceding with the king in having a decree of extermination of the Jews revoked. The Jews are saved and the Jewish feast of Purim celebrates their deliverance. The story illustrates God's fidelity to his people in helping them overcome insurmountable difficulties through the instrumentality of a woman.

Judith comes from the second century BC and is, again, the account of a woman vanquishing an enemy force through the power of God. Originally written in Hebrew, it has come down to us only in its Greek form and is therefore absent from the Jewish canon. It is a didactic piece, not intended to be historical, celebrating God's fidelity to his people. When attacked by Assyrian forces under Holofernes, Judith (the name means "Jewess"), after prayer and fasting, gains access to the Assyrian camp and beheads the drunken Holofernes. This results in chaos in the Assyrian camp and gives the Jews the upper hand. Victory is achieved and Judith leads a hymn of thanksgiving.

Both Judith and Esther come from a period when strong nationalism was on the rise. Insignificant numbers matter far less than an unqualified dedication to God. Both books are inspirational and gave renewed confidence to a downtrodden people now called to restore their former traditions.

The *Book of Jonah* is actually an antidote to postexilic exclusivism. In the absence of the monarchy, Judaism placed great emphasis on religious observance in Temple worship and the law as the center of moral life. For a monotheistic faith to remain intact, separation from polytheistic cultures was seen as necessary. The Jewish community celebrated its "apartness," as moments like the decree of Ezra (Ezra 9) illustrate all too well.

It was in reaction to this that certain books in the postexilic period began to appear. They take a decidedly different stance. As we have seen, Ruth, a faithful Moabite woman, was an ancestor of David himself. This meant that pagan blood flowed in the veins of the great monarch himself. This spirit of universalism or recognition of other peoples and cultures is particularly strong in the short book of Jonah. Although presented as a prophet, Jonah is not really one of the classical prophets. This is a story about a prophet in what might be termed an extended parable. It was never intended to be a historical presentation. The reluctant prophet Jonah is clearly connected with the spirit of exclusivism and does not have the will to carry out Yahweh's injunction to go and preach repentance to the people of Nineveh, the capital of Assyria. The fact that Nineveh had ceased to exist centuries before Jonah's time is irrelevant and has no bearing on the story's lesson. The prophet travels westward to avoid reaching Assyria. He boards a ship only to encounter a serious storm. Because he sees his presence on board as the cause of danger, he prevails on the crew to throw him overboard. He is then swallowed by a large fish and is finally spewed out—yes, on the shores of Assyria. Angrily and reluctantly, he goes to Nineveh and calls for conversion to God and sees a massive conversion of the population from nonbelief to faith in the one God. Totally upset and frustrated by what has occurred, the prophet is told of Yahweh's unqualified love for the Ninevites, one of Israel's most hated enemies.

As we can see, the author has given ample evidence to conclude that his account is not history. We do not have to look for traces of massive conversion to Yahwism in Assyria, nor for a fish large enough to accommodate a person for a three-day period. Jonah, even in its humor, rejects the "ghetto" mentality of postexilic Judaism and makes a major contribution to the spirit of universalism.

Third Isaiah (cc. 55–66) comes from a period after the resettlement has taken place. The strong expectations that accompanied the return have not provided the expected results. Much had been realized in the reconstruction of the Temple, the rebuilding of Jerusalem, and the reintegration of sacrifice and worship, although it was not long before an empty formalism surfaced once again. Third Isaiah is another attempt at correction. Continuing the spirit and work of the Isaian school, it lacks the full-throated optimism of Second Isaiah, while still upholding a strong sense of confidence and sense of the future. In the spirit of universalism, Third Isaiah sees a worship open to all people (c. 56); there is marked concern for the downtrodden and brokenhearted (61:1–3). Jerusalem remains the center of future hope (62:6–12), but all of this is offset by lying and falsehood, even murder, which have taken their toll. "Truth is lacking, and whoever turns from evil is despoiled" (59:1–15). Illicit worship and violations of dietary law have become common place (65:1–5). Religious practice must look to overcoming injustice, not simply carrying out ritual (c. 58). The outcome will ultimately mean punishment for the malicious (65:11–16) and salvation for the just (65:8–10). The end result will one day be a renewed and faithful Israel, inhabiting a new heaven and a new earth. As in First Isaiah, creation will no longer be made up of predator and prey in a redemption that is both human and cosmic.

Ezra 1, 9
Nehemiah 8
Judith 8–9, 13
Esther 4, 5–8
Jonah 1–4
Third Isaiah 56; 58; 59; 65:17–25; 66

XII.

WISDOM

The Old Testament Wisdom literature is contained in seven books according to the Catholic designation. They are Proverbs, Job, Psalms, Ecclesiastes (Qoheleth), Song of Songs, Sirach, and Wisdom. We have treated the psalms when speaking of Israel's worship. *Songs of Songs* is likewise a work in a class by itself. Although attributed to Solomon, it is actually a postexilic composition. The book is a collection of exotic, even at times erotic love songs, extolling the love between a man and woman, which may have found its original setting in a marriage ceremony. The question is often asked if the Song's message does not go beyond human romance. Is it not a metaphor for the love between God and Israel? Or Christ and the church? The songs themselves give no indication of such a meaning; in fact God is not named once. It would seem that its attribution to Solomon (1:1) helped find the book a place in the canon, much as in the case of Proverbs and Wisdom. The celebration of authentic human love, even with its erotic features, would have been no obstacle to the book's being seen as sacred. What must be admitted is that Song of Songs represents some of the finest poetry in the Hebrew scriptures.

The heart of the Wisdom tradition is its concern with questions of life, and this began on a very basic day-to-day level. *Proverbs* is a classic example: although a postexilic composition, it is a book with a lengthy history, parts possibly dating back to the Solomonic era. It is a book largely made up of what we would call today maxims or what is termed in Hebrew the *mashal*. These sayings offer a key to proper conduct in the course of daily living.

They are "proverbs" that cover everything from table manners to sexual mores in setting forth the norms for a good life. These are very concrete precepts and, at least in their origins, avoided the lofty plain of speculation.

The origins of the Wisdom literature are often identified with court circles where young men were trained in the discipline and skills of royal life. Israel was not alone in this; we have many examples of this type of wisdom in other Near Eastern cultures. The frequent "father-son" references were easy substitutes for "teacher-pupil." This rule-of-thumb type of education was seen as being permanently valid and applicable to much of life's circumstances, as suitable to postexilic conduct as to that of the early monarchy. It was in this period after the exile that the "proverbs" were collected and edited.

The genre of the *mashal* took different forms. It could be a simple statement of fact in verse form:

> An estate quickly acquired in the beginning
>   will not be blessed in the end. (20:21)

In other instances the teaching may repeat itself in two lines in a synonymous fashion:

> When wickedness comes, contempt comes also;
>   and with dishonor comes disgrace. (18:3)

Or even more engagingly, the second part of the maxim may express the same point but in a contrary sense:

> Some friends play at friendship
>   but a true friend sticks closer than one's nearest kin. (18:24)

The greater part of Proverbs is made up of this practical, experiential type of *mashal*. The same is true of *Sirach*. A second-century composition, the book was originally written in Hebrew and translated into Greek in about 132 BC by the author's grandson. In recent times a large part of the original Hebrew has been rediscovered. Because for most of its history, Sirach was known only in its Greek translation, it is not part of the Jewish or Protestant Bible; Catholics, however, have always seen it as inspired.

The author Ben Sirach (Son of Sirach) is steeped in the tradition of Israel and stays close to the theological positions of earlier times. His sayings parallel closely those of Proverbs. In his speculative moments, Sirach sees human wisdom as having its heavenly counterpart in God's creation and direction of the universe. Human wisdom is, in fact, a participation in that same attribute as found in God. This leads to the logical conclusion that the beginning of all human wisdom is the fear of the Lord (1:9–18). Divine wisdom is personified in Sirach and is present with God from the beginning, serving as his blueprint in the design and execution of the universe (cf. c. 1).

Of particular interest (as well as a good chance for review) are the final chapters of Sirach, written in praise of the great figures of Israelite history (cc. 44–51).

In the course of time wisdom wrestled with the major problems of life. It deals with questions of theodicy, the human future, retribution, suffering, sin, and death. Although this approach is more speculative, it never distances itself from the burning questions of daily life. Prime examples of this development in Hebrew wisdom are found in Job, Qoheleth (Ecclesiastes), and Wisdom. The "proverbs" of Proverbs and Sirach served as a springboard for this type of reflection, which carried wisdom in a new direction.

At this point, rather than look at the books singly or in a detached fashion, we shall consider one issue that is dealt with in all of them: the problem of evil.

Song of Songs 1–3, 7
Proverbs 1–3, 10–11
Sirach 44–51

SIN, SUFFERING, AND DEATH

No problem vexed the human spirit in antiquity more than the question of evil in both its daily manifestations and its origins. How are suffering and death to be reconciled with belief in an all-good God? The basic answer is given in Genesis 2–3, wherein sin explains both suffering and death. Thus, it is the fault of humans not of God. Death is now the common lot of all humankind with no exemptions. By association, then, an early or untimely death, as well as suffering in its many forms become linked with sin. The moral norm then becomes evident: the pursuit of virtue and the avoidance of sin lead to happiness, wholeness, and bliss, whereas a life of evil conduct is a certain invitation to disaster.

> Whoever walks in integrity walks securely,
>> but whoever follows perverse ways will be found out.
>> (Prov 10:9)

> The LORD does not let the righteous go hungry,
>> but he thwarts the craving of the wicked. (Prov 10:3)

This pursuit of true wisdom is validated by the fact that of Lady Wisdom it is said: "Long life is in her right hand; in her left hand are riches and honor" (Prov 3:16). Evil, from this perspective, has something of a "boomerang" quality: once released it will produce its effect but inevitably come back to haunt the perpetrator. Or as the conservative Sirach has it:

> Do no evil, and evil will never overtake you.
>> Stay away from wrong, and it will turn away from you.
>> (Sir 7:1–2)

He is also sure that the lot of the arrogant is rejection and loss (10:12–18), whereas those who fear God are bedecked with honor (10:19–23). Retribution is almost mathematically worked out. Evil brings its sorrowful company, whereas virtue brings certain bliss.

In a world with no true afterlife belief, this principle had to make sense. If God be just, how else could retribution be seen? It was this solution of "good for good" and "evil for evil" that prevailed through a great part of Israelite history.

This does not mean, however, that the principle was not contested. It was, and the Bible itself bears witness. The position was valid as long as it moved from cause to effect; it was an excellent tool of moral instruction. The problem arose when one began with the effect and worked back to the cause. If one wronged his neighbor, serious consequences could be expected. But what is to be said of one who suffers and is conscious of no deliberate sin? Is every sufferer a sinner? Is every affluent person virtuous? Aye, there was the rub! Two books of the Bible take serious issue with this traditional position: Job and Qoheleth.

Sirach 1–2, 38, 40, 44

Job

Written in the early postexilic period, Job is considered a world classic, especially noted for its soaring poetry. It is the story of a wealthy Oriental landowner, upright and devout, who suffers a series of disasters. He loses family and property, is reduced to indigence, and is seriously affected by bodily ailments. All of this he accepts philosophically as God's will. This is all part of the book's prologue (1:1—2:13). What he does not know is that God is permitting him to be tested. To complete the story in its original form, the reader must go directly to the book's epilogue (42:7–17). Because of his unquestioning acceptance in the presence of his three close friends, Job's losses are restored twofold. He now has property, family, and friends and is granted many years of life. The traditional picture has won the day. Virtue is inevitably rewarded, although the questioning Job has not yet had his say.

In the midsection of the book (cc. 3–42), the author takes relentless issue with the traditional position. The three friends of Job—Eliphaz, Bildad, and Zophar—ply Job with questions about his personal conduct. Each of them has three cycles of speeches

160

with a long-windedness that only compounds Job's suffering. Eliphaz states that no one suffers for nothing; in fact, all humans are guilty before God (4:1–9, 17–19). At one point, he even litanies Job's alleged sins (22:5–11). Job simply claims his innocence. Bildad is clearly on God's side and assures Job that it is never too late to repent (8:1–7). Zophar, never lost for words himself, accuses Job of being a man of many words (11:2f). Each time his accusers speak, Job replies and upholds his innocence. His friends' hypotheses find no echo in his life. He can only conclude that he has been wrongly treated:

> "Know then that God has put me in the wrong,
>   and closed his net around me.
> Even when I cry out, 'Violence!' I am not answered;
>   I call aloud, but there is no justice." (Job 19:6–7)

In total frustration, Job makes his final plea of innocence. He is guilty of no wrongdoing and even pursued virtue at every turn. He makes a final impassioned request for Yahweh to step forth and vindicate him (cc. 29–31).

At this point, the reader is ready for Yahweh's response, although in what is best described as a literary letdown, a new actor is introduced, who really has little that is new to add. Elihu goes on for six long chapters, repeating what the three friends have already said. He is clearly a witness in Yahweh's defense.

At this point, Yahweh makes a very dramatic appearance (cc. 38–40). Expectations run high and are not about to be fulfilled. To Job's questions he offers no answer and does not for a moment descend to the level of discussion that has been at center stage. In fact, it is God who does the questioning. The response centers wholly around the overarching wisdom and power of God. Where true wisdom is to be found is in the creation and ordering of the universe. Of his human interrogator, the Lord asks: "Who is this that darkens counsel by words without knowledge?" (38:2). Where was Job when the whole of the universe was set in order? There is too much evidence of God's intelligence for mundane and foolish discourses. The final answer is that God is mystery, and it is in the vast field of that unknown that the problem of suffering rests.

The prologue and epilogue show that Job's suffering was a test of his fidelity. This is unknown to him nor does it play a major part in the lengthy discussion. The book ends where it begins, with an unresolved problem. As even Job admits, humanity must submit before the unknown in God. Although there is no satisfactory answer given, Job does move away from the traditional answer of simple retribution. A sufferer is not necessarily a sinner, but the ultimate solution is part of the mystery of God.

Job:
Prologue and epilogue: 1:1—2:13, 42:7–17
The discussion: 4, 8, 11, 29–31, 38–39

Qoheleth (Ecclesiastes)

Known mainly by its Greek name, Ecclesiastes, the Hebrew Qoheleth means "assemblyman" or one who convokes an assembly. The book is hard to date with certainty but a fourth-century date is probable. With its inherent skepticism about almost every issue, the book was not readily accepted into the Hebrew canon. This hesitancy was finally overcome in view of the book's broader message. Qoheleth has little time for philosophical speculation on the meaning of life. The only reasonable approach is to accept life as it is, with all of its enigmas as well as its pleasures, and to live as a God-fearing person. The reason for this is that inquiry into the meaning and purpose of life is doomed to failure. It is a "vanity," a mere wisp of smoke with nothing of substance. Humans enter on the drama of life, play their part, and then exit, as unknown afterward as before. The rhythm of human existence provides for "a time to be born, and a time to die…a time for war, and a time for peace" (3:1–8); it goes on independent of human direction with an endless monotony over which we exercise no control.

When it comes to the question of retribution, Qoheleth would have us know that we are no better off. There too contradictions abound; the just are treated as if they had done evil, and the wicked, as though they had acted justly (8:14). Are not evildoers often treated as people of honor? And then, at the end, the lot of everyone is the same. Sheol is no safe haven; it is a place of emptiness, with no reward or punishment. Although he holds on to the belief in sanctions, Qoheleth feels the discussion and speculation will never resolve the anomalies. In life one does not pilot his or her ship. Thus it is best to accept life as it comes and be grateful for the happiness it provides. It is useless to strive to understand things too great; "for a living dog is better than a dead lion" (9:4).

Qoheleth: 1, 3, 5–6, 9, 12

Both Job and Qoheleth are examples of the direction the wisdom literature gradually took. We have gone beyond the simple maxim to inquiries on the meaning of life, in this case the question of suffering and death. As we have seen, the limitations of Israelite thought, even in the postexilic period, offered little new insight into an ancient problem; however, this does not mean that there was a willingness to settle for the tried and the true. Both Job and Qoheleth moved away from simple acceptance of a traditional explanation. This is clear evidence that biblical revelation is not a monolith. Teachings change and are subjected to challenge. Thought develops, even God-directed thought. One cannot stop at a given moment and claim that everything has been said. There are clear differences in things taught in one book over what is said in another. Revelation is a process, and its development can be traced in the scriptures themselves. The case of the problem of evil is certainly a case in point.

IMMORTALITY

It is with the clear appearance of life beyond the grave that the problem of suffering and death takes on new meaning. The idea of human immortality did not appear until two centuries before the dawn of Christianity. Although there may have been vague allusions theretofore, there was nothing substantive or marked by clarity. In addition to being understood as sanction, suffering could be seen as testing and, with the Servant of the Lord in Second Isaiah, as vicarious. However, it is unquestionably the belief in an afterlife, especially as presented in Daniel and Wisdom, that sheds the greatest light on this centuries-old problem.

Daniel

Written in the time of the Seleucid domination of Palestine by Antiochus Epiphanes, Daniel is a book of hope and exemplary courage. Written between 167 and 164 BC, it is not a book by a prophet but rather one about a prophet. During a period of severe persecution and major attempts to paganize the land of the Jews, it is the story of a man whose life and predictions stirred hope in the hearts of the Jewish population.

The story is one of a sixth-century prophet, a devout Jew who lived in Babylon in the times of the kings of the captivity. This is the account of Daniel and his three companions whose unflagging courage in the face of persecution, whether historical, legendary, or a mixture of both, served to motivate the second-century Jews, suffering as well at foreign hands. What we see here, then, is a second-century author retrojecting his story by four centuries to the time of the Babylonian captivity.

The first part of the book deals with Daniel's experiences in Babylon (1:1—6:20). Always faithful to their religious heritage, David and his companions are subjected to various ordeals by their captors. In whatever circumstances—observing the dietary laws (c. 1), being cast into a fiery furnace (c. 3), or thrown to the lions (c. 6), Daniel is resolutely faithful to his God.

The second part of the book (cc. 7–12), with its visions of the future, is written in the language of *apocalyptic*. This genre, quite simply, deals with revelation (*apocalypsis* means revelation) but in a different "unearthly" language, a symbolic language in need of being deciphered. In Daniel, the prophet is presented as living in sixth-century Babylon and, peering down the corridors of time, sees the fall of Babylon, Medea, Persia, and Greece. This is all done in highly symbolic language. It is, of course, a literary fiction because all these events have already taken place. When the prophecy reaches the rule of Antiochus Epiphanes, the author's present tyrant, everything becomes very precise. The persons and events being experienced at the time are presented in sharp relief. In the vision of the beasts, for example, the "small horn" of the beast is Antiochus himself (cc. 7–8). Various features of this Seleucid regime, known well to the author's contemporaries, are symbolically portrayed, although there is always the dominant note of hope. The final frieze in the symbolic vision points to the final outcome of God's plan; it is a note of salvation.

It is in the latter part of Daniel that immortality appears clearly for the first time. When the "time" of foreign domination has been completed and the period of trial has passed, the just shall be delivered and those who have fallen will be vindicated.

> "But at that time your people shall be delivered, everyone who is found written in the book. Many of those who sleep in the dust of the earth shall awake, some to everlasting life, and some to shame and everlasting contempt." (12:1, 2)

In context this is not a general resurrection; it deals with those faithful Jews who have died in persecution. They will rise and join their living countrymen, whereas the lot of the evildoers will be condemnation. This is the recognition of resurrection, however, even if viewed restrictively. Moreover, it is not a rising of the soul but of the whole-body person, in keeping with traditional Jewish anthropology. Nothing is said about postresurrection life, but the afterlife affirmation is made.

The idea continues. In the second book of Maccabees, the story is told of the heroic Jewish Maccabees, who revolted against the Seleucids in the final days of their oppressive reign. In one part, as the sons of a Jewish mother are martyred in succession, they witness individually to their belief, including the resurrection (2 Macc 7). Again, when a sacrifice for Jews who had died with pagan amulets on their bodies was offered, Judas Maccabeus affirms that it is done in the interests of their future resurrection (2 Macc 12:38–46).

Daniel 1–3, 5, 7–8, 12
2 Maccabees 7, 12:38–46

Wisdom

A Greek composition, Wisdom was written at the beginning of the last century before Christ and is probably the last Old Testament book to be written. It was composed in Alexandria in Egypt by a devout Diaspora Jew. As a Greek composition, it is not found in the Jewish or Protestant Bibles but has always been part of the Catholic tradition.

Alexandria was a city of Greek learning and culture, which had its effect on the resident Jewish community. The author is identified as Solomon to give added stature to the book; he is a man fully acquainted with Hellenistic culture and is not really at home with it. The pursuit of wisdom in philosophical terms cannot begin to compare with that true wisdom found in Judaism. Thus this pseudo-Solomon is at pains to show that the wisdom so evident in the creation of the universe and its organization was imparted to him by Yahweh himself (7:17–22). Was it not in fact the wisdom of God that first overpowered the Egyptians at the time of the exodus (11:1–16)?

Personal sentiments apart, the author of Wisdom is no stranger to the Hellenistic philosophical trends. Indeed, he has been conditioned by Greek learning more than he would probably like to admit. Although Wisdom is, for example, a personified attribute of God, her qualities of intelligence, multiformity, and all-pervasiveness are shared with the Greek *nous* or world soul.

Wisdom's understanding of immortality goes beyond any other Old Testament book. The author certainly knows the Hellenistic human composite of body and soul, with the immortality of the latter clearly affirmed. This would seem to have been a part of his anthropology; it is not the Hebrew anthropology of an animated body, with a life breath shared with all animate life. Rather for Wisdom, "a perishable body weighs down the soul" (9:15). Humans are endowed with "active souls" and "a living spirit" (15:11), an endowment "on loan" that must one day be returned to its maker (15:8).

Greek anthropology has unquestionably conditioned Wisdom's thinking. He understands body and soul well, but his immortality, interestingly enough, is not based on the immortal soul. Immortality is wholly based on justice. The afterlife is not everyone's destiny, rather "the righteous live forever and with the Lord as their recompense" (5:15). As an attribute of God, "righteousness is immortal" (1:14). To live a just life is to share in that divine quality, which is eternal.

> For to know you is complete righteousness,
> and to know your power is the root of immortality. (15:3)

The meaning of the verse is clear. To know or experience God is to live a life in accord with his will. This is justice. Because the creative force of God finds death (16:13) and Hades (17:14) powerless, the person who lives a life of justice has the key to immortality. This is the answer rather than any inherent property of human nature, although the Greek understanding of the human composite no doubt served as a catalyst to the author's thought.

There is no mention of a future resurrection in Wisdom, an idea that had no currency in the Greek world. In Wisdom there is no future for the evildoers. They are struck down as "dishonored corpses," "utterly dry and barren, and they will suffer anguish, and the memory of them will perish" (4:19). The eternal blessedness of the just neither includes nor excludes the presence of the body. Their future is a share in the lot of "the holy ones," the children of God whose lot is "among the saints" (5:5).

The impact of eternal sanctions on the problem of retribution is incalculable. It is now the evildoers who must eat, drink, and be merry for tomorrow they must die. With a life that goes beyond the present, past problems now dissipate. The accursed childlessness of the past now appears differently. "For blessed is the barren woman who is undefiled,...she will have fruit when God examines souls" (3:13). And what of the person who dies young? He shall be at rest. "For old age is not honored for length of time" (4:8). It is no longer gray hair that is a sign of virtue. It is a question of justice not age. Only with the passing of many centuries did biblical thought reach this point on one of the most important issues in human life.

> But the souls of the righteous are in the hand of God...
> For though in the sight of others they were punished,
> their hope is full of immortality.
> Having been disciplined a little, they will receive great
> good,
> because God tested them and found them worthy of himself;
> like gold in the furnace he tried them,
> and like a sacrificial burnt offering he accepted them.
> (3:1, 4–6)

Wisdom 1, 3, 4

THE NEW TESTAMENT

XIII.

THE FINAL AGE

With the Roman destruction of Jerusalem in AD 70, the existence of the political or national Israel came to an end. Its patrimony from that point on was exclusively religious. The scriptures were effectively closed, and the sacred books were seen as normative in the life of the people. The last major revolt against foreign power was that of the Maccabees, who opposed the Seleucids in the second century BC. The Hasmonean rulers then came to power in Palestine (142–63 BC), ushering in a period of limited independence, under a relaxed Syrian control. All independence ended with the coming of the Romans; authority over the Jews was exercised either by Jewish puppets or direct Roman governorship.

Judaism at the dawn of Christianity, however, was no longer solely a Palestinian phenomenon. The Diaspora had carried Jews to many parts of the ancient world, although "end time" hopes were strongest in Palestinian Judaism. There was a strong hope that God's reign would finally come, together with a ruler or messiah, who would inaugurate a period of justice and peace. The Essene community at Qumran expected two messiahs, one davidic and one priestly.

A mixture of disappointment and expectation marked those final days. Disappointment in a history that had often seen Israel unfaithful, then subjugated and oppressed. Hope that the promises of the Lord, begun with Abraham two thousand years before, would soon be realized. There was a deep religious heartbeat in that country then occupied by the most formidable empire in world history. It was on this scene that Jesus of Nazareth emerged, at the dawn of a new and final era, with a message that would revolutionize the known world but one that would always remain deeply indebted to a centuries-old patrimony of belief that began with a man named Abraham, the first to answer a heavenly call.

> At that time appeared Jesus, a wise man, if one may call him a man at all. For he was a doer of wonderful works, a teacher of men, who received the truth with gladness, and he attracted Jews as also people of the Greek sort in great numbers. This was the Christ and when on the denunciation of our leading men, Pilate had punished him with crucifixion, those who had loved him formerly did not cease therefrom. He appeared to them alive again on the third day, for the godly prophets had foretold this and innumerable other wonderful things concerning him. And even now the race of men called Christians has not died out. (Josephus, *Testimonium Flavianum*, art. 18.33, #63–64)

For Christians, Jesus Christ is the fullness of God's revelation, the fulfillment of scriptural prophecy, the inaugurator of the final era, and the redeemer of God's people. With all of this said and affirmed, it is surprising that the Jewish sources of the first century, outside of the New Testament, give him such little notice. The above quotation from the Jewish historian Josephus is a notable exception. He at least gives Jesus one paragraph. Although the quote has undergone Christian editing at a subsequent date (e.g., "if one may call him a man at all," "he appeared on the third day"), there is no doubt that the substance of the quotation come from Josephus in the 90s of the first century.

One of the earliest Roman witnesses attests to the Christians' regard for Christ. Pliny the younger, governor of Bithynia, in about AD 112 speaks of Christians "who sing a hymn to Christ as to a God."

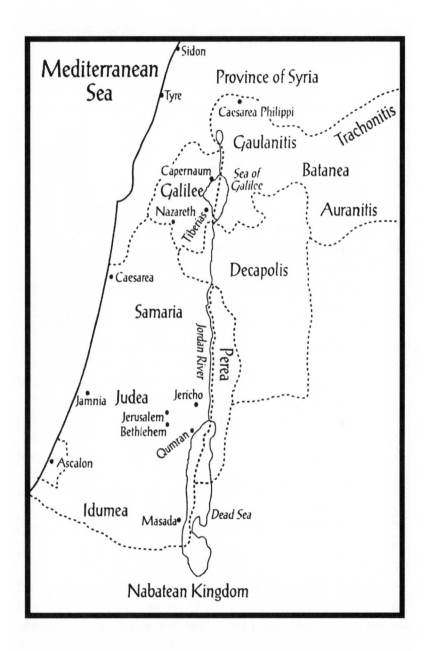

The fact is that the greatest part of our knowledge of the historical Jesus comes from the New Testament. The problem with that is that we are not dealing with unbiased historians; these were writers who, for whatever reason, were convinced that Jesus was not only the messiah but the Son of God and view his life in the light of this conviction. They were not disinterested or largely objective historians. The evangelists responsible for this fourfold witness wrote, not biographies, but the first catechisms of Christianity. Because their primary objective was to build faith, their writings must be accepted on that basis.

THE POLITICAL AND SOCIAL CONTEXT OF CHRISTIAN BEGINNINGS

During the life of Jesus and the period of early Christianity, Rome controlled Palestine and the Hellenistic world. During Jesus' life, the family of Herod the Great administered Palestine, at the pleasure of the Roman authorities. The New Testament attests that Jesus was born during the reign of Herod the Great, who died in 4 BC. (An early mistake misjudged the actual year of Jesus' birth by four years; the date must be adjusted to correspond to the period of Herod's life.) At Herod's death, his kingdom was divided among his three sons. The areas that most affected Jesus' life were the region of Galilee, governed by Herod Antipas, and Judea, ruled by his brother Archelaus, who was later removed by Rome, at which time Judea became an imperial province directly under Roman rule. Herod continued to rule in Galilee and, according to the Gospel witness, was responsible for the death of John the Baptist and met with Jesus during Jesus' trial in Jerusalem.

During the childhood of Jesus, there was a revolt against Rome that was quickly put down. There were moments of insurrection but Rome's control was largely unquestioned under the procuratorship of Valerius Gratus and Pontius Pilate, both of whom ruled for a ten-year period.

In the social order, the first adherents to Jesus' message were Palestinian Jews, and it was in Jerusalem that Christianity first took root. There was considerable contact between Palestine and other parts of the Near East because of the country's strategic location on a major trade route. The Jews occupied the northern and southern parts of the country, with the Samaritans occupying a fair part of the central region. Contact between the Hebrews and the "heretical" Samaritans was minimal because of questions of heterodoxy and an ethnically mixed Samaritan population.

A later Jewish insurrection against Rome at the time of the emperor Vespasian resulted in the quelling of the revolt and the final taking of Jerusalem by the emperor's son Titus in AD 70.

THE LIFE OF JESUS

Our attention in this book is centered principally on faith in Christ and the living of his message. However, we are understandably concerned with what we can know of Jesus in a historical sense. We are not involved in mere myth or historical construct; such would give us no adequate explanation of how Christianity became the religion it did. People did not give their lives for a symbol. By the same token, we are fully aware that the Gospels are faith documents. Not every account or assertion is to be taken at face value in a historical or factually reliable sense; we know that other factors were at work. Scholars, however, generally converge around a basic outline of Jesus' life.

The gospel proclamation begins, not with the infancy of Jesus, but with his baptism by John, the point at which Mark's Gospel opens. Three of the four Gospels speak explicitly of the baptism, even in the face of certain competitive attitudes regarding the baptisms of Jesus and John. Jesus was a Jewish layman residing in Galilee where he exercised most of his ministry. He was a rabbi or teacher, a healer and wonder worker, who restricted his activity to the Jewish population of Israel. Largely because of his teaching, controversy arose between Jesus and the Jewish authorities. This eventually led

The Jordan River

to his being handed over to the Roman rulers who ordered his execution. He was crucified under Pontius Pilate, with the religious movement that he inaugurated continuing after his death.

JESUS IN THE NEW TESTAMENT

The greater part of the New Testament was written between the early AD 50s and 100. Within these books the Jesus of history has become the object of Christian faith. If we were dealing with a simple historical personality whose life was to be recorded for future generations, we would begin where two of the gospels begin, with his birth and childhood. However, because he is a person to be accepted in faith, we are led to begin where the first believers began, with his death and resurrection. It was in the faith acceptance of this fundamental truth, with the aid of God's Spirit, that one was led into a consideration of his life and teaching. This proceeded from a series of questions to be answered for the believer, not a systematic presentation of

176

Jesus' life. This largely disparate collection of works and teachings of Jesus was finally woven into a written gospel. This means that the gospels are a retrojection, a looking back into the life of Jesus, from a faith position wherein his divine status and authority are already affirmed.

THE KERYGMA

After the resurrection, the first Christians were called to believe in the central salvific act of Jesus' life. The formula centered on a few basic truths, which are in fact recorded for us in the New Testament. This constitutes what is known as the *kerygma*, from the Greek word *kerussein*, to proclaim or preach. This was done before any type of teaching regarding Christ and his mission, partially because the return of Christ at the *parousia* was expected soon. When this did not occur as expected, a more extensive catechesis was seen as indispensable.

The kerygma consisted of belief in: (1) the salvific death of Jesus; (2) the resurrection; and (3) the post-Easter apparitions of Christ. Although this could be slightly expanded upon with a brief reference to his ministry, these three affirmations were essential. Writing to the church of Corinth in the mid-fifties, Paul already speaks of the kerygma as an integral part of the church's life.

"For I handed on to you as of first importance what I in turn had received; that Christ died for our sins in accordance with the scriptures, and that he was buried, and that he was raised on the third day in accordance with the scriptures, and that he appeared to Cephas, then to the twelve. Then he appeared to more than five hundred brothers and sisters at one time...." (1 Cor 15:3–6).

In this proclamation, the death and resurrection of Jesus are clearly salvific ("died for our sins") and preordained ("in accordance with the scriptures"). With the acceptance of these fundamental truths in faith, baptism was conferred, with the accompanying conferral of the Spirit and the forgiveness of sins. Christ is recognized as Lord and Savior and thus in a position to be the agent of forgiveness and salvation. This kerygmatic formula recurs repeatedly in the Acts of the Apostles as a fixed datum of the early church.

This procedure strikes the modern Christian as unusual, given that today baptism follows a period of rather lengthy catechesis. In early Christianity, the catechesis followed baptism. The kerygma is vitally important for an understanding of the early church because the Gospels are written within the kerygmatic framework.

Acts 2:22-36, 3:13-19, 5:30-32, 10:36-41

DIDACHE

After baptism further explanation was needed on the life and teaching of Jesus. This was probably not as necessary in the earliest period when the return of Christ and the close of history were seen as imminent. As this expectation receded and the church came more to the fore, there were questions that arose regarding the Christian life. Now that the Jewish law has been surpassed, what was the specific ethic of Christianity? What observances from Judaism were to be retained? What of the food and dietary laws? Sabbath observance? What was to be said of contact with nonobservant Jews or with nonbelievers in general? What was the proper attitude toward the Roman authorities? What was to be said of divorce? In short, what was the teaching of Jesus on these and many other questions?

Then there was the question of the life and mission of Jesus himself. What was his relationship to John the Baptist? The nature and circumstances of his miracles? Who were his earliest disciples? How could his ministry among the Jews be best described? His attitude toward the Gentiles? Most important, how did it happen that his own people rejected him and brought him to death? What was the role of the Romans in his execution? How was his resurrection known?

These were some of the questions that led the early church to reflect on Jesus' life and ministry in the light of its belief in him as Lord and Savior. This led to the *didache*, from the Greek *didaskein*, to teach. This collection of teachings regarding Jesus and his life began while the apostles still lived and were in a unique position to determine the credibility of what was taught. They were the accredited witnesses of his public ministry (cf. Acts 1:21f). Although this catechesis was supervised and directed, it was not an oral or written replay of past events. On the contrary, the events of Jesus' life were often "fleshed out" in the light of Resurrection faith with its clearer understanding of Jesus' true nature.

The didache or teaching did not hesitate to adapt the instruction of Jesus to developing circumstances in the early church. There were differences that arose in the life and culture of believers separated in time and place from the historical Jesus. According to Catholic belief, this collection and adaptation of data were done under the Holy Spirit's guidance; therefore, constituting part of Christian faith. Its truth lies in the fact that it was in this way that the Spirit led the church in its reflection on the historical Jesus.

As necessary features of Jesus' life and ministry were collected, they were tailored to fit accepted forms of expression. These were initially oral and only eventually consigned to writing in ways that allowed them to be easily committed to memory. In attending Mass today, we are struck by the fact that the Gospel reading has been excised from the Gospel as a whole and makes complete sense in itself. The reason is that this was the way that these episodes or pericopes originally came into existence. They were short teachings or events from Jesus' life, succinctly expressed, which circulated in the primitive church. This is similar to the way in which lessons are set into rhymes today for children to commit them more easily to memory; this was particularly important in early cultures in which memory was more to the fore than the written word.

Authors today generally categorize the gospel literary forms into pronouncement stories, miracle stories, logia, and legends.

Pronouncement Stories

Pronouncement stories are responses of Jesus to specific questions, which then become normative principles. The usual form is a question and response; in some instances, there may be more than one question offered by the questioner or respondent (Jesus). The response then gave the church a direction in dealing with some issue facing the early church. Various examples of the pronouncement story are found in Mark, chapter 2.

To cite an example: because Christians observed Sunday and not Saturday as their sabbath, they had much freer attitudes toward laws regulating Jewish Sabbath observance. Did the teaching of Jesus give any direction in this matter?

> One sabbath he was going through the grainfields; and as they made their way his disciples began to pluck heads of grain. The Pharisees said to him, "Look, why are they doing what is not lawful on the sabbath?" And he said to them, "Have you never read what David did when he and his companions were hungry and in need of food? He entered the house of God, when Abiathar was high priest, and ate the bread of the Presence, which it is not lawful for any but the priests to eat, and he gave some to his companions." Then he said to them, "The sabbath was made for humankind, and not humankind for the sabbath; so the Son of Man is lord even of the sabbath." (Mark 2:23–28)

In addressing the question of Christian observance of the Sabbath, a threefold response is given: a comparable case from the Hebrew scriptures (David), a priority of values (sabbath for humankind), and Christ's authority (lord of the sabbath). The pericope reflects the customary form: a question from opponents, a counterquestion in response, and a climactic statement of Jesus.

Similar pronouncements are had on the question of fasting (Mark 2:18–22), table fellowship with sinners (read: Gentiles) (Mark 2:13–17), the paying of taxes (Mark 12:13–17), and marriage and divorce (Mark 10:1–11), to cite but a few examples. In each case, the church fashioned a short and simple answer in an almost stereotypical form for a didactic purpose.

Miracle Stories

In his own day Jesus was recognized as a wonder-worker. He would hardly have been acknowledged as a divine emissary were he not. There was interest in retaining the memory of these events because they were the prelude to the eventual exaltation and lordship of Jesus. They were also signs of the End Time with its final vanquishing of the Evil One, the underlying cause of sin, suffering, and misfortune. In addition, the final days as envisioned by the prophets were to be a period of consolation and comfort for the afflicted (Isa 61:1f, Luke 4:16–21).

Jesus' miracles were of various types: healings (the ten lepers), exorcisms (the Gerasene demoniac), nature (the stilling of the storm), and restoration to life (the widow's son). The stylized miracle form had a very basic structure: a description of the circumstances or symptoms; the action of Jesus; and indication of the completeness of the outcome. A clear illustration of the form is seen in the account of Peter's mother-in-law.

> As soon as they left the synagogue, they entered the house of Simon and Andrew, with James and John. Now Simon's mother-in-law was in bed with a fever, and they told him about her at once. *He came and took her by the hand and lifted her up.* Then the fever left her, and she *began to serve them.* (Mark 1:29–31; emphasis added)

This succinct account describes the illness, the action of Jesus, and the completeness of the cure.

Logia

These were the "wisdom" sayings of Jesus. Rather than being seen as part of a narrative, they stand by themselves as the teaching of the Lord. At times they are simple statements, as, for example, in the beatitudes, or they may be expressed in synonymous or antithetic parallelism. When synonymous, the second half of the verse repeats the first half in a different way. It may go beyond a single verse and become a parable or extended teaching but with the basic structure remaining intact. In antithetic parallelism, the single point is made by making the second half of the verse say the opposite of the first. The following examples will illustrate the form.

Synonymous parallelism:

"Ask, and it will be given you;
search, and you will find;
knock, and the door will be opened for you." (Matt 7:7–10)

Antithetic parallelism:

"So, if your eye is healthy, your whole body will be full of
    light;
but if your eye is unhealthy, your whole body will be full of
    darkness." (Matt 6:22f)

The simplest form of the logia, as we have said, is the direct "one liner":

"In everything do to others as you would have them do to you." (Matt 7:12; cf. also Matt 5:3–10, Luke 6:20–23)

It is not difficult to appreciate the original forms of these sayings, which could easily be committed to memory.
**Miracle stories: Mark 1:14–45, 5:53–41, Luke 7:11–17
Pronouncement stories: Mark 2:13–28, 3:31–35
Logia: Matt 5–7**

In some instances the hand of the early church is thrown into strong relief. This happens when the narrative is somewhat altered or expanded by the authors. For example, in the fasting narrative that exempts Jesus and his disciples from Jewish fasting practices (Mark 2:18-22), there is the obviously inserted statement that fasting has subsequently returned to church life (2:20). There is a further instance when the church has combined a miracle story and a pronouncement story in the case of the healed paralytic (Mark 2:1–12), which "stitches in" a vindication of Jesus' power to forgive sin. In the Greek text, this is a rather uneven insertion (vv. 5–11), which illustrates that the one who has power over suffering also has power over sin.

Mark 2:1–12

Legends

This category is not as easily determined or identified as the other three. Although they are not numerous, the legends play an important part in the Gospel narratives. The legend is primarily a theological statement centering on the person of Jesus. Hence, it is elaborated as an interpretation and has a strong supernatural overlay. This makes the underlying historical event, if such there were, very elusive because the truth being expressed is of a different order. Examples of the legend are found in the trinitarian theophany after the baptism of Jesus (Mark 1:9ff) and the transfiguration, with its strong emphasis on the direction and outcome of Jesus' earthly mission (Mark 9:2-8).

Another example of the legend appears in the threefold temptation of Jesus (Matt 4:1-1, Luke 4:1–2). Here there is a literary triptych dealing with the various types of temptation to which Jesus was subjected during his earthly ministry, such as to being the bread provider or miracle worker, to manifest himself in his God-given power, and to be recognized as king. These were all temptations, particularly evident in John's Gospel, which came from human sources. Here they are brought together in three dramatic scenes in which Jesus is whisked from temple top to mountain top by Satan himself. The didactic aspect of the legend is to point out for the believers the dangers inherent in lust, power, and wealth.

THE PERIOD OF COLLECTION (AD 40–65)

As if making a string of pearls, these accounts of Jesus' ministry expressed in the aforementioned forms were eventually brought together in small collections. As the church continued to grow, these various accounts passed from oral to written form, whether as miracle or pronouncement stories or logia. There was no attempt to retain a strict chronological sequence from Jesus' life; very often particular themes determined the sequence. An example of this type of collection is found in Mark 1:16—2:28, wherein a series of miracle stories and pronouncement stories have been brought together in a single unit. In being given church approval as authentic expressions, they were used in the formative development of the Christian life, not only in Palestine, but in the various churches of Asia Minor and Greece.

This period before the written gospels was a time of considerable significance in illustrating how the teaching of Jesus was not only authenticated but adapted to the various cultures of early Christianity. Many of the gospel pericopes tell us as much about the early church as they do about Jesus himself, as his life was refracted through the ecclesial experiences of people who had never known Jesus of Nazareth. Many of these early church concerns are presented in the Acts of the Apostles. They centered on the failure of the Jews to accept Christ and then the whole question of the role of the Jewish law in a Gentile culture. There were, moreover, tensions between the conservative Jewish Christians of Palestine and the more progressive trends of the Gentile Christians. There were both negative and positive attitudes toward the Roman authorities. All of these issues had to be viewed in the light of Christ's own teaching.

This was the period when the gospel material was being formulated, under the guidance of the Spirit, not only for first-century Christians but for all future ages.

XIV.

THE THREEFOLD GOSPEL

Two questions arise with reference to this chapter heading. What is the meaning of *gospel?* Why is it termed "threefold" when there are actually four gospels, Matthew, Mark, Luke, and John?

The word *gospel* is related to its Greek antecedent *euangelion,* which means "good news." This centered initially, not on the final written documents, but on the kerygma, the heart of the Christian proclamation, the great good tidings of salvation through the death and resurrection of Christ. So when we read in the first verse of Mark's work that it is the "good news of Jesus Christ, the Son of God," the emphasis is on the gospel's climax, the vindication of Jesus as God's son in his death-resurrection. In the course of time, however, the term "gospel" was applied to the entire account of Jesus' public ministry.

The present chapter is concerned with the threefold gospel of Matthew, Mark, and Luke. Even a cursory examination of the three shows their interrelatedness. All three of them follow the same basic outline of Jesus' ministry. Many of his works and words are found in all three, sometimes almost word for word. There are certainly differences as well as likenesses, as we shall see, but the lines of convergence among the three is incontestable. John's Gospel, on the other hand, follows a completely different and distinctive line. Although he evidences a certain awareness of the threefold gospel, he does not make use of it nor does it play any real role in his composition. Of the many miracles found in the other gospels he presents only that of the loaves and fishes, and the miracles he does present—the wine at Cana, the man born blind, the cripple at the Bethesda pool, and the raising of Lazarus—are not recounted in the threefold gospel at all. For these reasons, as well as his highly developed theological perspective, the Gospel of John must be studied on its own.

The first three gospels are commonly called *synoptic*. The reasons for this become obvious when the three are lined up side by side in three separate columns. When this is done, likenesses, differences, and areas of convergence and divergence become immediately evident. This makes it possible to read them together or "to synopsize" the three. In fact, this is the best way to study the three by using what is called a *synopsis*, wherein the narratives and sayings are seen together. Commonality appears at once as well as the distinctive concerns of each evangelist.

This then brings the student to the final step: a study of each evangelist and his overall theme. We have already spoken of the two antecedent steps: the consideration of the event or teaching in the life of Jesus himself, as closely as this can be ascertained, and the use made of the event or teaching in the life of the early church during the period of oral and written catechesis. The third step, then, is to see the way each evangelist has fashioned the material in the composition of the canonical gospel.

Why were the gospels written? The first and obvious reason was one of practicality and usefulness. In the latter part of the first century, the church was expanding throughout the Western world. There was a need to ensure the accuracy of what was being preached and taught as the word was carried throughout the Roman world. Because Greek remained the common language of the far-flung empire, it was the language of the original gospel texts. Just as the Spirit of inspiration had been present in the earlier stages of gospel development, it was present as well as the final documents were taking shape. The gospels, once authenticated, were then clearly separated from other "gospels" that were beginning to appear, some of them Gnostic in their origins, which were seen as spurious and deceptive by the early church but as bonafide by some early Christians. The most celebrated of these is probably the "gospel of Thomas" with its presentation of a clearly Gnostic Jesus. In the interests of separating the heterodox from the orthodox, the early church was at pains to establish the normative character of the four gospels.

THE TWO-SOURCE THEORY

We have had occasion to speak of the likenesses and differences that appear in the threefold gospel. There are many instances in which there is a strong convergence among Mark, Matthew, and Luke. For example, the broad outline of the public ministry in the three gospels is the same. Many of the transcribed events of Jesus' life are in almost word-for-word agreement. There are also divergences, however, some of which continue to evoke interest. For example, Matthew and Luke will converge in matter not found in Mark and will sometimes have material peculiar to themselves.

The commonly accepted explanation of likeness and divergence is the "two-source" theory. This position holds that Matthew and Luke have used Mark, and this explains their common convergence. In addition, Matthew and Luke had another common source known as Q (from the German *Quelle*, "source"). This would explain common material not found in Mark. Finally, both Matthew and Luke have sources of their own that are not shared, here designated M and L.

This theory has won a broad measure of acceptance as the most reasonable explanation of interdependence. Although it does not answer every question, it is more reasonable than any other. Its only noteworthy competitor is the *Griesbach Hypothesis*, named after its eighteenth-century proponent, J. Griesbach, which argues for the priority of Matthew. Luke then follows Matthew and Mark then uses both Matthew and Luke. The sequence thus is Matthew-Luke-Mark. Griesbach's theory is in line with an ancient tradition of Matthew the apostle as the author of his gospel and thus being the first gospel written. There are a number of problems with this

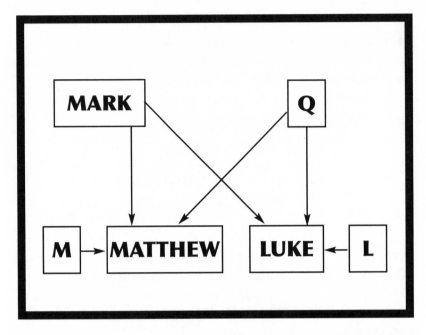

hypothesis, the most noteworthy being Mark's gospel as the last. This would mean that he used the two longer gospels and excised large sections of both. This would include important sections as the infancy narratives, the beatitudes, and the Lord's prayer, all of which would have had significance for early Christian communities.

Even with its shortcomings, the two-source theory offers the best solution of the interdependence of the threefold gospel.

AUTHORSHIP

The four gospels claim the names of two apostles (Matthew and John) and two prominent Christians (Mark and Luke). The question is how much do the names tell us. We have no actual proof that any of these is the author of the work ascribed to him. If Mark is primitive and was not an eyewitness himself, but was subsequently used by Matthew and Luke, we are removing Matthew ever farther away from being an apostle and companion to Jesus in his ministry.

In fact, all of the gospels were written in the postapostolic age, at a point in time when most if not all of the apostles were already dead. John's gospel comes from the end of the first century and is farthest removed from the eyewitness apostolic age. What significance then do the names have? None of the names was uncommon and could have belonged to any early Christian. Furthermore, no gospel makes any claim to have been the work of an apostle or his companion. Only John makes a connection between the "disciple whom Jesus loved" and the author of the gospel (John 21:20–25) but leaves the beloved disciple unidentified.

It would have been logical, however, to link the gospels with prominent members of the early church, just as it was important to attach Moses to the Pentateuch. Moreover, the gospels of Matthew and John may very well have sprung from authentic traditions of these apostles that were retained in the early church; however, such would require a period of gestation during which time the original traditions grew and evolved over a period of decades.

The question of authorship will also be treated with each gospel but it always remains a secondary issue. Whoever may have stood behind any of these writings did not give the text its definitive status. It is the gospel itself that is recognized and accredited as a work that accurately reflects the belief of the church. As it passed into the life of the church, each gospel became a normative rule of faith. In time they became part of the scriptural canon. It is its formal recognition that led to full acceptance as inspired and normative.

THE GOSPEL OF MARK

Often identified with John Mark, who was a companion of Paul and later present with Peter in Rome (Col 4:10, Acts 12:25), the author remains disputed and cannot be affirmed with certainty. If the scales were to be tipped in any direction, however, it would be in favor of John Mark. The gospel draws on different sources and therefore makes single authorship hard to establish.

In various ways he seems to lack a clear knowledge of Palestinian geography and customs and is perhaps best seen as someone from the developing church in the Roman world. In fact, Rome remains a likely place of authorship, with a date of somewhere between AD 65 and 70, that is, before the destruction of Jerusalem.

Literary Structure

The gospel has two major divisions: the Galilean ministry (1:1—9:50) and the events of Judea and Jerusalem (10:1—16:8). The first part includes:

- Introduction (1:1–13)
- Galilean Activity (1:14—8:26)
- Events at Caesarea Philippi (8:27—9:29)

The second part includes:

- The Jerusalem Journey (9:30—10:52)
- The Jerusalem Ministry (11:1—14:42)
- The Final Stage of Jesus' Life (14:43—15:47)
- The Empty Tomb (16:1–8)

It should be noted that the abrupt ending of the gospel with the women fleeing from the tomb underwent a certain amelioration in the course of time with the addition of a longer (16:9–20) and shorter ending. Although the original is not satisfying from a literary point of view, it is probably the original conclusion.

The Major Themes
"Who Is This Man?"

The literary and theological perspective through which Mark fashioned and ordered his material is best seen in the disciples' question after the stilling of the storm: "Who then is this, that even the wind and the sea obey him?" (Mark 4:41). Throughout the gospel there is a gradual self-disclosure on Jesus' part, which includes moments of faith as well as misunderstanding. This process has two important apogees, both of them pre-announced in the opening verse: "The beginning of the good news of Jesus *Christ, the Son of God*" (1:1).

In the course of time "Christ" became a surname for Jesus, although its original meaning was "anointed one" or "Messiah." The Christ was the expected emissary of God, a descendent of David, who was to inaugurate the reign of God, a reign of peace and justice. This hope for the king-Messiah, after centuries of subjugation to foreign powers, was particularly strong at the dawn of the Christian era. "Son of God," however, said much more than Messiah. By the time Mark's gospel is written, it is a clear recognition of Jesus' unique relationship to God the Father.

Two distinct moments in the gospel narrative give dramatic presentation to Mark's opening verse. At the gospel's midpoint, at Caesarea Philippi, Jesus asks his disciples who people say that he is. Peter responds: "You are the Messiah [the Christ]" (8:27–30). In seeing Jesus as the promised One of God, Peter has taken an important leap forward, but it still says less than the full truth enunciated by the pagan centurion at the Gospel's end. Looking upon the dead Jesus, he says: "Truly this man was God's Son!" (15:39). In this he is presented as acknowledging Christ's oneness with the Father, a profession of faith in divinity possible only in the power of the Holy Spirit.

It is within this framework that Mark has built his account of the life and ministry of Jesus. His miracles, usually healings or expressions of compassion, are acts of self-disclosure; his teaching is a call to discipleship, for which he is often referred to as "Teacher." His preaching centers on the reign of God, that is, the era of Yahweh's sovereignty. There are no claims to divinity nor mention of a future church. In short, unlike the other gospels, there is in Mark no strong postresurrection theology. His identity is gradually unfolded to those who come to him in faith (4:10–12). His disciples are selected and commissioned to be messengers of the reign of God as well. The entirety of Jesus' public ministry in Mark lasts about one year.

The Messianic Secret

Closely connected with the identity of Jesus in Mark's gospel is an unusual feature often designated the Messianic secret. This is seen especially in those instances where a given source would try to make claims as to his true identity, only to be silenced by Jesus himself. It occurs in the case of the demons (1:24f, 34; 3:12), as well as his disciples (8:30, 9:9). Various reasons are assigned for this strong emphasis, but it is probably attributable more to the evangelist himself than to Jesus. From the Marcan perspective it is important that Jesus be recognized only in terms of faith in his mission, which was one of suffering and death. Even Peter's recognition of him was open to misinterpretation because Jesus immediately moves his attention to the fact that this will be a Messiah who must suffer and die (8:27–33). It is only through a slow process of faith, and not through miracles and wonders, that the true nature of the Son of God will be understood.

The title for Jesus closest to Mark is Son of Man. It is used with frequency and has strong eschatological overtones. Originating in Daniel chapter 7, where a certain Son of Man is depicted as coming on the clouds of heaven in the final days, representing a renewed and restored humanity, the title fit Jesus well and yet was neutral enough to avoid notions of kingship or divine sonship. It also pointed to the true humanity of Jesus, one like us in everything but sin (Heb 11:15).

The Jesus of Mark's gospel is bound by a certain sense of urgency in what is almost a feverish activity. He is constantly involved in healings and preaching, almost as if he recognizes the limitations of time. He is literally besieged by the crowd. The people press around the door of his dwelling (2:2), surround him at the water's edge (4:1), and follow him to places of solitude (1:35–37). Jesus was called to a life of service over a relatively brief period of time, and as Mark makes clear, it was a self-giving that began well before his crucifixion.

Mark 1–2, 4:35–41, 8:14–16

THE GOSPEL OF MATTHEW

Matthew's gospel had a primacy of honor and of use in early Christianity. Because i   ked with the apostle of the same name (cf. Matt 9:9–13   ed as the first of the gospels and is the one most quoted   Christian circles. Although most authorities today do n   in its present form, as authored by an apostle or as the e   the four gospels, its importance in linking Judaism and e   tianity is widely rec   This is not to deny the possib   it some early stage   ae form it might have stood in   to the apostle; h   e book in its final form comes f   er date and is re   number of later sources. Even th   author remair   a, its origins are generally linked with Antioch of Syri   considerably large Jewish Christian population. It was   after the fall of Jerusalem (cf. 22:7) and after the Gospel   as in circulation, probably to be dated between AD 80 and 9..

The audience for whom Matthew is written is largely a Jewish Christian one. This is seen clearly in his reverential attitude toward the Jewish law and his audience's presumed familiarity with it. He is marked by a broad sensitivity to Jewish law and custom. In making this assertion, there are two qualifications to be made. First, the community had a mixed population in which Gentile Christians were also present. Second, by the time Matthew is written, the split between the church and the synagogue had become pronounced. Thus, although respectful of his Jewish patrimony, he often reflects the hostile attitudes prevailing at the time between Christians and Jews.

Literary Structure

The first gospel follows basically the outline of the Marcan narrative in highlighting Jesus' ministry, death, and resurrection. Like Luke, he begins with the stories of Jesus' birth and early childhood, generally termed the "infancy narratives." In neither gospel do these form a part of the earliest preaching but serve more as a theological overture to the two gospels. These accounts will be treated separately at a later point in this book.

The outline, then, of the Matthean gospel is quite simple:
• The Birth of Jesus (1:1—2:23)
• The Public Ministry (3:1—26:2)
• The Death and Resurrection (26:3—28:20)

Section 2 is the major part of the book, combining the teaching of Jesus with miracle accounts and other activities. This is subdivided into five subsections, each concluded with variations of the clause: "Now when Jesus had finished saying these things" (7:28, 11:1, 13:53, 19:1, 26:1). The arrangement reflects the Torah or five books of Moses with each section containing major teaching, together with accompanying narrative:
• The Higher Ethic (3:1—7:29)
• The Call of Discipleship (8:1—11:1)
• The Reign of God (11:2—13:53)
• The Kingdom as Church (13:54—19:1)
•The Final Time (19:2—26:1)

The Major Theme: Fulfillment

For Matthew it is the actualization of God's saving plan as foretold in the Old Testament and realized in Jesus of Nazareth that stand as the centerpiece of his gospel. He has in mind especially his Jewish Christian audience and so emphasizes continuity with the former dispensation in a way that the other gospels do not. He will repeatedly draw on the Hebrew scriptures as they point to Jesus and his mission. The gospel opens with a genealogy that is clearly geared to link Jesus with his two important ancestral figures, David and Abraham (1:1–17). Like other biblical genealogies, it suffers from a certain historical inaccuracy, although its nonnegotiables are the link established with David, the father of Jewish messianism, and Abraham, the earliest patriarchal figure. In countless contexts of the gospel where some word or event suggests an Old Testament parallel, Matthew does not hesitate to quote the earlier text. The earthly ministry of Jesus is exclusively directed to the "sons of Israel" and his disciples' mission is limited to the Jews as well (10:5f).

None of this is to say that there is no universalism in the first gospel. The post-Easter Jesus commissions his disciples to carry the gospel to the ends of the earth (28:18f). The four women mentioned in the genealogy (Tamar, Rahab, Ruth, and Bathsheba) are all types of Mary inasmuch as their offspring are all conceived in an exceptional fashion, but it is also worth noting that they all have close ties with the pagan or Gentile world.

The infancy narratives (cc. 1–2) are full of Hebrew typology as Jesus emerges as the new Moses and the new Israel. His Sermon on the Mount (not on the plain as in Luke) is clearly related to Moses and Sinai. In the same discourse there is a clear emphasis on the permanent and lasting character of the Torah (5:18), something found nowhere else in the gospels but readily accepted by those early Christians deeply attached to the Jewish law (cf. Gal 1–2, Acts 15). So as the new law builds on the old, it surpasses it and does not abolish it (5:21-48).

Any careful reading of Matthew's gospel shows why it is termed the most Jewish of the four. The author views Jesus against the background of Old Testament prophecy and personalities, making fulfillment a dominant theme of his writing. By the same token he is keenly aware that persecution in Jesus' life, as well as that of the early church, was inspired by Jewish animosity. It is he alone who cites the words of the Jews at Jesus' trial, "His blood be on us and on our children" (27:25), words that were used to stoke the fires of a strong and undeserved anti-Semitism through the centuries.

The Sermon on the Mount

Matthew draws on both Q and his own particular sources in giving us the "magna carta" of the Christian ethical life in the sermon on the Mount (cc. 5–7). It has long been seen as a summation of the Christian way of life. From the new Sinai, Jesus as the

The Church of the Beatitudes

new Moses expresses a new Torah with an unquestioned authority. He forthrightly modifies the Decalogue and other prescriptions of the Law.

Matthew shares the beatitudes with Luke but gives them a more inclusive thrust. Where Luke has four (6:20–23), Matthew has eight. Whereas Luke's blessings look to a poor and disadvantaged people, Matthew gives emphasis to moral dispositions. Thus Luke's "poor" become Matthew's the "poor in spirit," the "hungry" become those who "hunger for righteousness," and Matthew adds the meek, the merciful, the pure in heart, and the peacemakers. The beatitudes point up the internal dispositions of citizens of the reign of God, looking mainly to a spirit of trust, confidence, and moral uprightness.

In the central ethical section (5:17–48) Jesus skillfully preserves the values of the Law in going beyond it. He even sees the Law as marginal in calling for a more radical moral response. He excludes not only killing but any form of anger, not only adultery but any type of lust, not just the fulfillment of oaths but any form of oath taking at all. The Mosaic dispensation for divorce is

196

abrogated by a norm of indissolubility. The Christian does not see the Decalogue as the ultimate norm of conduct but an adherence to God's will that goes beyond it.

In speaking of traditional Jewish practices (6:1–18), Jesus does not abrogate them in warning of the danger of pride and self-seeking. His presentation of the Lord's prayer, taken from Q, differs from Luke 11:1–4 in its strong eschatology, which prays for the full implementation of God's reign, with an accompanying spirit of uprightness of life, and a sharing in the "end-time" banquet (the "bread of tomorrow"). The final period will seek God's forgiveness of our "debts" and a deliverance from the end-time battle with the "Evil One." This short prayer, presented as the single prayer given us by Christ, is a remarkable compendium of "end-time" values that are to characterize our present life as we prepare for that which is to come.

The teaching of the new Law is encased in a framework of total trust and dedication (6:25–32). It is a trust that avoids judgment of others or a disregard for the sacred, and finds confidence in prayer. Its solidity and permanence of will and heart make of its adherents a "house built on rock" (7:24-27).

Matthew 5–7

The Believing Community

The Matthean community was already becoming structured and defined. Of the four gospels only in Matthew does the term "church" *(ekklesia)* appear and there in three different instances. The church is constructed on the believing Peter at Caesarea Philippi (16:16ff), with the profession of Peter therein "You are the Messiah, the Son of the living God" going far beyond the synoptic parallels with their belief in "the Christ." The term also appears in the injunction to have recourse to "the church" in cases of litigation (18:17).

This is a transition from the earlier "reign of God" thinking to a more structured form of community life. Here as well the role of Peter and the apostles takes on added significance. The power to set forth binding legislation given to Peter (16:19) and the disciples (18:18) makes the Matthean structure distinctive and sets it on a new course. Although Peter is clearly seen as the leader or chief, the other apostles, representing the twelve tribes of Israel, are clearly given a share in that authority.

In a very distinctive way Matthew gives attention to ecclesial polity (18:1–35), directing his attention to issues that arise inevitably as a community becomes structured. There is a serious warning against ambition and the desire "to climb the ecclesial ladder" (18:1–5), the danger of scandal especially on the part of religious leaders (18:6–9), and a strong injunction to seek out the one who wanders from the faith community (18:15–18). Above all there is the importance of avoiding judgment in a forgiving and accepting community (18:21–25).

The accounts of Jesus' trial and sentencing are strikingly similar in all three gospels, although each has its particular nuances. Matthew, for example, will strongly underscore the guilt of the Jewish leadership. The resurrection accounts are more varied. Mark's Gospel ends in frightened flight as the women are alarmed by the news. Matthew, on the other hand, has Christ return to Galilee once more where he appears to the apostles and commissions them to bring the news of the new covenant to the nations. Christ is not only the redeemer and savior but the one who has brought sacred history to its climactic moment.

Matthew 16–18, 22–23

THE GOSPEL OF LUKE

Luke's gospel differs from the others in that it is part of a two-volume set. The Acts of the Apostles is its companion, authored by the same person. For completeness, then, the two should be read together. The gospel deals with the life and ministry of Jesus and, in addition to its own particular sources, uses both Mark and Q. It takes Jesus from his early ministry in Galilee and journeys with him to Jerusalem where his mission is to be accomplished. In Acts the teaching of the dead and risen Christ is carried under Paul's leadership to "Judea and Samaria, and to the ends of the earth."

Author, Time, and Place

A number of early Christian sources identify Luke as the companion of Paul mentioned in the epistles (Col 4:14, Phlm 24, 2 Tim 4:11). Many authors hold that position today, although the question of authorship remains here, as elsewhere in the New Testament, a complex question. Luke's gospel was not written before the ninth decade of the Christian era. He was not present with Jesus during his earthly ministry, and he is dependent on circulating sources for much of his material. If he was the companion of Paul, he makes no reference to such and in some of his views shows an ignorance of Paul's own thought and movements. Even though the gospel in its earliest form may well stem from Luke, Paul's companion, it is better to see its final form as the gospel that we know today coming from a hand that remains anonymous.

Luke was written in about AD 90. As the gospel itself indicates, Jerusalem had fallen, the church's Gentile mission was already advanced, the church was under duress from within and without, and end-time expectations were diminishing. The more difficult question is determining where it was written. Antioch in Syria has long been a prime contender because of its largely Gentile composition and the important role Antioch plays in the Acts of the Apostles. However, Luke-Acts, although clearly a product of a Gentile-oriented church, could well have been written anywhere in Asia Minor or Greece. It is very difficult to pinpoint a particular locale and a general background or milieu serves us just as well. This Gentile orientation explains why Luke often avoids details of Jewish law; in fact he seems to be ignorant of certain laws and customs. For this reason critics today would maintain that the author may have been a Jewish proselyte, who converted to Christianity and was therefore familiar with Judaism but was not himself born and raised as a Jew.

Luke's attitude toward Rome is generally positive and respectful, whereas the hostility of the Jewish population, especially in Acts, is much to the fore. There is the added question of Christians beginning to fall from the faith, which is why Luke places such emphasis on the cost of discipleship.

Luke's gospel is written in a fine Greek style, and the author is unquestionably a man of letters. Themes are well developed; literary parallels are well drawn; nuances are subtle and refined. This is not eyewitness reporting but a fine-tuned theological treatise, selecting narratives that highlight the meaning of Jesus' ministry. There were many questions to be faced. The failure of the Jews to accept Christ, the expected return of the Messiah, the relationship between Jewish and Gentile Christians, the "fall-away" Christians, the acceptance of all peoples. These are questions dealt with honestly while always highlighting the "good news" of Jesus, which was destined for the entire world.

Literary Structure

- Prologue (1:1-4). This is written in a classical Greek style with the author addressing his work to a patron (here Theophilus) and summarizing briefly the content of his opus.
- The Infancy Narratives (1:5—2:52). The childhood of John and Jesus
- Beginning of the Public Life (3:1—4:13). Baptism and temptations
- The Galilean Ministry (4:14—9:50). Capernaum, Nazareth, full ministry
- The Journey Narrative (9:51—19:28). Ministry and teaching combined in the journey to Jerusalem
- Passion, Death, and Glorification (9:24—4:53). Last supper, trial, death, burial, resurrection, and ascension

The Garden of Gethsemane

Major Themes

Savior of the World

The Gospel of Luke opens with Jesus present on a world stage. He is born during an alleged census ordered by Caesar Augustus for the entire empire. Later he interacts with Samaritans and Jewish outcasts. In Acts, the Word makes its way from Palestine to Asia Minor and Greece and finally reaches Rome, the heart and center of the empire. This highlights Luke's major theme. Jesus is not simply the Jewish Messiah; he is in truth the Savior of the world. Although remaining rooted in Judaism, it is with the Gentile or pagan world that Luke-Acts shows a dominant concern.

In the gospel, Jesus' outreach to the outcasts of Judaism, as well as non-Jews, is clearly evident. In the genealogy of Jesus (3:23–8), Luke traces the origins of the Messiah to Adam, well beyond Matthew's David and Abraham, thus underscoring the universal mission. In various subtle ways, for example, Simeon's mission to the nations (2:30–32), Luke points up the universal character of the faith.

The Samaritans

A people generally despised by the Jews serve Luke's all-inclusive theme very well when treating of Jesus' Palestinian ministry. Not only are they spoken of with deference and respect, they also illustrate the dispositions proper to the reign of God. Of the ten lepers whom Christ healed, only the Samaritan returns to express gratitude (17:11–19). In the parable of the Good Samaritan, it is this foreigner who brings solace to the unfortunate wayfarer (10:29-37).

It is people like this, generally outside the view of the Jewish population, who are favored in Luke. This includes the tax collectors, the shepherds, the outcast, the widow who gave to God of the little she had. Early in his ministry, Jesus quotes Isaiah in pointing up the heart of his mission, which was directed toward the most needy (4:16–20). In addition, when considering the generally inferior status of women in the society of the times, it is interesting to see the attention Jesus gives them. This is true not only of Mary and Elizabeth, but Mary and Martha and the women who accompanied him. There is, moreover, the parable of the persistent widow (18:1–8) and the woman of the lost coin (15:8–10).

Jesus' concern for sinners appears repeatedly during his ministry, nowhere more strikingly than from the cross. There he speaks with the criminal crucified beside him and assures him a place in the kingdom. It is only Luke who has preserved for us the parables of the lost son and the lost coin (c. 15).

Luke 4, 10, 15, 17

The Journey (9:51—19:27)

In the ninth chapter of Luke, Jesus takes his leave of the Galilean ministry and begins journeying toward Jerusalem. This journey constitutes a major part of his gospel and serves as the time for Jesus to present a major part of his teaching. The journey terminates in Jerusalem at the end of the gospel. This is the geographical highpoint of his life and ministry; it is from there in Acts that the disciples will carry the message from Jerusalem to Antioch and finally to Rome.

The journey is a literary expression for the spiritual journey to which every Christian is called. By incorporating within the journey the teaching of Jesus, Luke has pointed out the way to the heavenly Jerusalem.

Finally, it should be noted that just as there are three major cities in the Lucan account of early Christianity—Jerusalem, Antioch, and Rome—so there are also three stages in the history of salvation. The first is that of the Old Testament, which for Luke includes Zechariah, Elizabeth, and John the Baptist (16:16); the second is the era of Jesus' ministry, which concludes with his ascension; the third is that of the Holy Spirit who is the principal figure in the Acts of the Apostles as the church is guided in its earliest years. Each of these remains very distinct while unified in the overall plan of God.

The Infancy Narratives

In the first two chapters of Luke and Matthew there are a series of narratives that treat of Jesus' childhood. We have waited until this point to treat both gospels so that the two narratives may be seen jointly. They are of a distinctly different genre than that of the remainder of the gospels, even though they form an integral part of them. They are not written to give a historical account of Jesus' childhood but rather as overtures to the respective gospels in which the major theological motifs are thrown into bold relief.

Luke's narrative highlights Mary as a principal agent. One of its major features is the comparison drawn between the conception and birth of John the Baptist and Jesus. This is carefully worked out in a literary schema.

JOHN	JESUS
Annunciation of birth	Annunciation of birth
(1:5–25)	(1:26–38)
Birth	Birth
(1:57–80)	(2:1–38)

Complementary Episodes

Visitation—Joining of Mary and Elizabeth, Jesus and John
(1:39–56)

Jesus in the Temple—Relationship of Jesus to the Father
(2:41–52)

Although there are similarities in the account of the two major figures, John and Jesus, there is strong emphasis on the differences between them. Gabriel's announcement to Zechariah points to conception at an advanced age; the announcement to Mary speaks of a conception without a human father. John is an Elijah figure (1:17), a forerunner or herald of the One to come; Jesus is clearly the Messiah and Lord (2:11). John is of the priestly line (Levi); Jesus is of royal origin (Judah and David) (2:4). When Mary and Elizabeth meet in the visitation scene, Elizabeth clearly defers to Mary as does John to Jesus, with both still in the womb.

In Luke, it is interesting to note that the Jerusalem Temple appears at both the beginning (1:9–10) and the end of the gospel (24:52). The singular character of Jesus as both Son of God and son of David is highlighted (1:32), with the loss of Jesus in the Temple illustrating the primacy of the former over the latter (2:41–52). Humility and lowliness, two key Lucan themes, are seen in the submissiveness of Mary (1:48), the circumstances of Jesus' birth (2:6-7), and the initial appearance of the angel to the shepherds, the poor of God (2:15–20). Also to be noted is the unity between the two Testaments in the respectful inclusion of Jewish personalities: Simeon and Anna (2:25–38), as well as Zechariah and Elizabeth. The relationship of Jesus to the Father takes precedence over human ties, even those of family (2:41–52), a point that echoes other gospel accounts (cf. 8:19–21, 11:27–28).

Jesus' Davidic and Jewish origins are seen in his birth at Bethlehem, with the universal Roman census at the time adding a sense of an all-inclusive mission.

There are three hymns or canticles in the Lucan infancy narrative, that of Mary (Magnificat) (1:46–55), Zechariah (Benedictus) (1:68–79), and Simeon (Nunc dimittis) (2:29–32). Simeon's hymn is more closely related to the context than the other two, which reflect the hymnody of the Old Testament and have little direct relation to the narrative. In fact, in both the hymn of Mary and that of Zechariah, only a verse or two relate to the event itself. In addition, the hymn of Mary bears a strong resemblance to that of Hannah, the mother of Samuel (1 Sam 2:1–10). These canticles were evidently drawn from early Christian liturgical sources betraying a strong dependency on earlier Jewish compositions.

The infancy narrative in *Matthew* (cc. 1–2) differs markedly from that of Luke. Joseph, not Mary, is the central figure. The five incidents recorded by Matthew are all punctuated by a quotation from the Old Testament, to which they are seen as being directly related. Jesus is being viewed against his Hebrew background, with Joseph serving as a prototype of the Old Testament patriarch of the same name. Jesus is the son of David through his legally recognized father, Joseph. This is further confirmed in his birth in Bethlehem, David's city, and the magi's star with its messianic significance (cf. Num 24:17). At the same time Jesus is God in the flesh (1:23).

The story of the magi is a theological statement, reflecting the early Christian experience of Gentile acceptance and Jewish rejection of Jesus. The Jews, to whom the promise had been made, stand aloof and unresponsive in the person of Herod and his advisers, whereas the Gentile magi make their way through Jerusalem to worship the child in Bethlehem. The flight into Egypt recalls the migration of Jacob and his sons to find refuge there in a time of famine (Gen 46) and in a special way prepares for Jesus' new Exodus, as he, like Israel of old, is called out of

Egypt (2:15). The slaughter of the innocent children parallels the slaughter at the time of Moses' birth, when he too was saved through God's intervention (Exod 1–2).

The Matthean stories want to see Christ against his Hebrew background by drawing parallels between him and important Old Testament events and personalities. At the same time he acknowledges the Jews' rejection of Jesus and the growth of the church in the Gentile world.

There are more divergences than convergences in the narratives of Luke and Matthew, making it impossible to pair the two as a whole. The areas of agreement are: the divine conception of Jesus, the marriage of Mary and Joseph, the birth in Bethlehem, the virginity of Mary, and the settling in Nazareth. Areas in which they differ include: Nazareth as the family place of origin, the sojourn in Egypt about which Luke is silent, the humble circumstances of Jesus' birth in Luke, the census, and the journey. The family ties between John and Jesus, so prominent in Luke, are something about which the Gospel of Matthew is apparently ignorant.

However, whenever we consider the scope of the infancy narratives, there is no reason why the two should match. In essentials regarding the nature and origin of Jesus, they are at one, but beyond that they have different objectives that go beyond historical fact. They highlight important religious themes that appear repeatedly in their respective gospels. Therein lies their importance.

Matthew 1–2
Luke 1–2

XV.

THE GOSPEL OF JOHN

The fourth gospel is notably different from its three predecessors. It does not have the historical progression of the others;
from the beginning Jesus is identified as the Son of God, indeed
as God himself (1:1). There is no indication of a developing presentation of himself and his mission. There is no sequence or literary progression in the works of Jesus, his miracles, or his
teaching. The miracles in John are basically signs of his divine origins and his mission. John is the last of the gospels to be written
and is theologically characterized as having a "high Christology,"
a profound awareness of Christ's divine nature. He is present to
the Father throughout; this unity of Son and Father permeates the
work as a whole. This gospel is a serious theological reflection on
the meaning of Jesus rather than an unfolding summary of his
earthly ministry.

There is no direct dependency of John on the other gospels.
He recounts only a few of the events that the synoptics present,
while introducing other events heretofore not mentioned (e.g.,
the wedding at Cana, the raising of Lazarus). Although he betrays
no literary dependency on the synoptics, he does share with them
some of the key happenings of Jesus' ministry (e.g., the encounter
with John the Baptist, the Last Supper, the trial, crucifixion, and
resurrection). It is safe to say that John used some of the traditions
about Jesus used by the synoptics, especially Mark, and, at the
same time, has fashioned them according to his own theological
and literary purpose.

The image often used to describe the fourth gospel is that of the eagle. It is an apt figure because the gospel soars into the realm of Jesus' divine origins. He is clearly seen as God's presence in the world to communicate the way of salvation. The evangelist's way of presenting this makes this gospel a very singular contribution.

DATE, PLACE, AND AUTHOR

The authorship of John's gospel presents a set of complex questions. From the second century until the eighteenth, the author was identified with John the apostle, the son of Zebedee and the brother of James. This position has been largely abandoned today for a variety of reasons. The time of composition is seen as separated from the time of the apostles by decades. There is the added fact that John, although present in the gospel, is never mentioned as the author, an identification saved for the "disciple whom Jesus loved" (21:20–24). Events for which John was present in the synoptics (the transfiguration and suffering in the garden) receive no mention in the fourth gospel. Today it is generally accepted that there were more hands than one at work in its composition. Although it traditionally carries the name of John, there is no further specification as to which John is meant.

The closest we come to identifying the author is the statement found in c. 21:20–24 where there is mention of the "disciple whom Jesus loved." This unnamed person appears at critical moments in Jesus' life: the Last Supper (13:20–25), possibly during Jesus' trials (cf. 18:15), the crucifixion (19:26f), the empty tomb (20:1–7), and the postresurrection appearances (21). This disciple serves primarily in a symbolic role as the faithful and constant follower of Jesus. However, this would not militate against his being an actual disciple of Jesus, otherwise unknown, whose influence on the community responsible for the gospel was pronounced. The historical character of the "beloved disciple" cannot be ruled out, even though he assumes a symbolic role in the gospel. He may well have been the first editor or redactor of the

208

gospel, which then continued to be refined within the community of origin.

As is clear from the above, the question of authorship cannot be separate from that of origins. Composed in different stages, the Johannine text probably grew out of a community experience. Originally made up of Jewish converts, including the "beloved disciple," and rooted in Palestine, it eventually found its home in the Gentile world, perhaps at Ephesus. By then its membership base was broader including Samaritans and Gentiles. Its members at one point had been excluded from the synagogue (cf. 9:23), accounting in part for its hostile attitudes toward "the Jews." They were decidedly favorable toward the Samaritans and the Gentile (Greek) world (cf. 12:20–25). Gnosticism eventually affected the community, especially as it touched on the true humanity of Christ. This appears especially in the three epistles of John, which came from the same school, and which strongly emphasize that Jesus came "in the flesh." Heresy seemingly carried many of the community members away from their moorings, although a certain number remained orthodox and by the end of the first century was clearly involved in the life of the early church with its recognized authorities. This appears clearly in the epilogue (c. 21) where the role of Peter and the apostles is strongly underscored.

The three epistles of John bear a striking resemblance to the gospel in both theology and style. However, differences in emphasis and style have led some authors to follow a middle path: although the epistles stem from the Johannine community, their authorship is different from that of the gospel.

As these suggested origins of the text indicate, John's Gospel went through various stages of composition. There are two endings of the gospel (cf. 20:30f, 21:24), the last chapter being a later addition. Other later "retouches" include highlighting the implicit sacramental illusions, such as baptism (3:5) and the Eucharist (6:52–58). The well-developed Christology of the gospel carries it beyond the early apostolic age. The date of composition in its final form is about AD 100. There is evidence from discovered fragments that the gospel was already well in circulation by the mid-second century.

In summary, the gospel of John is a late first-century composition, about AD 100 rooted in an early Christian community, and probably written at Ephesus. Its attribution to "John" may be purely literary to give it apostolic authority or point to an otherwise unidentified John, connected with the community in its origins and seen as the gospel's earliest source.

LITERARY STRUCTURE

- Prologue (1:1–18)
- The Book of Signs (1:19—12:50)
- The Book of Glory (13:1—20:31)
- Epilogue (21:1–25)

The literary structure of the fourth gospel is uncomplicated but requires explanation in terms of John's overall objective.

Prologue (1:1–18)

In the fourth gospel Christ is eternally present with the Father. He is identified as God's Word, a concept rich in Judaic and Hellenistic thought. In some ways it is akin to our own usage wherein our words are acts of self-disclosure. It is through words that persons are identified in their strengths and weaknesses, their joys and sorrows. Christ gives us insight into God, a window, as it were, on God's invisible nature. Through the life and teaching of Jesus we are better able to understand the Father. In Hebrew thought, God's word is also synonymous with his power. In Genesis it is the word of God that effects the work of creation. When the prophets are empowered to proclaim a message it is said that the word of God came to them. In John, the Word is Christ himself, present in the act of creation (v. 3) as well as the maintenance of the created order.

John unequivocally identifies Christ as God. This is a high Christology, which came to the early church's understanding only by degrees. In the other gospels, he is spoken of as God's Son, Messiah, Savior, and Son of Man, but to speak of him simply as God would be to identify him as Yahweh, for whom that term was reserved exclusively. It was only as the concept of deity broadened, that the term God was seen as equally applicable to Yahweh (Father) and Christ (Son). Thus, Christ is referred to as God at the beginning and the end of the gospel (20:28).

The prologue goes on to speak of Christ's engagement in the world in both creation and redemption. He was heralded by John the Baptist and received by many in faith, disciples who were then empowered by the Spirit to become sons and daughters of God. There is a shadow side as well, however. Jesus suffered rejection at the hands of his own people, who refused to accept him or his teaching. In speaking of Jesus' coming "in the flesh," John underscores his total humanity, one who was like us in everything except sin.

It is this notion of acceptance in faith that characterizes the first half of the fourth gospel.

John 1:1–18

The Book of Signs (1:19—12:50)

In this first section of the gospel, Jesus reveals himself in a series of events that serve as signs. In each narrative, many of them miracles, the event becomes a sign of Jesus' nature and mission. This is done in a series of concentric circles, wherein the same basic theme is repeated in various forms: Jesus is truly God's Son and acceptance of him is the key to salvation. Rejection means to continue in a life of darkness. Examples are helpful at this point. In chapter 6, there is the account of the feeding of the people with the loaves and fishes. The feeding becomes a sign of Jesus himself as "the bread of life" whose teaching nourishes his followers and is also a sign of the Eucharist. In chapter 9, the sight given to the blind man becomes a sign of the enlightenment given through faith in Jesus. Hence, the wedding at Cana, the cleansing of the Temple, the Samaritan woman, the miracle of the loaves, the cure of the blind man, and the raising of Lazarus—all point to Christ himself as God's Son and Savior of the world. They are signs that lead to acceptance or rejection.

John 2, 4–6, 11

The Book of Glory (13:1—20:31)

This part of the gospel is directed mainly to the disciples and indicates the fruits of acceptance. The ever growing faith of the disciples centers wholly on Jesus, who is the way, the truth, and the life (14:6). The book moves through the arrest, death, and resurrection of the Lord, through which eternal life becomes accessible. Christ passes through death to glory and then makes glory the lot of his followers. The risen Christ confers the Spirit upon the apostles (20:19–23), who are then to embark on their mission.

The Epilogue (21:1–25)

This is a chapter added to the already completed gospel (20:30f). The chapter reflects developing church structures and the role of authority. There is the missionary role of the apostles (1–14), the singular ecclesial role of Peter (15–19), and questions arising from the death of the beloved disciple (20–23).

John 21

MAJOR THEMES

Identity and Eschatology

The identity of Jesus in John's gospel is not progressive. He is clearly presented as God's Son from the beginning, even though it was only through the conferral of the Spirit after the resurrection that such an affirmation could be made. Indeed, he is spoken of as God in this first-century document of the church. The fourth gospel is not a chronologically progressive narrative; in fact the same idea is repeated in each chapter as Jesus presents himself under various signs. The gospel is Christocentric because it repeatedly returns to Christ at the center of each concentric circle as each narrative unfolds.

There is both a realized and future eschatology in John. This appears clearly in the Lazarus story. As Martha speaks of resurrection in the end time (11:24), Jesus speaks of an end time that is already present (11:25). It is the gift of the Spirit that confers eternal life; it is a life that has its beginning here but will continue uninterruptedly into eternity (cf. 4:13–14). To believe in Christ as Lord and Savior is to have eternal life, not only in the future but in the here and now. It should be noted that the resurrection, ascension, and Pentecost blend together as one in John. With his rising, Christ goes at once to the Father and returns the same evening to confer the Spirit on the disciples.

Signs and Symbols

None of the gospels is as rich in signs as is John. Concrete experiences and features of daily life become symbols of the nature and mission of Jesus. The wedding at Cana (2:1) symbolizes the marriage between Christ and his church with the abundance of wine and feasting mirroring end-time expectations. The temple is related to the dead and risen Christ (2:13–22). The water in the Samaritan well is to be surpassed by the "living water" of the Spirit (4:1–42). The bread of life is symbolic of Christ himself (c. 6); physical sight, the light that comes through faith. The raising of Lazarus stands for the personal raising up of everyone who believes in Christ (c. 11). It is through the understanding of the signs and the acceptance of their message that discipleship is realized.

The elements of daily life appear as signs of new life. Wine, bread, water, light—all are seen as signs of Christ's grace and the work of the Spirit.

Sacraments

Both baptism and Eucharist appear in John's Gospel, a clear indication of their importance in the life of the early church.

Some of the clear sacramental references have been added to an earlier text to make explicit a further meaning of the text. This is the case in the reference to baptism in the Nicodemus discourse (3:5) and the eucharistic development at the end of the bread of life discourse (6:51–59). Authors also see a baptismal reference, at least implicitly, in the conversation with the Samaritan woman about "living water" (c. 4), the blind man washing in the pool of Siloam (9:7), and the blood and water that issue from the side of Jesus at his death (19:34). Eucharistic allusions are suggested in the post-Easter meal at the lakeside (21:12ff). It is interesting to note, that despite John's sacramental concerns, there is no mention of the Eucharist at the Last Supper, nor is the meal a Passover supper.

LEVELS OF UNDERSTANDING

The signs in the fourth gospel can be understood only when we penetrate their meaning in faith. Failure to move in faith occurs when the person engaged in conversation with Jesus understands only on a very basic human level. Thus, Nicodemus is incapable of understanding the rebirth of baptism, as he struggles with a literal understanding of a second birth (c. 3). The Samaritan woman understands Jesus' "living water" as spring water and moves beyond it only as her faith increases (c. 4). Some of Jesus' disciples understand the "eating of flesh and blood" in a cannibalistic sense and thus walk with him no more (c. 6). The opponents of Jesus in the story of the man born blind understand nothing of what he says and thus dash about from person to person like "blind mice" (c. 9). These two levels of understanding are referred to as that of the "flesh," which is the concrete, human grasp and that of the "spirit," which is the higher or faith level. This is a strong characteristic of the Johannine literature.

Clearly the Gospel of John is very distinct and unique. It does not follow the outline of Jesus' life and ministry as found in the other gospels but is rather a profound reflection on the unique identity of Jesus and the call to faith which is entailed. Although it is certainly different from the synoptics, it shares key features with them, notably the events leading up to Jesus' death and resurrection. It emerges from a community, reflecting on the meaning of Christ in the midst of struggles from within and without. Although possibly springing from the "disciple whom Jesus loved," responsible for its early written form, the gospel has developed and flowered over the course of time. It points up very clearly that the Word become flesh has shown the way to the Father.

John 19–20

XVI.

EARLY CHRISTIANITY

THE ACTS OF THE APOSTLES

The spread of the gospel after the ascension was viewed as essentially the work of the Holy Spirit, accomplished through the apostles. Our first and most important insight into the life of the early church is to be found in *The Acts of the Apostles*, the companion volume to Luke's gospel, composed between AD 80 and 90. In our basic presentation, only a summary presentation of early church life can be given. Here we will present the broad historical background provided by Acts and then visit the life of the early church as it appears in the Pauline literature.

If there is any central figure in Acts it is the Holy Spirit. Conferred on Pentecost (2:1–13), it is the Spirit that takes the lead as the church moves forward in the missionary work of the apostles. The Spirit gives the direction and is the quiet force throughout, even to the point of indicating which road should be taken (16:7). The destination of missionary activity in geographical terms is outlined early in Acts. The apostles are to carry the message to "Judea and Samaria, and to the ends of the earth" (1:8). Thus, there is the mission in Jerusalem (2:14—8:3), Judea and Samaria (8:4—9:43), and then the broader Gentile mission (10:1—28:31). There are three main cities around which the work of the Spirit rotates in Acts: Jerusalem, with its Jewish Christian community; Antioch, with its converts from the Jewish Diaspora and some Gentile Christians, the city where the disciples were first called Christians (12:26); and Rome, where the church is present at the heart of the Roman empire.

The two principal human actors in Acts are Peter and Paul, with the latter receiving the lion's share of attention. Peter serves as a link between Palestinian Christianity and Paul's mission to the broader Gentile world. It is a somewhat different Peter from the Peter we had met in the gospels, now more resolute and determined. At Pentecost he gives two major addresses to the Jews, proclaiming Jesus as Lord and Messiah (2:34—3:26). Taken before the Sanhedrin, he remains strong in his convictions (4:1–3, 5:17–42). He is early convinced of the Gentile mission in receiving the pagan Cornelius and his household as converts to the faith, after a vision that convinces him of the universal character of Christianity (10:11–26). He supports Paul's position on Gentile freedom from the Jewish law at the Jerusalem assembly (c. 15), even though he sometimes wavered in his conviction, much to Paul's chagrin (Gal 2:11–14).

After his conversion (9:1–30), Paul assumes the central role in Acts. The one who once persecuted the church becomes its principal exponent. In three missionary journeys he carries the gospel and establishes the faith in Asia Minor and Greece. After his arrest he is taken to Rome, where, as the book ends, he is still proclaiming the gospel.

Once Paul make his appearance, the outward thrust of the church is much to the fore. The conversion of Cornelius serves as the linchpin for the church's subsequent endorsement of the Gentile mission (c. 15). The three missionary journeys of Paul (13:1—14:28, 15:36—18:23, 18:24—21:14) bring Christianity to Asia Minor and southern Europe, and as mentioned earlier, even under surveillance in Rome, Paul continues his missionary efforts (27:1—28:31). There is no mention of Paul's death. As Acts ends the gospel has reached Rome, the "ends of the earth"; the scope of the book has been realized. Paul's death occurred in AD 62.

Acts 1–2; 9:1–9; 10

ISSUES AND TENSIONS

The reading of Acts brings us into contact with the issues that faced the church in its infancy. In its passage from a Palestinian congregation to a predominantly Gentile one, the church had to negotiate some difficult curves in matters of considerable importance for the future of Christianity.

Jewish Response

There was always a certain tension between Jewish and Gentile Christianity. There is also indication of some difficulties between Palestinian Christians and those from the Jewish Diaspora, the Hellenists. One of the earliest, which is recorded in Acts, was the neglect felt by the Hellenist Christians on the part of the Jerusalem church in the question of food distribution. Many of their widows were evidently not being provided for by church leadership, and this led to the designation of seven men, including Stephen, to "wait on tables" and provide for material needs (6:1–7). This is often interpreted as being the institution of the diaconate, although the text never refers to these men as deacons.

As an outgrowth of Judaism, the first members of the church were Jews from Jerusalem. Under the leadership of James, "the brother of the Lord," these first Christians retained a strong attachment to their Jewish traditions and customs, while recognizing Christ as the Messiah. They soon emerged as the conservative wing of the early church. They belonged to a church that held a primacy of honor; it was there that the Twelve resided, and, as far as the New Testament is concerned, there they remained. At least there is no scriptural evidence of their preaching in other parts of the world. Shortly after Pentecost, the church began to spread among Greek-speaking Jews of the Diaspora. These were the Hellenists, who, as we have mentioned, found themselves at odds with the Palestinian community over the question of providing for material needs. With the passage of time, the influence of

Palestinian Christianity began to diminish, as attention became more centered on the growth of the church in other areas of the ancient world. The importance of Antioch as a center of the faith emerged as the spread of the church through Judea and Samaria became more pronounced (c. 8). From being a religion steeped in Judaism, Christianity to an ever greater extent leaned toward Gentile concerns. It was at Antioch that the followers of Jesus were first called Christians (11:26).

Even with prevailing difficulties, it was never expected that the Jews would reject Jesus as the Messiah, the promised one of Israel. For this reason Jerusalem Christians did not see the division between themselves and their former coreligionists as being definitive. Christians continued many of their Jewish customs, including Temple worship, which served as an adjunct to their own distinctive practices (2:42–47). As we have seen, Matthew's gospel is clearly sympathetic to Jewish interests in a number of areas. However, despite the importance of Jerusalem, the faith did not continue to grow there, especially once its centrifugal force had begun. The apostles experienced considerable hostility from the Jewish leaders, who soon saw Christianity as a major threat.

Despite these difficulties, Christianity never divorced itself from its Jewish roots, realizing that Christ had come primarily as a savior for the Jews. As Paul makes his missionary journeys, he first visits the Jewish community in a town or city before making overtures to the Gentiles (cf. 13:16–43). He generally fails to make inroads there, whereas the Gentiles respond positively in ever greater numbers. The Jews stirred up animosity toward the apostles, even inflicting physical harm (c. 14). They eventually accused them before the Romans, thus endangering a Christian future within the empire (c. 22). Paul claimed his Roman citizenship, and when accused, called for a trial before Caesar; this claim eventually brought him to Rome.

The rejection of Christianity by the Jewish world was the first setback experienced by the apostolic church. Its Jewish beginnings soon diminished in importance and were no longer a dominant force. Its growth among the Gentiles gave it a very different outlook and ethos, something that the apostles had not originally envisioned.

Acts 3–4, 13

The Question of the Law

As long as the church had a dominantly Jewish constituency, the issue of Law observance was not of great importance. As long as Jesus was seen as the fulfillment of the Law and the prophets, there was no immediate thought of its abolition. As the church became increasingly Gentile in its makeup, however, problems inevitably arose. In addition to their acceptance of Christ as their Savior, were Christians to be expected to accept circumcision and observance of the Torah as well? This was the first major decision the church had to make, and on its outcome the whole mission of the church to the world depended. Paul was the first major spokesman for Gentile freedom from the Law, whereas the Jerusalem community remained convinced of its necessity. With God as its author and a tradition of centuries in its favor, how could the Law be abandoned? Paul felt that the Law compromised the singular path to salvation, faith in Christ alone. Peter stood somewhere in the middle (cf. Gal 2:1–14), but Acts shows his unequivocal consent as a supporter of Gentile freedom after his experience with Cornelius (Acts 10).

At an assembly of church leaders in Jerusalem, the issue was publicly addressed and solved (c. 15), with Paul speaking forcefully in favor of freedom. The conservative wing of the church had previously shown opposition, but at the assembly, under James's leadership, they recognized the validity of Paul's position and expressed agreement. From that point on, the Gentiles were not held to the observance of the Law, with the exception of a few precepts. However, there is no indication of any change in the prevailing discipline for Jewish Christians. The problem was completely solved with the passing of time and the overall Gentile orientation of the church.

The Fortress of Antonia

The Greek and Roman World

It was inevitable that early Christianity would encounter
Greek philosophical thinking, which permeated so much of the
Near Eastern world. It comes to light in Acts with Paul's speech at
the Areopagus in Athens (17:22–39). His approach on that occasion differs notably from his other addresses to nonbelievers.
Greek philosophy was widely esteemed and considered a major
intellectual accomplishment. Paul is more than aware of this and
begins by finding a common ground in the "altar with the inscription, 'To an unknown god'," which had been included with altars
to the Greek gods. He speaks on behalf of that "unknown god" in
making an appeal for monotheism and the exclusion of competing
deities. The only likeness to this God is to be found in his human
offspring, who, in the light of Christ, bear a distinct resemblance.
In philosophical terms, he sees human existence as circumscribed
by God's presence. "In him we live and move and have our being"
(v. 28). Paul is followed with interest by his audience until he
touches on resurrection of the dead. He goes no farther. His words

had won a few adherents, but the majority found Greek speculation superior to Paul's thought. Little more is said about inroads among the Greek intelligentsia. At a later point in history there was a convergence of Christianity and Greek philosophy, representing a major positive development in the life of the church.

Roman authorities generally did not interfere with the diverse religious beliefs present within the empire. People were left undisturbed in religious matters as long as there was no conflict with Roman authority. It was only when emperor worship became a bone of contention for early Christians that the inevitable conflict erupted. In the period of the Acts of the Apostles, difficulties with Roman authority grew mainly out of Jewish incitement. Paul was committed to Roman hands only after the Sanhedrin tried to kill him. Paul demanded to stand before a Roman court because he was a Roman citizen. In Acts, Rome treats the accused apostle favorably, and he is authorized to make his appeal in Rome. There is no mention of his death in Rome; the final record finds him preaching there. In accordance with Acts' theme, the gospel had reached the ends of the earth. As far as Acts is concerned. Rome acts civilly without any real evidence of heavy-handedness.

The picture of the early church that emerges in Acts is one of ongoing development. It has its roots in Judaism but clearly has a universal mission. All people, without exception, are called to experience salvation in Christ. It is the Spirit that guides and directs the church in its courageous and even controversial undertakings. Conflict and opposition are woven into the future of faith, with perseverance leading to ultimate vindication.

Acts 17, 23–25, 28

XVII.

THE LETTERS OF PAUL

If by the end of the first century Christianity had become an important religious force, it is attributed in no small measure to the work of St. Paul. It was he who, while respectful of its Jewish origins, moved the Christian faith into a position where it was no longer bound by Jewish law and was able to embrace people of any cultural background. After his own conversion, Paul worked tirelessly to carry his message from the Palestinian world through Asia Minor and southern Europe to Rome, the heart of the empire. Toward the end of his career it was his hope to use the church of Rome, which he had not founded, as a base for the evangelization of other parts of Europe. From his writings we know that his was frequently a difficult road. He was often in conflict with the Jews, his former coreligionists, and also with Roman authorities. There were also difficulties with members of the Christian community who at times found themselves at odds with the apostle's position.

The culture of Paul's time was Greco-Roman. In the fourth century BC, Alexander the Great dominated the Near Eastern world and was a strong devotee of Greek culture. He promoted philosophy, literature, architecture, and athletics. He brought the Greek language to the Eastern world, a tongue that became the *lingua franca* of early Christianity. All of the canonical writings of the New Testament are in Greek. Later the Romans conquered most of the world formerly dominated by the Greeks and brought with them a political and economic security. Trade and governmental structures linked the empire, and roads were constructed to connect as far as possible a very far-flung empire. It was a peaceful era, often known as the period of the *pax Romana*, initiated by Caesar Augustus, which lasted from 37 BC to about AD 130; it substantially facilitated the spread of Christianity.

The religious world of Paul's time was complex. It included the polytheism of Greece and Rome, the cult of the Roman emperor, the mystery religions of the ancient world, and Gnosticism. It was evident from the start that Christianity was not compatible with any other form of religious belief. As a strictly monotheistic faith, it found the worship of many gods an anomaly. Rome generally did not interfere with the diverse religions of the empire; difficulties arose only when there was conflict with official policy. Christians, for example, could not accept emperor worship. When this became a test of loyalty, Christians found themselves at odds with Roman authority.

The mystery religions were common in the Near Eastern world, with their female gods and male consorts responsible for the seasons of the year. They were "mystery" cults inasmuch as adherents were bound to secrecy in any cultic matters. Gnosticism (from the Greek word *gnosis*, "knowledge") was well known in the world where Christianity took root. It called for spiritual release from everything material or earthly through the acquisition of a special knowledge of the divine, which alone brought about redemption. This disdain for matter found Gnosticism at odds with Christianity, but this did not prevent certain segments of the church from attempting to reconcile the two. Such efforts ultimately failed, although this was a matter of considerable concern as the church moved into the Greco-Roman world.

THE LIFE OF PAUL

Sometime between the years AD 5 and 10, Paul was born in Tarsus, the capital of Cilicia, at the eastern end of the Mediterranean, in present-day Turkey. It was not unusual at the time for one to have both a Roman and Jewish name, in this case,

Paul and Saul, respectively. There was a considerably large Jewish community in Tarsus and it was there that Paul received his education in Judaism and its traditions. At the same time, his Hellenistic education was not lacking; he was fluent in Greek and acquired good rhetorical and writing skills. There is reason to doubt the accuracy of Acts' mention of his Jerusalem education under Gamaliel (Acts 22:3), given that this would have found him in Jerusalem during the time of Jesus' ministry, when in fact he gives no indication of knowing of or being acquainted with Jesus during his public life. Moreover, Gamaliel belonged to a liberal school of Judaism, quite different from the conservative direction of Paul's thinking. As in other instances, Luke may be taking historical license in keeping with his own objective of emphasizing Paul's knowledge of Jewish law.

There are various references to Paul's persecution of the early church, which put this part of his life beyond question. The same is true of his unexpected and sudden conversion to the cause of Christ (AD 32–33). He then set out for Arabia and Damascus and made his first visit to Jerusalem as a Christian in AD 36. This was followed by his first and shortest missionary journey to Syria, Cilicia, and Galatia. There was then a trip to Jerusalem in AD 49 to settle definitively, in full assembly, the issue of the binding force of the Jewish law for Gentile converts. The second missionary journey carried the apostle to the early centers of Christian life—Corinth, Ephesus, Thessalonica, and Galatia, all of which became destinaries of his letters. In fact it was during this period that most of his epistles were written. After his third and final missionary journey to Ephesus and Greece, Paul was arrested in Jerusalem in about AD 59. He was ultimately taken to Rome for his trial "before Caesar" and remained there under house arrest until his death in AD 62 or 63.

THE LETTERS

There are thirteen letters or epistles, as they are frequently called, attributed to Paul. The word *attributed* here is important

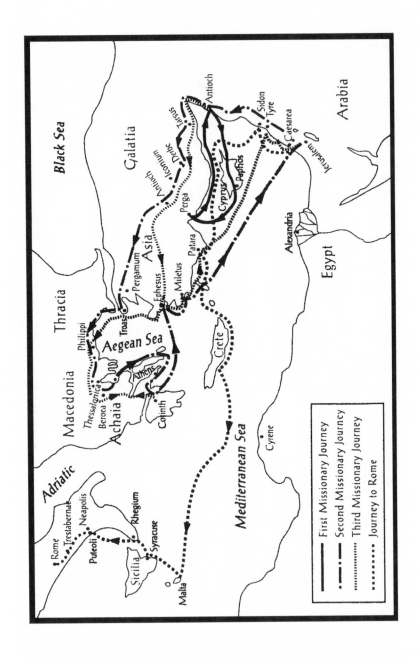

because there is no unanimity among scholars regarding Paul's personal authorship of all thirteen. Excluded from consideration here is the Letter to the Hebrews, which, on the basis of style and content, does not stem from Paul. Beyond that, there is considerable discussion and nothing like total agreement. We shall here avoid a lengthy appraisal of the question and deal with what might be termed the prevailing opinion among scholars today.

The letters that are considered authored by Paul personally are: 1 Thessalonians, Galatians, 1 and 2 Corinthians, Philippians, Philemon, and Romans. Those that are questionable or disputed, on the basis of both content and style, are 2 Thessalonians, Colossians, Ephesians, Titus, and 1 and 2 Timothy. These are called Deutero-Pauline or Pseudonymous epistles. They are viewed as being written by someone other than Paul. Because many of them build on Pauline thought, the authors are often thought to be of a "school of Paul," or people closely related to him in ministry and thinking. They are seen as applying Paul's thought to new circumstances. Another point of view would see attribution to Paul as giving authority to the work; linking it with the apostle would add to its credibility and acceptance. In this view, the authors may have had no direct relation with the apostle. It was simply a question of literary attribution such as is found frequently in the Old Testament. The *pastoral epistles* to Timothy and Titus, which appear to be quite a distance from Paul in time and theology, are often placed in this category of simple literary attribution.

Whatever the case, it should be noted that authorship has no affect on the inspired and authoritative character of any of the letters. Regardless of who wrote them, they are all part of the canonical scriptures and recognized by the church as being inspired and normative.

Here we shall examine only the letters generally agreed upon as being Pauline, giving an overview of their contents. In a subsequent chapter we shall consider themes from the Deutero-Pauline literature.

The Parthenon

1 Thessalonians is the earliest of Paul's letters written about AD 50. Thessalonica was the provincial capital of Macedonia and it was there that Paul founded a small community early in his ministry. One of the issues that the letter addresses was harassment of the community by outsiders, presumably Jews who had been earlier antagonists. There had also been a questioning of Paul's own authority. Paul defends his position and urges the community to stand firm in the face of opposition. The return of the Lord (the parousia) was close at hand, at which time persecution would pass and those who were faithful would share in Christ's victory.

Both the time and the destinaries of the letter to the *Galatians* are unknown. There was a northern and southern Galatia in Asia Minor, with the exact location of the Christian community remaining uncertain. However, the importance of the letter lies in its being Paul's first treatment of Christian freedom from the Jewish Law, an issue to be treated later in this chapter. Certain Judaizers from the larger Christian community strove to convince the Galatians to accept circumcision and the Law. These intruders also attacked Paul's authority, with the

228

argument that he could not be an apostle because he was not one of the Twelve. Paul's anger is evident throughout the letter as he sets forth his reasons for Christian freedom and his own apostolic authority.

For a sampling of the different issues that touched early Christianity, a reading of *1 and 2 Corinthians* is indispensable. In the *first letter* to this important coastal city, the capital of the province of Achaia, the ethos of the locale is evident. With its variety of religions and a markedly libertine seaport morality, there were a number of problems facing the Christian community, largely from internal sources. These included factions within the community (1:10—4:21), questions regarding marriage and sexual morality (cc. 6–7), the difference between license and Christian freedom (cc. 8–11), matters related to worship (cc. 11–14), and belief in the resurrection (c. 15). This letter is also written with the prevailing belief that the return of the Lord was proximate.

There is no letter that gives us better insight into Paul's personality and sentiments than *2 Corinthians*. However, it is the unity of the letter that is disputed. The difference in tone between the first and second parts of the letter argues forcefully against an original unity. The first part of the letter speaks warmly of Paul's peace and reconciliation with the Corinthians; it is positive and approving in tone (cc. 1–9). The second part is reproving and severe in tone (cc. 10–13). Were these originally two letters written on different occasions, which have been stitched together? This may well have been the case because it at least accounts for the very distinct differences in tone.

In this letter Paul is fully aware of the continued opposition to his present position in Corinth. He speaks of his total dedication to his mission as well as the humiliation he has endured. His credentials and sincerity can hardly be questioned (cc. 1–4). He speaks of a former letter, corrective in character, which may well be preserved in cc. 10–13. He derides his opponents on their pride and arrogance and speaks of the importance of lowliness in the life of a true apostle. Human weakness enables the power of God to emerge.

According to Acts 16, Paul's first visit to Philippi occurred during his second missionary journey. Encouraged by a vision to visit Macedonia, Paul and his company crossed the Aegean Sea and soon thereafter reached Philippi in AD 50/51. The date of his *Letter to the Philippians* is uncertain. We know that it was written during one of his imprisonments, but that could have been Rome, Caesarea, or Ephesus. He and Silas were brought before magistrates and imprisoned for a time in Philippi as well. The growth of the small church in that city is also recorded in Acts 16.

In spite of the difficulties, Paul writes one of his most positive letters to the Philippians, dwelling on the riches of friendship and community. It contains as well one of Paul's most celebrated hymns. Probably drawn from the liturgy of the early church, this hymn (2:6–11) highlights the self-abasement of Christ who, from his exalted position, descends to a level of humble human service, culminating in his death. Glorified, he then returns to his place with the Father and is accorded the title Lord. The hymn is recognized as a Christian classic.

The message of Philippians is simple and direct. Paul expresses gratitude for the kindness of the community toward him and instructs them on the importance of faithfulness, unity, and humility. He also warns against outsiders who would attempt to reinterpret the faith they had received. Finally, he urges all to rejoice and to continue to grow in Christ. The letter contains only four chapters and is often referred to as the "letter of joy."

The *Letter to Philemon* is also a captivity epistle written during one of the imprisonments. Only one chapter in length, it is a plea on behalf of a certain Onesimus, a slave belonging to Philemon, whom Paul has befriended in prison. Onesimus was a runaway slave who had converted to Christianity during his stay with Paul. He also served as an aide to the apostle. Onesimus is now returning to Philemon and Paul requests that he be received as a "brother in Christ" (v. 16).

This is an appeal by Paul for an individual slave; he has no known position on slavery itself. It was an accepted reality of his time; many centuries would pass before the Christian conscience matured on the question. Suffice it to say that in view of the short period of time before the final days that Paul envisioned, he did not intend to change the structures of society. However, it is equally true that in his repeated emphasis on the intrinsic worth of the human person he sowed the seeds for a matured understanding of the question in the future.

There is no writing of Paul that has had the impact on Christianity that matches his *Letter to the Romans.* In the early Christian centuries it was widely commented on. At the time of the Reformation in the sixteenth century, it was the New Testament work that created the greatest conflict between Lutherans and Roman Catholics, especially with respect to its teaching on justification through faith. The letter was written from Corinth in AD 57/58 to a Roman community of Christians that Paul had neither founded nor visited. The letter is a well-ordered presentation of the major teachings that Paul had expounded in his career. The Roman church was made up of Gentile and Jewish converts, with the former probably being in the majority. Paul shows a special sensitivity to the concerns of Jewish Christians in his treatment of the Jewish covenant and the destiny of the Jewish people.

Why did Paul write at length to a church with which he had had no direct contact? The first reason that suggests itself is the importance of Rome as the capital of the empire; Christians there may well have enjoyed a certain preeminence. Second, Paul intended to visit Spain after his return to Jerusalem to deposit a collection for the poor. He would first visit Rome and then proceed west (15:26–29). As a result of his subsequent imprisonment his plans were never realized; however, if he felt that his future missionary efforts would be expended in Europe, he may well have seen Rome as the center, just as Antioch had been in the past.

The main body of the letter extends from chapters 1 to 15. Initially it sees sinfulness as prevailing among both Jews and Gentiles in pre-Christian times. None was deserving of God's goodness because all lived in opposition to his will and were in no way in tune with his righteousness (1:18—3:30). With God's intervention in Christ, however, righteousness is now offered to all who believe that God raised Jesus from the dead. This results from the gift of the Spirit, which is in no way merited and is conferred solely through the goodness of God, working through the faith of the believer. The former dispensation under the Law was to no avail; it was an era of sin and death and in no way achieved righteousness. Justice is realized solely through the saving action of Christ. As widespread as sin may have been in the former era, it in no way compares with the abundance of grace in these final times (cc. 5–8).

Paul then addresses the lot of the Jewish people (cc. 9–11). In respectful terms, he regrets the failure of his former coreligionists to accept Christ, especially in light of the favor that God had shown them in the past. However, God's fidelity is irrevocable and before the end the Jewish people, children of the promise, will accept Christ and be grafted, as branches on the cultivated vine, into the new covenant.

In the final chapters (12–15), Paul reflects on the meaning of life in Christ in practical terms. He speaks of the proper attitude toward Roman authority, the primacy of love, conditions at the end of time, and the relationship between the "strong" and the "weak." Greetings and admonitions make up the final chapter.

Here we have dealt solely with the generally accepted Pauline letters. Consideration of the Deutero-Pauline corpus will appear in the next chapter on developments in the early church.

MAJOR PAULINE THEMES

Jesus

As distinguished from the gospels, Paul tells us nothing about the events of Jesus' earthly ministry. There are no narratives to give us any historical profile of Christ. His whole focus is centered on the paschal mystery, the death-resurrection of Christ as the eschatological event of salvation, achieved in compliance with the Father's will. For Paul, this says everything. Regardless of what may have happened before his death, the real meaning of Jesus is seen in this "saving event" from which Paul's gaze never departs.

In what terms does Paul speak of Jesus? He is first of all the *Christ*, a title that appears in the opening line of his letters (Rom 1:1; 1 Cor 1:1; 2 Cor 1:1; Gal 1:1). The title means "the anointed one" and translates the Hebrew *messiah*. It was a title that enjoyed broad currency in the intertestamental period, based as it was on the promise of God (cf. 2 Sam 7) and the belief that it was the messiah who would deliver God's people from oppression and inaugurate the reign of God. In itself the title had no divine connotation. It was, however, aptly applied by the early Christians to Christ, as the promised liberator of God's people, even if in a sense quite different from the political hopes of the time. Paul certainly understood Christ in this authentic sense, although by his time the title had become equivalently a surname for Jesus.

The title *Son of God* appears in the Hebrew scriptures to indicate someone enjoying a special relationship with God, as the king (Ps 2:7). In its Greco-Roman use it pointed to one endowed with divine prowess to effect exceptional deeds. In the case of Jesus, however, it points to a unique relationship with God and for Paul is reserved for the risen Christ, who is endowed with the life-giving Spirit (Rom 1:4). This is not a denial of sonship at an earlier stage because the very context of Romans 1 indicates, "his Son, who was descended from David according to the flesh," and the prevailing notion of preexistence in Paul (Phil 2:5f). However, true sonship is experienced only with the resurrection, whereby Christ becomes the singular and effective agent of salvation. It is this understanding of being Son that makes Christ worthy of the worship given to the Father.

Much the same can be said of the title *Lord*. In the Hebrew scriptures this is a surrogate for the unpronounced name Yahweh. With Christ's resurrection, the title is now accorded him (Phil 2:9–11), with special regard to its cultic use. Jesus is also referred to as *Savior* and *Servant*, underscoring once again his salvific mission. It is this notion of Jesus as the world's savior that underlies any title accorded him in Paul.

Romans 1–3, Philippians 2

Justification by Faith

No theme in Paul's writing is more important, or has stirred more controversy, than that of justification. It has to be accorded a certain priority if for no other reason than the role it has played in the history of Christianity. Closely related to the titles of Jesus, this is the doctrine that deals with human salvation and is found primarily in the letters to the Galatians and the Romans. There are different terms that Paul uses in explaining the action of Christ on our behalf, as justification, redemption, salvation, and expiation. "Salvation" is probably the easiest for us to understand because we know what it means "to save" someone, to bring someone back to safety from the brink of disaster. Paul teaches that, before the coming of Christ, all people were in the state of sin and death, both physical and moral (Rom 1–3). By Christ's saving death, however, we have been cleansed of sin and through grace brought into the household of *Abba*, God our Father (Gal 4:1–7). "Justification" is related to God's justice in its biblical sense. God is just and righteous inasmuch as he is holy and incapable of wrongdoing. In Old Testament thought, the concept was related primarily to his fidelity to the covenant. Even in the face of Israel's repeated failures, God never wavered in his commitment to his people. In that light, humans are just insofar as their conduct mirrors that of God, avoiding sin and alienation from God.

For Paul justification is humanly unattainable. It cannot be attained through personal initiative, as the history of humanity from the time of Adam clearly attests. Even with the giving of the Law to Moses, justice was not attained. The Law was good in itself, but humans were incapable of observing it. The Law succeeded only in specifying evil; it was now possible to label each sinful act. Throughout history, three forces have been at work: Sin, Law, and Death (physical and moral). All three served the cause of evil and human degradation. Justification remained beyond human grasp (Rom 5:12–14).

Justification has now become real in Christ (Rom 5:15–21). Fully human he stands as our representative before God. With a totally obedient spirit, he has reversed the tide of Adam's disobedience and in so doing has drawn us out of sin to a new life in the Spirit. Now a reality, justification is attained only through faith. Faith is a gift, not something acquired by human effort. Its beginnings were found in Abraham who was justified because he believed, not because of his good works (Rom 4:1–5). In the belief that God raised Jesus from the dead, with a faith that is vibrant and active and not a mere passive acceptance, justification takes place.

This justification, according to Paul, is now open to Jew and Gentile alike. Former barriers have fallen; before God there is no shade of partiality (Rom 3:29f). Justification then produces its own works, those of the Spirit (Rom 5:16–25), which make superfluous the demands of the Law. For against the works of the Spirit, there is no law. The Christian attains justification through baptism. As one descends into the pool of water and ascends after baptism, the symbolism itself reflects Christ's entrance into the tomb and his subsequent resurrection to newness of life (Rom 6:1–4). Works now proceed from justice and are no longer an avenue to attain it (Gal 5:16–26). Now there is nothing to fear. There is no human experience from the heights or the depths, whether sad or joyful, that can separate us from the love of God that comes to us in Christ Jesus (Rom 8:37–39).

Redemption is a term derived from the social context of the liberation of slaves from bondage. Their freedom was quite literally bought for them. Christians too have been "bought" from the slavery of sin and led to freedom by the goodness of Christ the Redeemer (1 Cor 6:20, Rom 3:24). Other terms such as reconciliation, adoption, and expiation, with their particular nuances, also appear in Paul, all pointing to the work of justification.

Romans 5–7, Galatians 3–4

Cosmic Redemption

In an age marked by environmental concerns, it is worth considering the Pauline and Deutero-Pauline teaching on the redemption of the universe. From the time of the human fall from God's favor in Genesis, sin has affected not only the God-human relationship but also the relationship of humanity to the world itself (Gen 3:17–19, 6:7–11). With sin, the relationship between Adam and Eve, as well as their descendants, and their natural environment was clearly altered. In Christ, then, this order is reestablished. Grace has not only a vertical component but a horizontal one as well.

It is the letter to the Colossians, frequently considered post-Pauline, that makes the clearest statement on cosmic redemption. Even though the letter may be written by a later author, the theme is not alien to Paul. Moreover, this teaching is found in the Colossians hymn, probably derived from a liturgical source, which emphasizes the preeminence of Christ (1:15–20). He is presented as eternally present with the Father and plays a part in the entire process of creation. Christ is the alpha and the omega, the one through whom and for whom all things are created. As the Wisdom of God, he is the blueprint by which God creates everything. In the order of redemption, he is the agent who brings about the salvation of humankind (v. 16). In addition, just as it is through him that the cosmos is created, so too it is redeemed

(vv. 19–20). All things, whether animate or inanimate, are related to him as both creator and redeemer: "…and through him God was pleased to reconcile to himself all things, whether on earth or in heaven, by making peace through the blood of his cross" (v. 20).

In the epistle to the Romans, Paul speaks of the present state of this redemption. Just as we are in transit, and while living in the Spirit are not yet completely transformed, so the universe itself is in an imperfect state of redemption (Rom 8:22–25). Caught up in the relics of sin and still hampered by the imperfections of this temporal order, all of creation "groans," as we ourselves, for final consummation. It is a concept that moves away from a purely utilitarian outlook on the world or one that sees us transients simply moving through creation. We are joined with all that surrounds us. If heaven is not a place but basically a relationship, then that which binds us to the universe must be factored in.

This is clearly an area of theology that calls for further study and consideration. The early rupture in creation found the soil difficult to cultivate as Adam tilled it by the sweat of his brow (Gen 3:27–29). After the flood, the animals fled from Noah in fear, with the human passage from the vegetarian to the carnivorous state (Gen 9:1f). These are poetic illustrations of a disordered world in which sin has taken its toll. The work of Christ has not only restored a primordial relationship; it has given it a sacredness as well. Christians are called to reverence the world that has been given to them and to be mindful of their connectedness. Or in the words of the poet: to "see his blood upon the rose."

Genesis 3, Colossians 1, Romans 8

The Body of Christ

In the account of Paul's conversion in Acts (9:1–9), Christ identifies himself with those who are being persecuted. This is a theme developed at length in the Pauline literature, pointing to an intimate spiritual relationship between Christ and the Christian. So close is this bond that it is asserted that what is done to the Christian is done to Christ. This, moreover, is not a mere figure of speech or some sort of metaphor touching on interconnectedness. There is a realism in Paul's teaching that points to a very concrete unity. Here we will treat of the major moments where this is treated in Paul as well as in the Deutero-Pauline letters.

The starting point is the relationship between Christ and the individual Christian. In *Galatians* (2:15–21) Paul speaks of the Jewish Law as no longer meaningful in the Christian life. In fact, it was through the Law that specified sin that one experienced only spiritual death, but it is in the state of death that life is attained. It is in dying to one's former self and to the Law that life in the Spirit is actualized. It is in experiencing death with Christ, which occurs in baptism, that one's life is restored in the vivifying power that comes from the risen Christ, and that same Spirit permeates one's being and forms a concrete bond with Christ. Paul says that his life is now no longer his own; it is Christ alive in him. As far as his bodily life is concerned, it is only a life of faith in the Son of God. This personal identification with Christ cannot be reduced to a mere manner of speaking. It is a real, albeit spiritual, oneness with the personal Christ.

This occurs in baptism wherein one is immersed "into Christ" (3:27). The Greek preposition used has a sense of motion or direction toward: just as the newly baptized emerged from the pool/tomb and was clothed in white, the symbolism pointed to a new life. Clothing in antiquity was an expression of the person, a symbol of status or rank. It was also intimately associated with the wearer. So too the newly baptized is at one with Christ himself. So close is this identification that all former distinctions vanish, be it ethnicity (Jew-Greek), gender (male-female), or status (slave-freeman). All barriers of distinction fall in the presence of this newfound unity.

Paul's only boast is the cross of Christ. Formerly Paul and the world stood on opposite sides of the cross. He first had to experience a crucifixion himself in dying to the world and "the flesh" that he might share in the new life in Christ (Gal 6:14f);

that which has passed away is to no avail (e.g., circumcision); the only thing that matters is the cross of Christ, which is Paul's solitary boast.

In *1 Corinthians* Paul deals with problems of sexual morality (6:12–19). He bases his argument for moral rectitude on the closeness of the Christian with Christ. On the question of prostitution, Paul argues that for a Christian to be intimate in a sinful sexual relationship is a betrayal of a higher intimacy that is his, the unity in the Spirit with the risen Christ. It is that bond that precludes any action that would betray the total belonging to Christ. Comparison of the two forms of oneness excludes a mere metaphorical understanding of the bond with Christ. Neither one nor the other is simply a "manner of speaking."

In the same letter, Paul returns to the "body" theme under various headings. One of these is the communal dimension, underscoring the new relationship that exists among Christians as a group. He calls the faithful "God's temple" (3:16f), a dwelling place of the Lord, giving them a sacredness reserved for places of cult. In another place, he uses the body image, seeing believers united to Christ as body parts united to the whole (c. 12). As the members of the human body are integral and diversified, so it is also with the body of Christ. This excludes any notion of superiority (12:14f) but also points to diversity of function, a collaborative working together for the good of the whole (12:4–11).

In speaking of the Eucharist, Paul treats of both bodies as closely related. The one loaf, or the one eucharistic body of Christ, is shared among many at the one table. The fact that all eat of the one bread or the one body is illustrative of the unity among the members themselves. Just as there are many pieces in the one loaf, the faithful, although distinguished as individuals, are also one as adhering in the person of Christ (1 Cor 10:14–17).

In this communal understanding, where then does Christ stand in relation to the body as a whole? For the answer we must look to the Deutero-Pauline literature wherein this concept is developed. In the Colossians hymn, which is probably drawn from a liturgical source, the role of Christ in the entire created order is given lofty poetic expression (1:15–20). The preexistent Christ is presented in his creative and redemptive role. As the icon of God himself, he serves as the primary agent and the blueprint, as well as the unifier, of creation (vv. 15ff). In redemption he is the first to rise from the dead and in the body of Christ, which is the church, he is the head (v. 18). With the fullness of divinity, he stands at the center of the whole created order, which he has reconciled to God through his saving death (v. 19f). In ancient times the head was the source of authority and vitality. As head of his body, Christ presides over and directs the church, as well as being responsible for its life and growth. In all things, then, Christ is preeminent (Eph 1:23).

This development in the Pauline literature then passes from the individual relationship to Christ to the collective unity of all the faithful. Then, in naming Christ's relationship to the body as a whole, he is the head. This is the heart of Pauline ecclesiology, which is totally Christocentric. It is this same understanding that is at the core of his ethics. It is Christ alive in the Christian that is always the dominant consideration in moral choices (Gal 5:16–26). With love standing at the center of Christ's redemptive work, it is clearly the primary virtue of the Christian life (1 Cor 13, Rom 12:9–19).

Galatians 2, 3:23–29, 5
1 Corinthians 6:15–20; 10:14–17; 12
Romans 12, Colossians 1, Ephesians 1

XVIII.

A DEVELOPING CHURCH

As the apostolic era faded with the passing of that generation of people who had firsthand knowledge of Jesus, a certain measure of that initial enthusiasm began to wane as well. The expected return of Christ had not occurred and there was the growing realization that Christianity as a religion was destined to play a part in the ongoing history of the world. With the death of the apostles, the question of authority and its exercise came more to the fore. There were new questions on the relationship between Jewish and Gentile Christians. Moreover, Christians were regularly being forced to rub shoulders with other philosophical and religious systems, which had to be judged in terms of their compatibility with orthodox belief. There was the added question of relations with the Jewish people, with whom a common past was shared but with whom there was growing conflict. What form should the authoritative direction of the church take? What was to be said of people who had desisted from belief and left the community? How was heterodox teaching to be dealt with? These were a few of the issues that faced late first-century and early second-century Christianity. They became the subject matter of important writings that constitute the final pages of the New Testament.

PRESERVING THE FAITH

The correction of what may well have been a misunderstanding of Paul's teaching on justification is found in the *Letter of James*. Pseudonymously identified with James, "the brother" of the Lord

(Mark 6:3), the leader of the Jerusalem Christian community, the letter dates from the last decade of the first century, with the actual author unknown. Paul had taught that it was faith alone that justifies and works are of no account (Rom 3:20–25, 9:30–32, 10:4–6). By the time James was written, faith had become more formalized and codified, constituting a body of teaching. There was a growing belief that a simple acceptance of the truths of faith was sufficient for salvation. This was a distortion of Paul's thought, who never denied the role of "works" once justification was realized. In fact, he speaks of "faith working through love" (Gal 5:6). However, there is little question that James wishes to correct a false way of thinking. "What good is it, my brothers, if someone says he has faith but does not have works? Can that faith save him?" (2:14). Although not at odds with authentic Pauline thought, James is a counterbalance to Paul's faith dominance. Although the two are not at odds, James contributes a qualifying and helpful note.

We have already spoken of Paul's First Letter to the Thessalonians. At this point we consider his *Second Letter to the Thessalonians*. There are, then, two letters to this community: one is the earliest of Paul's writings; the second, coming from a later date, is more questionable in terms of its authorship. It bears some striking similarities to the first, even to the point of using the same expressions, although its content and overall style make a later author more likely. It may have been a companion of Paul, who is writing to correct earlier misunderstanding. In 1 Thessalonians, Paul had dealt with the delay in Christ's return, a vexing problem in light of the fact that some Christians had already died (4:13–17). Paul reassures the community but indicates that the exact time of the parousia remains uncertain (5:1ff).

In the second letter, the problem resurfaces with some people holding that the second coming was already present, arguing from a letter allegedly written by Paul (2:1f). The present author denies this and speaks of the present moment of expectation in apocalyptic terms. This, he says, is a time of a sinful presence, called "the lawless one." He is currently restrained, in a possible reference to the period of evangelization, but he will be finally revealed and destroyed at the return of Christ (2:7–11). In short, in nonPauline apocalyptic language, the author is asserting that there is still unfinished business before the end.

Written probably between AD 80 and 100, 2 Thessalonians casts light on the consternation created by the expectation of the Lord's return. Although the expectation never dies, it is much less a focal point in other late New Testament writings. In John's Gospel, for example, much greater emphasis falls on the Spirit-filled present era and less on the Lord's return.

Gnosticism, derived from the Greek *gnosis*, was a philosophical and religious system that validated the spiritual, while finding the material sinful at worst and irrelevant at best. Although Gnosticism was a post–New Testament phenomenon with which the church had to grapple, its beginnings were dealt with in early Christianity and a number of New Testament writings, with the epistles of John, Jude, 2 Peter, and Colossians reflecting that early stage. Docetism was an early heresy that claimed that the humanity of Christ was not real, but only apparent. This emphasis on illusion saw God in human form as incompatible with the prevailing heterodox view on the evil of matter. These religious currents played a significant part in eliciting the late New Testament writings.

The *Letters of John* are in many ways related to John's Gospel in vocabulary, style, and content. Whether they were authored by the same person, they are clearly related to the Johannine school. In some ways they are a corrective to overaccentuated features of the gospel. For example, in the gospel, there is a strong emphasis on the divinity of Christ. He is the Lord from the gospel's beginning to its end. Within the Johannine community, there were people creating doctrinal difficulties who eventually took their leave of the community and were seen as outsiders or "antichrists" (1 John 2:18–22, 4:2f). Their failure consisted in an unwillingness to accept the humanity of Christ, the fact the Son of God "came in the flesh" (1 John 4:1f). Emphasis on Christ's humanity is a consistent theme in the Johannine letters.

Second John, authored by "the Presbyter" without further iden-tification and only one chapter in length, decries the "deceivers" who fail to accept the full humanity of Jesus (v. 4). The letter gives great emphasis to the need for mutual love (v. 5), which obviously does not include the "deceivers," who are not even to be provided lodging (v. 11). Those guilty of this departure from the faith were evidently well known in the community. *Third John,* also from "the Presbyter," actually singles out one of the dissenters, Diatrophes, who has set himself against the Presbyter and the community.

Although it is not clear as to how they deviated from the truth, the *Letter of Jude,* also from the late first century, treats its opponents with bitter invective. They are blemishes, carousers, empty clouds, and dead trees. They are scoffers who are to be avoided at all cost. This also may have been some early form of Gnosticism, but we have no certainty in the matter. It is significant to note the extent to which deviant teaching was affecting the church only a half century after the death of Christ.

In *2 Peter,* opponents of the truth are again to the fore. This letter, one of the last of the New Testament writings, comes from the second century and is pseudonymously attributed to the apos-tle. Although there is an evident concern with the delay of Christ's return, the author vigorously defends the belief. The delay is ascribed to God's mercy for a sinful people, but the end will come "like a thief" (3:3–10).

The *Letter to the Colossians* carries a strong polemical tone without clearly identifying the forces opposing authentic belief. It may have been early Gnosticism or ideas coming from the ancient mystery religions that were prevalent in the Near East. Seemingly there were also Jewish customs and rituals being imposed on the community. The letter also speaks of angel worship and a direc-tive power connected with "the elemental spirits of the universe" (2:18ff). The latter may be identified with cosmic forces that were capable of being influenced by human effort. All of this is rejected by the author, who emphasizes the centrality of Christ in the whole of the universe. In preeminence and authority he has no competitor; to him alone is due worship and allegiance (1:15–23).

These writings of the early church reflect the dangers to which authentic belief was subjected in a world where philosophy, mystery religions, and polytheism were prevalent. Deviant teaching was affecting the church in its fledgling years. This was at a time when the structures of authority were only beginning to emerge and a clear presentation of orthodox teaching was not easily attained. It was a critical moment but one that moved the church from its charismatic beginnings to institutional forms.

> **James 1–2; 1 Thessalonians 4:13—5:11**
> **2 Thessalonians 2**
> **1 John 2–4; 2 John 1; 3 John 1; Jude 1; 2 Peter 2–3**

STRUCTURING THE FAITH

The inbreaking of the reign of God in the gospels has very little to say about structures of belief. The Twelve were the closest to Jesus, later seen as the reconstituted twelve tribes of Israel. They followed closely the activity of Jesus and were sent on mission by him. Peter held a position of primacy among them and in Matthew's gospel is clearly given a role of authority (Matt 16:15–20), an authority that was also shared with the other disciples (Matt 18:18). Matthew is the only gospel to show this ecclesial concern, and many authors today see this as coming from a post-Easter era. The New Testament indications are that the earliest community of believers was largely charismatic and unstructured.

The Acts of the Apostles recounts the election of a substitute for Judas among the Twelve (1:15–26), as well as the appointment of seven members of the community to look after temporalities (6:1–7). As the faith spread, there was a ritual of continuity and unity, signified by the imposition of hands. In the course of time, however, as ministerial needs grew and there was an increased danger of false teaching, the faith community became more structured.

The key to this development is found primarily in the *pastoral epistles, 1 and 2 Timothy* and *Titus*, so designated because they center on the spiritual needs of the faithful and the need for shepherds or pastors to exercise leadership.

The pastorals are attributed to Paul, writing to two of his colleagues, Timothy and Titus, who have roles of authority within their respective communities and who appear elsewhere in the New Testament. Timothy, son of a Christian mother and pagan father, was already a Christian when Paul met him in Lystra (Acts 16:1ff). He became a close companion and aide of Paul in his missionary work (1 Thess 1:1; 1 Cor 4:17; Phil 2:19–24). Titus, never mentioned in Acts, appears in the epistles (Gal 2:1–10; 2 Cor 7:5–16, 8:6). In the pastorals the two have responsibilities in Ephesus and Crete, respectively.

The great majority of scholars today would argue that the pastorals are Paul's only by attribution. The letters are absent from the oldest Greek manuscripts; the theological perspective, as well as the language and style, are distant from that of Paul. By the time the pastorals were written, probably in the early second century, the church had progressed well beyond the period of Paul himself. Again, though, it should be remembered that the question of authorship has nothing to do with the authenticity and importance of the letters themselves.

There are three categories of ministry mentioned in the pastoral: bishops *(episkopoi)*, elders *(presbyteroi)*, and deacons *(diakonoi)*. The bishops and elders shoulder the major responsibility and at times the terms are used interchangeably (Titus 1:5–9). If this is viewing a single group from different angles, then the bishops may have been considered "overseers" or directors, whereas the term *elders* or *presbyters* looked more to status or seniority within the community. In a given city or town, there were a number of presbyters appointed (Titus 1:5), who evidently acted as a group in the supervision of the community. Only people of good reputation were to be named to the office of bishop/presbyter (Titus 1:5–10), the position being confirmed through the laying on of hands

(1 Tim 5:22). Qualities are also outlined for the office of deacon (1 Tim 3:8–13), but nothing is said about their duties.

It is clear from the pastorals that the chief duty of the hierarchy was the preservation of the faith. There is no indication that the single bishop had yet emerged in the church; the authority of preaching, ruling, and teaching resided in the body of bishops/presbyters (1 Tim 3:4f, 5:17). There is no indication of any of these offices being linked to a liturgical or cultic role.

All of the pastorals speak to the existing dangers to the faith. There may have been elements of Gnosticism in the forbidding of marriage and the emphasis on food abstention (1 Tim 4:1–3). The incursions of wealth and the desire for it were present dangers (1 Tim 6:5–10). Three of the dissidents are named—Hymenaeus, Philetus, and Alexander—as falsifying the truth of the resurrection (1 Tim 1:20; 2 Tim 2:17f). The scriptures are upheld as the certain source of the truth, and to the Word of God must be given unwavering fidelity (2 Tim 3:16f). Respect for civil authority is underscored (Titus 3:1). Although doctrinal concerns are present in the pastorals, it is attention to good morals that receives major consideration.

The emergence of leadership in the person of bishops/presbyters arose from the church's concrete experience. They acted in a supervisory capacity; the deacons probably exercised a ministry of caring for community needs. How widespread these ministries were in the early church remains a matter of speculation. Other local churches may well have been structured differently. The Spirit guiding the church from its inception provided for a maturing appreciation of needs and the structures to accompany them.

1 Timothy 3–4, 5:17–25; 2 Timothy 2:14–26; Titus 1–2

ENCOURAGING THE FAITHFUL

The *Epistle to the Hebrews* is called by its author "a word of exhortation" (13:22). It is one of the most stirring and scripture-filled books of the New Testament, although unfortunately nothing is known about its origin, its author, or its audience. In fact, it is a letter only in the broad sense of the term because it does not follow the epistolary form; it may more properly be called an essay or a homily. About Hebrews the most we can offer is a series of "may have beens." It may have been written before AD 70, given that its strong Temple concerns make no mention of its destruction. It is certainly not later than AD 90 because it is cited by Clement of Rome at that time. In early Christianity there was a limited attribution of the book to Paul, especially in the East, but that position has been almost universally abandoned. Both in style and content it is distant from Paul. Its theology and vocabulary, as well as its concern with Jewish ritual, are clearly non-Pauline. The author received the Christian message from others (2:3); Paul did not.

The question of authorship, then, remains unresolved. The "may have beens" regarding those for whom the epistle was written range from Jerusalem to Rome. Because there is much emphasis on Jewish cult and belief, there is considerable likelihood of its being written for a community with a large Jewish Christian component. Its largely impersonal character argues for its eventually being used as a homily in various churches.

Regardless of these secondary considerations, Hebrews remains one of the finest theological and literary works of the New Testament. The author has a masterful and fluent command of Greek. He is both an accomplished writer and an excellent rhetorician. His comparisons of Jewish and Christian elements are masterful. The centrality of Christ in all things manifests a person of a deep and constant faith. His scope was to give courage to people who were wavering in their convictions (2:1, 6:11f, 10:32–36). With the return of Christ delayed, the presentation of Christ the High Priest interceding for the faithful was geared to convey strength and consolation.

In fact, this concept of the high priesthood of Christ is one of Hebrews' strongest images (8:1-6). In our former discussion of the various ministries present in the early church, there was no mention of priests. Although there were undoubtedly members of the church who were designated to preside at the Eucharist, there is no indication that they were known as priests. One of the main reasons for this was to avoid any confusion or cast any doubts on the singular priesthood of Christ. He is the mediator between God and humanity, a position that could not be qualified or in any way compromised.

This priesthood of Christ is framed within the fulfillment theme, which is so much a part of Hebrews, chapters 3–10. After speaking of Christ as the ultimate expression of the Father, the One exalted above all of creation (1:2–14), the author highlights Christ's humanity, the divinely ordained vehicle of salvation. It was as man that he was able to identify with and bring hope to an alienated humanity (c. 2).

Christ proceeded from the former dispensation while surpassing it in every way. His mission embraced and went beyond that of Moses (c. 3), the High Priest and his sacrifice (c. 5), Melchizedek (c. 7), the covenant (8:7—9:28), and sacrifice in general (c. 10). Moses "was faithful in all God's house"; Christ is the one placed "over God's house," which is the community of the faithful (3:1–6). Jesus is also the compassionate High Priest, chosen by God just as his former counterpart (5:1–10). He interceded before God during his earthly life "with cries and tears" and now continues in that role in his glorified humanity. The Old Testament priest offered sacrifice in an earthly sanctuary; Christ has entered the heavenly sanctuary where he remains forever. The High Priest entered the Most Holy Place only once a year, on the Day of Atonement; he offered animal sacrifice that had to be repeated annually. Christ offers not animal blood but his own, not repeatedly but once only, sufficient, as it is, to atone for the sins of humanity forever (9:1–5, 23–28). In fact, the former sacrifices were ineffectual, whereas that of Christ, offered in obedience to the will of the Father, has an efficacy that is perpetual and nonrepeatable. Christ is now seated at the Father's side waiting for the final cessation of evil (10:1–18).

How can Christ be termed a priest when he was not of the line of Levi? It is because he belongs to the priestly line of Melchizedek (c. 7), an unknown priest-king who appears briefly in Genesis (14:18ff). Although he is spoken of as a priest of "God Most High," he was actually a Canaanite priest whose major deity also had the same title. He blessed Abraham and Abraham gave him a tithe of what he possessed. No more is said of Melchizedek, except in Psalm 110 where the role of king and priest is again mentioned (v. 4). Christ, then, is a nonlevitical priest of the line of Melchizedek. The ancient priest-king is a type of Christ in his "eternal" character, "without father, without mother, without genealogy," just as Christ had eternal origins. Moreover, he was "king of Salem," a place name close to the Hebrew word for peace; Christ, then, is "king of peace." Finally, he blessed Abraham and through him his future descendants, thus placing him in a superior position to that of the Hebrew patriarch and his offspring. This points to the superior position of Christ as well. His priesthood is superior to that of the Levites who were already present "in the loins" of Abraham when he was blessed by Melchizedek, the type of Christ.

The earlier Sinai covenant was inaugurated by sacrifice, so too the new covenant established by Christ (8:7—9:28). Evoking Jeremiah's promise of a new and better covenant (31:31–34), Hebrews clearly sees the prophecy as fulfilled in Christ, who offered not the blood of goats and calves, but his own blood. By his death, Christ removed the guilt of past sins incurred under the former covenant and has at the same time established the new and lasting covenant.

For Hebrews, the main features of the past—priesthood, sacrifice, sanctuary, and covenant—are now brought to perfection. Former institutions were but a shadow of what was to come. Christians, rather than feeling disheartened, should derive courage from the fact that in Christ they have the eternal Priest who unceasingly intercedes on their behalf. In a final exhortation, the author pleads for constancy and trust. He cites biblical examples of persons—Abel, Enoch, Abraham, Jacob, and Moses—who in their faith were found pleasing to God (c. 11). Far more privileged are the Christian faithful who have access to the heavenly Jerusalem in "Jesus the mediator of a new covenant" and the sprinkled blood that "speaks a better word than the blood of Abel" (12:24).

The *First Letter of Peter* is probably an extended baptismal catechesis, which is also meant to encourage the new Christians in their faith. It is written for the people of Asia Minor (1:1) from Rome (the "Babylon" of 5:13). Many claim that it is authored by Peter himself or through his secretary, Silvanus (5:12), seemingly preceding any major persecution (2:13–17), and showing a certain familiarity with Jesus' words. The greater number of authors favor a pseudonymous authorship on a number of grounds, such as developed church organization (5:1) and a possible persecution in the reference to a "fiery ordeal" (4:12), factors that follow the life of Peter. If Peter is the author, the composition would come from the early 60s; a post-Petrine authorship would place it between AD 70 and 80.

The emphasis on baptism in the letter (1:3, 1:23, 2:2, 3:20f) argues in favor of this being a baptismal letter reminding the newly baptized of their responsibility. Their anxiety proceeds from their separation from former companions and way of life. They are "aliens and exiles" (2:11), who now live in fear of persecution for their belief (3:13–17, 4:12f). They are not to lose sight of their heritage as "a chosen race, a royal priesthood, a holy nation" (2:9; cf. Exod 19:6). Regardless of their state in life as free people (2:13–17) or slaves (2:18–25), married persons (3:1–7), or church authorities (5:1–4), their conduct should be exemplary. The capstone is mutual love, the clear sign of their discipleship, and a sense of confidence and trust in the face of hardship. They must always remember that the Lord "called you out of darkness into his marvelous light" (2:9).

Hebrews 3, 5–7, 9–11
1 Peter 1–3

XIX.

THE APOCALYPSE

The final book of the New Testament marks the end of time. The book was long known as The Apocalypse until such time as the word lost its meaning in the English-speaking world. At that point it became known by its English equivalent, the book of Revelation. Ironically, today the word *apocalypse* has reentered the modern vocabulary, and largely because of media hype, has regained a considerably high level of understanding. Even though the word may have common usage, the literary form or genre is much less understood and for many people this is a book that remains a mystery.

GENRE

Although the word *apocalypse* means "revelation," it is a revelation of a particular type. It is almost wholly expressed in images or figures that have to be decoded to gain access to the message. In the case of this biblical book, the images are almost entirely drawn from the Old Testament. Ugly and terrifying beasts, cosmic upheaval, ethereal splendor, and liturgical props—all play a part in conveying the author's message. Neither evil nor good is presented in the abstract; they are always vividly depicted in unseemly and in comely form, respectively. It is precisely because of the vivid imagery found in Apocalypse/Revelation that the book is often considered incomprehensible. Nothing is farther from the truth. This is not the first appearance of apocalyptic in the Bible. It plays a major part in the Old Testament book of

Daniel. Written during the time of Greek oppression of the Jewish people, Daniel is a book of consolation and hope in time of distress. There is also the "little apocalypse" of Isaiah (cc. 24–27), a postexilic addition to the work of the earlier prophet.

Repetition plays a key role in this type of literature. The same idea is repeated several times under different images. Thus, although it is true that the message of Apocalypse/Revelation is not immediately comprehended, once it is decoded it is not only easily grasped, its repetitive character can make it more than a bit tedious. There were different reasons that explain the use of the genre. One was the uncertainty that surrounded the "end time." Neither the day nor the hour could be predicted with certainty; hence, apocalyptic shrouded it with the aura of mystery and lifted it out of the realm of human determination. Another was the need for a cryptic type of communication. This was particularly necessary in a time of persecution when what was written or said could easily rebound and be used against its proponents. Apocalyptic literature did not allow easy access. The earliest Christian readers of this book were able to understand its message or had it explained in homiletic settings. As time passed, it became less understood and vastly unappreciated. What is perhaps even worse was the extent to which the book was misinterpreted and applied to people and settings that were far from the author's mind.

In the present text, the book will be referred to by its English title, Revelation, as has become common in recent times. However, the reader is encouraged to keep in mind that the word "revelation" has a broader meaning in religious circles, and therefore is to be here understood in the sense of "apocalyptic" revelation.

AUTHOR, TIME, PLACE

Persecution places such a dominant role in Revelation that its time line is best identified with one of the early Roman persecutions, probably that of Domitian (AD 81–96). Its place of origin was Asia Minor where many Jewish Christians had emigrated after the destruction of Jerusalem in AD. 70. The audience was made up of largely Jewish Christian congregations as seems evident from the use of the apocalyptic genre that was more familiar to the Jewish world. The author appears to have been of the same Jewish background. Although he writes in Greek, the work has many semitisms, which point to one more familiar with Hebrew than the Greek in which the book is written. He is identified as one John of Patmos, an exile living on the island of Patmos, a Roman penal colony in the Aegean Sea. Nothing is known of the author; it is suggested that he was of Palestinian origin and had later emigrated to Asia Minor. He is not to be identified with John the apostle nor with John the evangelist. He clearly distinguishes himself from the Twelve (21:14). His Greek with its semitisms argues forcefully for his not being identified with the author of the fourth gospel whose Greek is much more refined.

The book, then, is authored by one John of Patmos, a seer and Jewish Christian, writing for a largely Jewish Christian audience in Asia Minor, sometime after AD 70, probably during the 80s or early 90s.

POLITICO-HISTORICAL SCENE

Revelation was written while Rome was the occupying colonial power in much of the Near Eastern world, as well as Asia Minor. A large number of Jews and Christian had settled in Asia Minor after the destruction of Jerusalem. Within a matter of years, before the end of the first century, Christians were beset by their own set of "woes." They were not as highly respected as the Jews, being a nascent sect that was seen as a Jewish offspring. While in its early stages, Christianity coexisted with Judaism, it was not long before a major split occurred. This resulted in marked hostilities between the two, with Christianity clearly suffering the most. At the same time, there were ongoing difficulties with Roman authorities, especially over such issues as emperor worship, with resultant major persecutions under Nero (AD

54–68) and Domitian (AD 81–96). The book of Revelation clearly reflects this animosity on the part of Jews and Gentiles alike. It was probably written as a pastoral letter to congregations known to the author, containing both admonitions and words of encouragement for the Christian minority.

STRUCTURE

Revelation has a relatively simple structure:

- Letters to the Churches (1:1—3:22)
- Judgment on the Evil Empire (4:1—18:24)
- Final Redemption (19:1—22:5)
- Epilogue (22:6–20)

The number seven plays a key role within the structure, as is evident in the accompanying more detailed structural outline **(structure outline).** Letters are written to seven churches. In a series of six apocalyptic visions, each vision contains seven signs. In conjunction with each of the six visions, there are intermittent visions that break the sequence by introducing prophetic insights.

MAJOR THEMES

As is characteristic of the apocalyptic genre, there is considerable repetition of the central theme in Revelation. The visions of seven are repetitive in their expression of punishment on the Evil Empire and the ultimate triumph of Good, all of this occurring under God's direction. John is the messenger, the legate of Jesus Christ and the one who conveys the revelation. Throughout it is God himself, "the one who is, who was, and who is to come," enthroned in the heavens, who is the ultimate source of all that is communicated. Christ is the "faithful witness" of God's will, the first to rise from the dead and now the sovereign of the universe (5:1–14).

BOOK OF REVELATIONS OUTLINE

THE SEVEN CHURCHES (cc. 1–3)

Ephesus	Smyrna	Pergamum	Thyatira	Sardis	Philadelphia	Laodicea

HONOR TO THE THRONE (GOD) AND THE LAMB (cc. 4–5)

THE SEVEN SEALS (c. 6)

War	Violence	Famine	Death	Martyrdom	Earthquake	Silence 8:1

SEALING OF THE ELECT (c. 7)

THE SEVEN TRUMPETS (cc. 8–9) (11:15–19)

Fire	Sea	Bitter Water	Falling Stars	Locusts	Horses	Glory

INTERVAL: Scroll, Measuring Rod, Trees, Lampstand (cc. 10–11)

Conflict (c. 12) ⟶ Beasts (c. 13) ⟶

SEVEN HARBINGERS OF FATE (c. 14)

ANGEL I	ANGEL II	ANGEL III	SON OF MAN	ANGEL IV	ANGEL V	ANGEL VI
Judgment	Fallen Babylon	Punishment	Harvester	Herald of Doom	Harvester	Final Recompense

APPEARANCE OF THE SEVEN ANGELS WITH SEVEN BOWLS (c. 15)

THE SEVEN BOWLS (c. 16)

Sores	Bloody Sea	Bloody River	Burns	Darkness	Invasion	Earthquake

THE FALL OF BABYLON THE GREAT HARLOT (cc. 17–18)

SEVEN FINAL EVENTS (cc. 19–22)

Lamb's Feast	Last Battle	Binding of Satan	The Millennium	Defeat of Gog and Magog	Last Judgment	New Jerusalem

The Seven Letters

The letters are addressed to the Aegean cities of Ephesus, Smyrna, Pergamum, Thyatira, Sardis, Philadelphia, and Laodicea. They are symbolized by the seven lampstands in the midst of which Christ stands, holding seven stars, representing the angels of the churches (1:12–16). The churches had relatively small communities in cities, about forty miles apart, which were centers of Roman life. In a prevailing Gentile culture, the Christians found themselves in difficulty in trying to live their newfound faith. Within the communities themselves, there were confusing currents of thought, perhaps Stoic in origin, which favored the adoption of pagan customs and rituals. Religion was seen as primarily internal, unrelated to external conduct. These wrongsayers and seducers are variously identified in the book as Nicolaitans, Balaam, and Jezebel, favoring forms of adaptation alien to the authentic Christian spirit. The two global forces in opposition are Jerusalem (good) and Babylon (evil); both are amply illustrated in Revelation.

Although each of the letters is written to a particular church, the message of each was applicable to any of the churches and was probably passed on to other audiences (2:7). The letters contain a mix of blame and blessing; only Smyrna and Philadelphia receive unqualified praise. The heart of each message is a call to conversion (Greek: *metanoia*) and endurance (Greek: *upomone*) in the midst of a very troubled world.

Judgment

Much of Revelation deals with the trials and punishment of the final era before the full inbreaking of the kingdom. A clear teaching of the Hebrew scriptures was that evil would have to be totally uprooted and destroyed before the final manifestation of God's glory. The picture that is given us in this section of the book (4:1—18:24) finds God placed at the center of the vision, enthroned and sovereign. He receives praise from the heavenly court, comprised of the four living creatures, the twenty-four elders, and the angelic choir. To them is added the elect of the earth, representatives of the old and new Israel. Central to the theme and standing "at the center of the throne" is the Lamb, representing Christ, who inaugurates the end time vision (4:1; 5; 14).

Judgment comes in sevens. In each presentation, the first six visions deal with catastrophe—famine, earthquake, violence, death, and the like. Examples are seen in the seals (c. 6), the trumpets (cc. 8–9), the angels of fate (c. 14), the bowls (c. 16), and the seven final events (cc. 19–22). Heavenly messengers inflict judgment on the forces of evil that are creating havoc in the world. Evil is seen primarily as the force of Rome, depicted in various forms—a dragon, a beast, a harlot; they preside over Babylon (Rome). Her overthrow is given various expressions from war to cosmic upheaval.

As we have indicated, these visions are cyclical, returning repeatedly to the same idea, always depicted in a different way. Only when the final battle is won is the way paved for the vision of the definitive triumph, the heavenly Jerusalem, the nuptials between the Lamb and his bride.

In all of this, the principal players remain the same: God, Christ, and the forces of evil, principally Rome, the members of the heavenly court, and the saved or elect. John of Patmos is the seer and witness who records the events for future retelling.

The Seven Seals

Among the concentric circles that depict the end time events are the seals, the trumpets, avenging angels, and the bowls. A single illustration, that of the seven seals, will serve our present purpose. The seals enclose a scroll held by God (5:1) and are to be opened only by the one found worthy. The lot falls to Christ, "the Lamb that was slaughtered" (5:9–12). With the breaking of the first seal, a rider and white horse appear, symbolizing invasion by a foreign power (6:1f). The breaking of the second seal, with its resultant red horse and rider, prefigures internal insurrection (6:3f); the third seal with its black horse, famine (6:5f). This

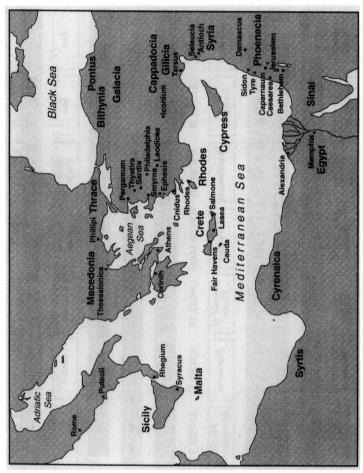

The seven lampstands are the seven churches of Revelation 2–3.

leaves the people without sustenance and impoverished. The pale green horse of the fourth seal signifies death itself and Hades, Sheol, or the underworld (6:7f). It is evident that many of these images—plagues, famine, and death—are reflective of the misfortunes inflicted on the Egyptians at the time of the Hebrew exodus. With all of these tragic events, one fourth of humanity was left intact.

With the fifth seal, the lot of the saved or elect is depicted (6:9ff). They were martyrs, now appropriately found near the altar where the blood of animal victims was gathered. These are those who died under Roman persecution; as sufferers, they cry out for the vindication of God's justice. Their presence only adds to the end-time drama. The sixth seal brings on an apocalyptic climax—earthquake (Joel 2:10, Isa 24:9), discolored sun and moon (Isa 13:10, 50:3, Matt 24:28), falling firmament and stars (Isa 34:4). All the peoples of the earth, regardless of rank or station, hide themselves from final judgment. The opening of the seventh seal is almost anticlimactic (8:1). It is marked by thirty minutes of silence, like that of Zephaniah before the Day of the Lord (Zeph 1:7). It is a silence full of awe, silence, and fear. It is prelude to the next set of woes, the trumpets.

In all of this end-time imagery, the justice of God is inflicted on the enemies of the just, with Old Testament imagery used extensively to illustrate what was viewed as an inescapable reality. This broad use of symbolism accented the fact that the justice of God would prevail.

The Final Nuptials

The conclusion of Revelation is one of glory (19:1–10) and praise (19:11–22). The great chorus of the elect sings of the final victory and the twenty-four elders and the four living creatures fall down in worship. The white horse and Christ, its rider, inflict the final blow on the enemy. The chorus then announces the joyful wedding day of the Lamb (19:7). There is a symbolic period of a thousand years during which Satan is to be chained and held immobile; the years are figurative, simply another expression of end-time imagery.

In the final period (21:1—22:20), there is the reward of the just and the renewal of the cosmos. God will dwell eternally with his people and death will be no more. Evildoers are definitively condemned. In a final vision, the heavenly Jerusalem descends in brilliance and transparency; she is the bride prepared for her spouse. She is both God's dwelling and the home of the elect. Her twelve gates stand for the twelve tribes of Israel and the twelve foundation pieces, the twelve apostles (21:12ff). There is no temple because God now permeates the whole of the city (1 Cor 15:25–28). The waters flowing from the throne of God evoke Ezekiel's end-time revelation (21:22—22:5, Ezra 47:1–12). Night no longer exists, nor is there any need for light, with the light from God all sufficient.

With evil overthrown, God presides over the nuptials of Christ, the Lamb and his bride, the elect. The drama of salvation draws to its close or, better still, it marks a new beginning. As we have indicated, the symbols of Revelation are largely biblical and are fairly easy to identify. The book is a drama, at once brilliant and frightful. In its denouement it carries us back to the beginnings in Eden. Much as the tempting serpent, evil has emerged repeatedly in history and has taken a deadly toll. It was opposed by the patriarchs, the prophets, wisdom writers, and Jesus himself. Yet the Bible points to one irrevocable truth: the final word belongs to God. That is the overriding message of Revelation, as well as of the two Testaments that recount our sacred history.

Revelation 1:1—3:22, 6:1—8:1, 21:1—22:5

SELECTED BIBLIOGRAPHY

INTRODUCTIONS TO THE BIBLE

Beasley, J. R., et al. *An Introduction to the Bible.* Nashville, TN: Abingdon Press, 1991.

Fant, C. E., D. Musser, and M. Reddish. *Introduction to the Bible,* rev. ed. Nashville, TN: Abingdon Press, 1979.

Hauer, C., and W. Young. *An Introduction to the Bible,* 2nd ed. Englewood Cliffs, NJ: Prentice Hall, 1989.

Hauret, C. *Introduction to Sacred Scripture.* De Pere, WI: St. Norbert Abbey, 1964.

OLD TESTAMENT INTRODUCTIONS

Anderson, B. *Understanding the Old Testament,* 4th ed. Englewood Cliffs, NJ: Prentice Hall, 1986.

Boadt, L. *Reading the Old Testament: An Introduction.* Mahwah, NJ: Paulist Press, 1984.

Eissfeldt, O. *The Old Testament: An Introduction.* New York: Harper & Row, 1965.

Hayes, J. *An Introduction to Old Testament Study.* Nashville, TN: Abingdon Press, 1979.

Kaiser, O. *Introduction to the Old Testament.* Minneapolis: Augsburg, 1975.

NEW TESTAMENT INTRODUCTIONS

Achtemeier, P., J. B. Caeen, and M. Thompson. *Introducing the New Testament, Its Literature and Theology.* Grand Rapids, MI: Wm. B. Eerdmanns, 2001.

Brown, R. *An Introduction to the New Testament.* New York: Doubleday, 1997.

Brown, S. *The Origins of Christianity: A Historical Introduction to the New Testament,* 2nd ed. New York: Oxford, 1993.

Childs, B. *The New Testament as Canon: An Introduction.* Philadelphia: Fortress, 1985.

Collins, R. F. *Introduction to the New Testament.* New York: Doubleday, 1983.

Fuller, R. H. *A Critical Introduction to the New Testament.* London: Duckworth, 1974.

Kee, H. C. *Understanding the New Testament,* 4th ed. Englewood Cliffs, NJ: Prentice Hall, 1983.

Koester, H. *Introduction to the New Testament.* Philadelphia: Fortress, 1982.

Kummel, W. *Introduction to the New Testament,* 17th ed. Nashville, TN: Abingdon Press, 1975.

Moule, C. F. D. *The Birth of the New Testament,* 3rd ed. London: Black, 1981.

Perrin, N., and D. C. Duling. *The New Testament: An Introduction.* Fort Worth, TX: Harcourt Brace, 1994.

Wikenhauser, A. *New Testament Introduction.* New York, Herder & Herder, 1960.

STUDY GUIDES

The Catholic Study Bible. New American Bible. New York: Oxford Univ. Press, 1990.

The New Jerusalem Bible. New York: Doubleday, 1985.

The New Oxford Annotated Bible. New Revised Standard Version. New York: Oxford Univ. Press, 1991.

HISTORIES

Aune, D. E. *The New Testament in Its Literary Environment.* Philadelphia: Westminster, 1987.

Bright, J. *A History of Israel,* 3rd ed. Philadelphia, Westminster, 1981.

Conzelmann, H. *History of Primitive Christianity.* Nashville, TN: Abingdon Press, 1973.

DeVaux, R. *The Early History of Israel.* Philadelphia: Westminster, 1978.

Noth, M. *The Old Testament World.* Philadelphia: Fortress, 1966.

Rogerson, J., and P. Davies. *The Old Testament World.* Englewood Cliffs, NJ: Prentice Hall, 1989.

DICTIONARIES AND ENCYCLOPEDIAS

Achtemeier, Paul J., ed. *Harper's Bible Dictionary.* San Francisco: Harper & Row, 1985.

Bromley, G., ed. *The International Standard Bible Encyclopedia.* 4 vols. Grand Rapids, MI: Wm. B. Eerdmans, 1979–88.

Buttrick, G., ed. *The Interpreter's Dictionary of the Bible.* 4 vols. Nashville, TN: Abingdon Press, 1962.

INDEX